VALIANT UNIVERSE™
THE ROLEPLAYING GAME

VALIANT

TABLE OF CONTENTS

CATALYST GAME LABS

Original Cue System Game Design
Matt Heerdt
Additional Game Design
Randall N. Bills
Valiant Cue System Game Design
Randall N. Bills
Project Development
Randall N. Bills
Philip A. Lee
Production Assistance
Bryn K. Bills
Writing
Randall N. Bills   Joel Bancroft-Connors
Aaron Cahall   Ken' Horner
Kevin Killiany   Philip A. Lee
Craig Reed   Geoff Swift
Editing
Philip A. Lee
Jason Schmetzer
Cover Artwork
Tom Raney
Cover Art Direction
Brent Evans
Graphic Design & Layout
Ray Arrastia
Graphic Assistance
David Kerber
Artwork
Diego Bernard   Doug Braithwaite
CAFU   ChrisCross
Will Conrad   Clayton Crain
Roberto de la Torre   Ming Doyle
Neil Edwards   Khari Evans
Tom Fowler   Lee Garbett
Manuel Garcia   Stefano Gaudiano
Robert Gill   Trevor Hairsine
Clayton Henry   J.G. Jones
Kano   Barry Kitson
Lewis Larosa   Arturo Lozzi
Emanuela Lupacchino   Álvaro Martínez
Cary Nord   Pere Pérez
Tom Raney   Brian Reber
Esad Ribic   Andrew Robinson
Bart Sears   Ryan Sook
Mico Suayan   Patrick Zircher

Dedication
To the various members of my original high school gaming group: Jeremy Cheek, Kater Pratt Cheek, Denby Cluff, Scott Crandall, Chad Dean, Amy Lewis, Tony Liddle, Shannon McLean, Jeff Morgan, Manu Sharma, Steve Pitcher, Cynthia Robinson, and Larry Yanez. I highly doubt I'd have had the chance to create this fantastic book without your great and wonderfully geeky friendships over the years. Thank you!

VALIANT ENTERTAINMENT

Chairman
Peter Cuneo
CEO & Chief Creative Officer
Dinesh Shamdasani
CFO & Head of Strategic Development
Gavin Cuneo
Publisher
Fred Pierce
Editor-in-Chief
Warren Simons
VP Operations
Walter Black
**Director of Marketing,
   Communications & Digital Media**
Hunter Gorinson
Sales Manager
Atom! Freeman
Production & Design Manager
Travis Escarfullery
Associate Editor
Alejandro Arbona
Assistant Editor
Josh Johns
Assistant Editor
Kyle Andrukiewicz
Logo & Trade Dress Design
Rian Hughes
Operations Manager
Peter Stern
Operations Coordinator
Robert Meyers
**President, Consumer Products,
   Promotions & Ad Sales**
Russ Brown
Vice Chairman
Jason Kothari

Thanks
To Brent Evans for being the right person, at the right time, in the right place at New York Comic Con 2013 to "stumble" into this opportunity…thanks for helping turn me to the dark-side.

To Peter Stern, Russ Brown, Robert Meyers, Hunter Gorinson, Dinesh Shamdasani, and the entire Valiant Entertainment team for leaping on board with us and making this whole experience so fantastic.

To our Demo Agent, Richard Brown, and the players at the Pax East 2014 demo that spawned the idea we used in our example comic

To Eric Petersen for bringing a longtime Valiant fan's eye—crossed with the expertise of long years of role-playing—to subtly enhance the rules with comics in mind and open my own eyes to the myriad possibilities of Powers.

To Philip A. Lee (and Craig Reed) for stepping way beyond the bounds of editing to help me wrangle this book through the final throes of development and layout.

INTRODUCTION

You and your friends are sitting around talking about comic books, 'cause that's what we do, after all …

You've just finished reading *Harbinger* #21 and are wondering about Peter Stanchek's powers. The key phrase that you're excitedly debating is from Peter: "You know … it affects me pretty hard. Every time I scan someone. The homeless I wipe to keep rumors of your apparitions from spreading. All those Foundation members during Harada's mind squall. Ax earlier today..."

One of you says, "Y'know, if *I* was Peter I'd simply anchor an invisibility shield to Monica Jim. Every time she leaves the Renegades' underground lair, Peter's psionic energy spikes on. That keeps Monica Jim hidden while alerting Peter to potential trouble while she's out. But this also gives her some leash so the kid doesn't go stir crazy."

Another one of you says, "Nah, nothing in any of the comics says Peter can anchor his powers, much less have them kick off subconsciously like that. That's going too far."

And another friend pipes up and says, "Yeah, I agree. Not to mention that doesn't solve Peter's problem of the psychic weight he's carrying. If I was Peter, I would've figured out how Harada's mind squall worked while it was scrambling all that brain juice. The comics have shown how fast he adapts, after all. Then, when he's scanning and erasing memories, he generates, well, let's call it a 'mind bubble.' A subtle pressure of memories spread into a wide area—a pressure valve relief sorta thing. Kicks off déjà vu for anyone in a certain radius. But no one's really hurt, no alarms sound, and Peter's not getting crushed because he's carrying the weight of everything."

A chorus of "Oh … that's good" flows around the room. Except for the original guy, who mutters, "I still like my idea better."

Who hasn't enjoyed those thought experiments as we've all put our imaginations to work in great debates to answer the questions that come out of reading the best comics? Well, that's exactly what *Valiant Universe: The Roleplaying Game* lets you do.

This is *your* chance to step in, suit up, and answer those questions for yourself! How would *you* do it?

WHAT IS VALIANT UNIVERSE?

Valiant Universe: The Roleplaying Game is set in Valiant Entertainment's brilliant superhero universe.

The universe is presented across numerous comic book titles, with new issues being released every month. The Valiant Universe was designed from the ground up to be a merged, unified universe that shares characters, organizations and so on across all of its titles. This approach creates a synergy among the comic titles, which allows for unparalleled, epic storytelling in individual titles but also in fantastic crossover events.

Ultimately the Valiant Universe spans millennia, where decisions made at the dawn of time ripple into the distant future and today's heroes can be tomorrow's villains when the hard choices are made. This universe provides a dark and gritty tapestry of stories that *you* join and bring to life at your gaming table!

COMICS VS. RPG PUBLICATION

Readers of the *Valiant Universe* comics might notice that some of the current storylines or characters from their favorite Valiant series don't appear in this book. Since new issues for Valiant titles come out every month, stories from the most current issues were unable to be included in this volume. Rest assured that if you don't see a particular character or story arc in this book, it will likely show up in a future *Valiant Universe* sourcebook or PDF exclusive.

In the meantime, feel free to use the Character Creation rules on p. 60 to create your own version of a favorite character that might not be in the Sample Characters section. Or you could use current issues of your favorite Valiant Universe title to inspire ideas for generating your own Events. The sky's the limit!

WHAT IS A ROLEPLAYING GAME?

If you've ever read a book, seen a movie, or watched a television show where, upon finding a character saying or doing something really dangerous or foolish, you thought, "I wouldn't have said/done *that*!" then you have a good idea of what makes up the core premise of a roleplaying game. While the actions of a character in a comic book, movie, or television program may be beyond your control, in a roleplaying game, *you* control the actions of your character. *You* determine the character's fate, through decisions and actions whose outcomes range from spectacular success to tragic failure.

A roleplaying game (RPG) is essentially improvisational theater: part storytelling and part game. A single player (called the gamemaster, or GM) directs the game for a group of players who assume the roles of characters in a fictitious setting. This setting could be a "mystery adventure" set in the forty-first century where the characters traverse the colossus that is a future Japan in search of treasure and intrigue, or a "fantasy" setting within the Faraway that can be inhabited by dragons, trolls and sword-wielding barbarians alongside dinosaurs, or even a "science fiction"-style setting complete with Vine aliens, spaceships and world-crushing weaponry. The players pick a setting that they find cool and want to play in. The players then craft their own characters, providing a detailed history and personality to bring each to life. These characters have a set of statistics—numerical values that represent skills, attributes, and other abilities. The gamemaster then explains the situation in which the characters find themselves. The players, through their characters, interact with the storyline and each other's characters, acting out the plot. As the players roleplay through scenarios, the gamemaster will likely ask a given player to roll dice, and determine the success or failure of a character's attempted action based on the roll's result, using the rules of the game as a guide.

Together, the players control the storyline (adventure), which evolves much like any movie or book, but within the flexible plot directed by the gamemaster. This gamemaster's plot provides a framework and ideas for potential courses of action and outcomes, but is simply an outline of what might happen; nothing is concrete until the players become involved. If you don't want your character to walk down those darkened stairs, your character doesn't. If you think you can talk yourself out of a situation in place of blasting away with your psionics, maybe your character can. Only the story into which the players are immersed is scripted; their reactions to it are not. And so the story can be changed based on the characters' actions and their responses, creating a constantly evolving adventure.

The best part is that there is no right or wrong way to play an RPG. Some games may involve more combat and dice rolling-related situations, where other games may involve more storytelling and improvised dialogue to resolve a situation. Each group of players decides for themselves the type and style of game they enjoy playing!

TRADING IN YOUR GAMEMASTER

While *Valiant Universe* is a roleplaying game as defined above, it's different in one key element: trading in a single gamemaster for a more pure improv experience.

While traditional roleplaying is usually defined as improvisational theater, it still has a single person channeling most of the creative energy of the group. *Valiant Universe* disengages that mechanism, allowing the entire gaming group to share in the responsibility of the gamemaster's role.

What's improvisational theater? This is a form of theater where actors improvise each of the scenes of play without recourse to scripts. Complete spontaneity and playing off of each other's lines and physical cues creates a fast-paced, vibrant experience that twists and turns as each person continues to build off of what has come before.

WHAT'S NEEDED TO PLAY

To play *Valiant Universe*, you need the following:

- A group of players and a place to meet
- The contents of this book
- Tokens (of any sort) to represent Plot Points
- Something for everyone to take notes with (tablet, laptop, notepad)
- D4, D6, D8, D10, D12, D20 (or a digital equivalent)
- Imagination (can be helped by mood music)
- Drinks and snacks

A Group of Players and a Place to Meet

While roleplaying games are flexible enough to allow any number of people, most gaming groups number around four to eight players. This number of people brings a good mix of personalities to the table and ensures great cooperative play without getting too chaotic or too focused on just one or two characters.

Once a group of players have determined to play *Valiant Universe*, they'll need to work out a time and place to meet. While most roleplaying groups meet locally and regularly, each group is different and should determine where, when, and how often they'll play. One group may decide they can only get together once a week, at a friend's house, library, or college common room for four-hour sessions, while another group might have to meet "virtually" via internet chat rooms, Skype, a Google Hangout and so on, synching up their schedules for a once-a-month six-hour gaming marathon.

When playing groups meet for the first time, the players should use this first session to determine which sample characters (starting on p. 74) will best fit together to form a group. While *Valiant Universe* is presented in a way that will allow the most outlandish combinations, players may find they don't want characters that are too different from, or even too similar to, each other. Or they may simply want to more closely follow a given comic title and not have, say, Woody from *Quantum and Woody* constantly showing up in their *Shadowman*-centered campaign. This also allows the more experienced roleplayers in the group a chance to help out those who may be newer to roleplaying.

The Contents of This Book

This book is specifically organized to present the information needed to start your own adventures in the Valiant Universe. Below you'll find a summation of each chapter of this rulebook.

Title Exposés: *Valiant Universe* is a roleplaying game immersing players into the world constructed via the Valiant comics. While players can fully enjoy the world with just this volume, the comics are what truly bring the universe to life. As such, this section provides an overview of the history, locations, and themes generally covered by a given title. This provides a firm foundation for players to start exploring the comics while also offering a solid base for a host of campaign ideas players can jump right into. Like a given style, character, location, or theme of a given Exposé? Then there's your first campaign—dive right in!

Organizations: As with almost any comics universe, organizations within *Valiant Universe* are incredibly important. They act as support and lifelines to almost all characters, provide links between plot lines and characters, and often act as the framework for unfolding storylines to build the fun at a game table. While not a comprehensive list, this section covers the most important organizations, and like the Exposés section, it serves as great fodder for campaign play.

Game Rules: This section details how the game mechanics of *Valiant Universe* mesh with the improv-style of play to create a fun gaming experience, as well as character creation. Who doesn't want to create their own superhero or villain?!

Sample Characters: A myriad of sample Dossiers allow players a wide variety of characters to grab and leap into the action of improv excitement. This section includes characters straight from the comics, and a whole host of foes to test your resolve.

Event Briefs: Numerous Event Briefs provide an instant evening of action, allowing player groups to easily select one of many starting points to leap into adventure. While they're perfectly good starting points, players can also mix and match as they wish or even spin off whole new adventures based on those elements of a given Event they find the most intriguing.

Tokens

The game rules of *Valiant Universe* make use of tokens (these can be pennies, poker chips, or whatever else you have at hand that'll work), as an easy way to track Plot Points while the game unfolds (see *Plot Points*, p. 50).

Something for Everyone to Take Notes With

Roleplaying can get pretty in-depth, even in an improv-style game like *Valiant Universe*. Each character has a number of statistics and other resources that must be tracked over time to maintain continuity in the game. For this reason, character record sheets (Dossiers) are provided in this book, and may be photocopied as needed to facilitate easy recordkeeping for characters. In addition, notepads (or word processing programs/apps) may be used to record any other information the players deem important.

Additionally, some groups enjoy a synopsis of each session that can be compiled and read at a later time in order to enjoy and share their exploits. This can be particularly useful for a quick recap that can get a player who missed the previous gaming session back up to speed on what he or she missed. The session scribe can be a shared responsibility or assigned, all based on what a given playing group finds works best for them.

Dice (or a Digital Equivalent)

As will be described in the *Game Rules* section (see p. 42), the following dice are needed for game play: D4, D6, D8, D10, D12, and D20. These are also known as "polyhedral" dice and can be found in almost any hobby store.

Dice are used to help resolve actions the characters may perform where the possibility of success or failure exists. For players gaming through an online medium such as chatrooms, Skype, and so on, dice-rolling programs (often referred to as "dicebots") are a common and accessible equivalent, providing similar randomized results to the clattering of physical dice.

Imagination

Last, but by no means least, a roleplaying game—especially an improv-heavy game like *Valiant Universe*—requires imagination. It's easy for someone looking at a pencil-and-paper RPG to be intimidated by the rulebooks and the numbers. But the core focus is to have fun, to delve into a fictional reality where control over the characters' actions—the characters' fates—lies in the hands of the players controlling them. Imagination—more than the game rules—is what truly brings the player into the game; without it, a roleplaying game would merely be an exercise in mindless dice-rolling.

Music can be very effective at setting the mood for anything you might be playing. When tackling *Valiant Universe*, music can be even more powerful in sliding players into their characters. Even just a laptop or MP3 player with some music playing in the background can do the trick. There's a huge swath of excellent "superhero" soundtracks for a range of great superhero movies, many of which are available for direct purchase and/or streaming. Do a little listening and research beforehand, and you'll be able to mix and match various songs to create a certain mood during an evening's gaming session.

While you can play *Valiant Universe* with just this volume, nothing will spark the imagination like the comics themselves. Playing Renegades? Then reading a few issues of *Harbinger* will help you more fully unleash your imagination in fantastic ways.

WHAT DO PLAYERS DO?

The possibilities for gameplay in *Valiant Universe* are literally limitless. You can be a H.A.R.D. Corps team hunting down dangerous psiots, or you can be a Renegade fighting against the "evil" Harbinger Foundation trying to conquer the world. Why not be a true believer of the Harbinger Foundation, dedicated to making the world a true utopia at any cost. Or Generation Zero psiots that have no memory of a childhood before the isolation and guinea pig testing of Project Rising Spirit and are suddenly free in the world. Or you could be a brand new set of heroes (or villains) that your group created, battling alongside (or against) your favorite characters.

If you don't have a specific setting or characters in mind but you do know your group wants a specific style of play—such as action, intrigue, guns, psionics, and so on—take a moment to flip through the Title Exposés, Organizations, and Characters Dossiers sections and review their Tags. That will provide some quick yet solid direction for where to start looking for the type of games you'd like to play.

If don't already have an idea of the style of game you want to play, then simply peruse various sections. The flavor of a specific title or organization or even a character should eventually grab your attention. For example, if you flip around, stop on Torque's Dossier (see pp. 136-137), and find him interesting, then you can work from there: knowing that he's a Renegade, you'll tackle the *Harbinger* Exposé section, then the Organization pages for the Harbinger Foundation and the Renegades, then perhaps review some more Dossiers for characters involved in the *Harbinger* series. If all of that looks good, then it's a matter of reading through the Event Briefs (perhaps you'll start with *Harbinger Event Brief: The Minds' Eye*; see p. 176) to find one your group would like to start with, choosing who'll play which character, and you're off!

Finally, as noted above, while this book is designed as a standalone volume, if you're still struggling for a flavor you'll enjoy, grab some Valiant Universe comics and see what storylines and characters speak to you and your group.

It's All About the Fun Factor

Valiant Universe is all about comic books and is not based or dependent on real-world science. Though the Valiant Universe prides itself on its realistic take on superheroes, don't be sheepish about rattling off cool-sounding technobabble to explain why something fun happened, such as why a character's telenecrotic Power turned an oncoming Vine soldier into a puddle of toxic goo. Much of the fun comes from building an exciting adventure with your friends. Try not to get caught up in technicalities or in mundane, real-world things. Unless, of course, you're a long-time Valiant Universe fan that enjoys exploring the more "realistic" nature of superheroes…then by all means!

Always remember this rule of thumb: if something makes the game more fun for players, do it (even if it sounds crazy or is technically against the rules)! Let your imaginations run wild!

WINNING, LOSING AND VAGUENESS

While *Valiant Universe* is a game, it's not a game dedicated to winning or losing. The characters players embody are extraordinary—they face a myriad of threats and usually come out on top. Whether that's due to courage, luck, or grim determination is up to the roleplaying to determine. So what if a team of heroes fails to achieve the objectives set out in an Event Brief? Keep going and weave that plot twist into the next storyline. Make it work!

Valiant Universe rules are intentionally vague on many points where a traditional RPG would be more detailed. As previously mentioned, Dossiers give many statistics for a character, yet some aspects are left to the player during gameplay, like a movement stat, for instance. There's no real limit on how far a character can move in a turn—it's entirely dependent on the current circumstances and what the player wants to do during his Narration.

If a player encounters a situation where there is no applicable stat or number, the player should consider the situation and what he wants to accomplish in his turn and check if there's an appropriate Cue on the Dossier to use in a Narration. There's really no right or wrong way to handle a situation.

If a disagreement does crop up during gameplay, just remember that the current Lead Narrator has the final say on what can and can't happen.

ARCHER & ARMSTRONG

TAGS/CUES

- assassin ● immortal ● the Sect ● the Boon ● the Faraway
- time travel ● aliens ● technology ● secret societies

THE ASSASSIN

The world is a lot stranger than one might think. Young Obadiah Archer thought he had always lived in the Promised Land theme park, a place of safety in a corrupt and dangerous world. Along with his twenty-two foster brothers and sisters, Obie

trained to hunt down and smite the Evil One, the Antichrist, He Who is Not to be Named. When the time came for him to fulfill his mission, his biggest regret was he had to leave behind his adopted sister Mary-Maria—the girl he dreamed would share his life—as he left the only home he remembered. Of course, Obie didn't know that Project Rising Spirit, a secret firm experimenting with psionic powers, had abducted him when he was very young, and he didn't remember the surgery that activated his fighting abilities or the weeks of training and testing in PRS's underground Nursery facility.

Archer knew the world could be dangerous, but he was certain holding fast to his belief in his God would keep him safe and focused. But that was before the Evil One turned out to be an immortal poet named Armstrong, a man who wanted nothing more than to enjoy life. That was also before Obie discovered his parents were part of the Sect, a secretive organization that pulled the world's strings from the shadows. And before visions of a mysterious man began giving him instructions, before he learned his "God-given" talent allowed him to access information stored in the mystical Akashic Record, before Mary-Maria seemingly came back from the dead, and before he was transported out of time and abducted by a flying saucer and … Well, you get the picture.

THE IMMORTAL

Aram Anni-Padda—a.k.a. Armstrong—witnessed firsthand the destruction that grief and despair could bring to the world. Literally. When Aram and his two brothers ventured into the Faraway, a land outside of time, Aram's youngest brother Gilad was killed while trying to retrieve a mysterious Faraway artifact known as the Boon. In his grief, Aram's elder brother Ivar triggered the artifact in hopes that it would revive Gilad, but instead, the Boon drew the life forces out of the inhabitants in the ancient city of Ur and infused them into Aram. For thousands of years the three Anni-Padda brothers suffered the consequences of Ivar's actions. Ivar was trapped in the time stream while locked in a timeless prison known as the Aleph, and Gilad was resurrected by the Earth and fought an unending war in its service. Aram, however, wandered the world alone, with the thousands of life forces from Ur trapped inside him. He watched civilizations rise and fall and saw people commit unspeakable acts of brutality and perform unimaginable acts of beauty. Aram came to trust the basic goodness of people and be wary of governments. For three millennia, factions of the Sect hounded him, bent on either torturing the secrets of power and immortality out of him or trying to kill him outright. So when a Sect assassin named Obadiah Archer tracked him to a New York bar, Armstrong expected a routine confrontation, a reasonable facsimile of the many that had gone before: he'd waste too much time trying to talk sense into his attacker before putting the idiot down and moving on.

Except Archer turned out to be different. Sure, the Sect had conditioned him to be full of his own self-righteousness—only a true believer would think he could take down Armstrong. And of course underneath it all was a good kid trying to do the right thing—only innocents could be twisted so completely. But there was something about the kid, a spark that reminded Armstrong of his brothers.

THE BOON

When Archer realized his parents were willing to kill him for the sake of their own ambitions to learn the secrets of the Boon and the immortality it would bestow, Armstrong expected the kid to throw out everything he'd been raised to believe. But Archer's faith remained strong. His parents exploiting God to do evil didn't make God evil, and as a servant of God, Archer's duty was to stop his parents' schemes. He proposed a partnership with Armstrong, and Armstrong accepted.

To activate the Boon, the device that gave Armstrong immortality, the Sect needed six artifacts: the Fulcrum, the Inclined Plane, the Wedge, the Torque, the Axle, and the Sphere. After finding the last few pieces of the Boon and recovering the rest from Armstrong, Archer's parents traveled to the La-Chen monastery high in the mountains of Ladakh, but Archer and Armstrong were not far behind.

At the monastery, the Sect faction known as the Green Dragon Lamas held the monolith into which the six simple machines must be imbedded for the Boon to work. In the short span of time between Thelma Archer activating the Boon and Obadiah Archer destroying it, the Boon was able to harvest the life forces of the Green Dragon Lamas, Obie's parents, and their children. However, the Boon's energy poured into Mary-Maria, giving her a tiny fraction of Armstrong's power, and the intact egos of Joseph and Thelma Archer were deposited in her brain. Their consciousnesses were autonomous—able to argue with each other and verbally abuse Mary-Maria—but they could neither control her body nor force her to obey them.

THE FARAWAY AND THE SECT CIVIL WAR

With her parents' help, Mary-Maria convinced the Sect Faction known as the One Percent to bankroll her raid on PRS to find a gateway to the Faraway and bring back another Boon. When she returned from the Faraway empty-handed, the One Percent sold her to another Sect faction, the Sisters of Perpetual Darkness, who intended to burn her at the stake. When the Black Bloc—yet another faction of the Sect—interrupted her execution, Mary-Maria took command of her captors and repelled the invaders.

Realizing fighting the Sect piecemeal was a waste of time, Archer set a trap—using the unwitting Armstrong as bait—to lure them all to an undersea pyramid for a single battle he hoped would decapitate and cripple the Sect factions. All but the Vine responded, but Mary-Maria and the Sisters of Perpetual Darkness sprang a trap of their own, flooding the pyramid and attempting to kill them all.

Archer saved the leaders of the Hashish Eaters, the Gnomes of Zürich, the Master Builders, and the Black Bloc, all of whom have sworn fealty to him as the leader of the Sect.

BLOODSHOT (AND H.A.R.D. CORPS)

TAGS/CUES

- Project Rising Spirit ● nanite technology ● military action ● regeneration
- lost identity ● false memories ● psiots ● bio-config implants

FALSE MEMORIES, REAL MISSIONS

The secretive security firm Project Rising Spirit sent a nanite-infused operative known as Bloodshot to eliminate a target in Afghanistan. Operating under the illusion of rescuing an old friend, Bloodshot infiltrated the terrorist base, but the mission was a trap intended to capture him.

Bloodshot awakened strapped to a chair, surrounded by equipment and technicians. Former PRS researcher Dr. Emmanuel Kuretich told Bloodshot that his memories of family and friends were all false: PRS was using these implanted memories as motivation to convince Bloodshot to perform missions for the organization. Unable to handle Kuretich's revelations, Bloodshot broke free and escaped, only to run into a PRS strike team that filled him with bullets.

On a PRS cargo plane, Bloodshot's nanite technology regenerated his body, and he awoke. Urged on by the ghosts of his false families, he escaped confinement, killed all the soldiers onboard, and crashed the plane before it could reach the nearest PRS facility.

NEW ALLIES, OLD ENEMIES

Bloodshot awakened in an ambulance and used his nanites' control over machines to stop the vehicle. He then forced the paramedic Kara Murphy to drive him to Albuquerque, New Mexico—where his memories were telling him "home" was.

In the Nevada desert, Dr. Kuretich extracted memories Bloodshot could not access and uncovered a buried PRS town whose population had been slaughtered by Bloodshot years ago to hide a major nanotech incident. Meanwhile, PRS brought a psiot prisoner, code name Pulse, into the hunt for Bloodshot. During the earlier town massacre, Pulse had been instrumental in recapturing Bloodshot, and PRS hoped she could repeat this feat.

In Albuquerque, Bloodshot discovered the memory of his wife was based on a woman whose image Dr. Kuretich had used. A mysterious, ghostly image of Bloodshot's "son"—a psychological manifestation of the nanites in Bloodshot's bloodstream—warned him that the enemy was closing, and the resulting confrontation left several PRS agents dead and Pulse on the loose. Bloodshot and Kara tracked Pulse down and offered her the chance for revenge against her former captors.

A NEW MISSION

Determined to learn his true identity since he did not have his real memories anymore, Bloodshot set his sights on taking the fight directly to PRS. With the nanites' direction and the help of Dr. Kuretich, Kara, and Pulse, Bloodshot infiltrated the PRS facility known as the Vault, in hopes of finding the mainframe that stored his identity. After he fought through PRS guards and a deadly, cybernetic combat team—code name Chainsaw—Bloodshot found himself not in the Vault, but the Nursery, where PRS held young psiots—humans with neurologically based preternatural abilities. Here he was forced to confront part of his past.

Over the years, PRS had used Bloodshot to kidnap children possessing psiot abilities. These abducted kids were taken to the Nursery, where they were subjected to cruel tests and training for their abilities. At first the psiot children ran away in fear or used their powers against Bloodshot, but he fought to protect the children from their sadistic psiot nanny, Gamma. Unfortunately Gamma broke Pulse's neck during the skirmish. With her dying breaths, Pulse extracted a promise from Bloodshot to look after the children. Bloodshot and the children fled into the desert, but another group of the psiot children managed to hijack a PRS helicopter and fly it out of the base.

Meanwhile, Dr. Kuretich kept his new employer, the incredibly powerful psiot Toyo Harada apprised of the situation, as Harada was interested in adding these children to his own collection of psiots.

THE HARADA PROTOCOL

Out in the Nevada desert, Bloodshot led the children to a ghost town, where he had left a small cache of supplies. There, Harada and a small team of psiots from the Harbinger Foundation, Harada's secret army of psiots, arrived to take the children. Upon seeing Harada in person, the nanites unexpectedly overrode Bloodshot's control of his body, enacting the Harada Protocol, deeply embedded nanite programming that PRS had designed to kill Harada at any cost.

Despite Bloodshot suffering horrific damage, the Harada Protocol forced Bloodshot to get close enough to Harada to spray him with nanites that would eat him apart from the inside, but Harada fought Bloodshot back. Moments away from death, Harada and used one of his Foundation students as a dumping ground for the malicious nanites before they could kill him. Harada survived—barely. As a diversion, Bloodshot detonated every building in the town with pre-planted explosives, and his companions used a stashed military vehicle to escape.

As Bloodshot slowly recovered, he learned that the second group of escaped psiot children had crashed their helicopter into the Bellagio in Las Vegas. The children accompanying Bloodshot convinced him to head to Vegas to reunite the two groups of psiots. Critically injured from the fight with Harada and desperately in need of protein to refuel his nanites, he entered a nearby slaughterhouse. The place was a trap. Kuretich and a small team of soldiers dismembered Bloodshot while a second team attempted to capture the children. Bloodshot Left for dead and moments from certain death, Bloodshot's nanites shut down the building's power. He then triggered a synaptic burst, which stunned Kuretich and his team. Bloodshot then enacted his revenge on his former partner and recovered his strength.

LAS VEGAS SHOWDOWN

Bloodshot and the children slipped past a military blockade to reach Las Vegas, only to run into the Renegades, a team of psiots led by former Harbinger Foundation member Peter Stanchek. The two groups clashed on the Vegas Strip in front of the Bellagio. During the battle, H.A.R.D. Corps, a PRS team of recently recommissioned psiot hunters, dropped on the resort. Using their implants, which allowed them to download psiot abilities from their Lifeline support station, H.A.R.D. Corps eliminated some of the psiot children before Bloodshot could reach them. The fight against the Renegades weakened Bloodshot to the point where a rejuvenated Harada beat him to a pulp and captured him to study the nanites.

ENTER H.A.R.D. CORPS

At the Harbinger Foundation, Harada extracted most of Bloodshot's nanites. Shortly thereafter, a H.A.R.D. Corps team infiltrated the headquarters, intending to retrieve Bloodshot for PRS, as Bloodshot was the one weapon that had come closest to actually eliminating Harada. The team fought its way out of the Foundation's El Segundo, California, headquarters but were forced to leave Bloodshot's nanites behind. Without his full complement of nanites, Bloodshot's abilities were inhibited due to an autoimmune reaction: Harada had affected the nanites' protein absorption, which meant Bloodshot required special nutrient baths to keep his nanites functioning.

PRS's new director, Morris Kozol, offered Bloodshot command of H.A.R.D. Corps for a mission to retrieve his nanites and thus keep them out of Harada's hands. Kozol sweetened the deal by promising to reveal Bloodshot's real identity, the driving force behind Bloodshot's personal war against PRS. Bloodshot agreed.

During the mission, most of H.A.R.D. Corps searched for the nanites while Major Palmer—H.A.R.D. Corps' second-in-command—and Bloodshot went after Harada. Harada sent Bloodshot several floors down in the facility, where Bloodshot discovered his missing nanites had become sentient. This artificial intelligence, calling itself Lysander, wanted to take the rest of the nanites from Bloodshot. Instead, the nanites in Bloodshot's body overwhelmed and absorbed the sentient nanites.

THE RETURN OF ORECK

During the Las Vegas showdown between Bloodshot, the Renegades, H.A.R.D. Corps, and the Harbinger Foundation, PRS Director Simon Oreck had fled the country, leaving the organization in the hands of Morris Kozol. Oreck later kidnapped Kozol in Nigeria.

When H.A.R.D. Corps landed in Nigeria to search for Kozol, they discovered Oreck has his own team of psiots, the Specialists. Bloodshot and most of H.A.R.D. Corps escaped into the jungle. While several team members rescued their captured teammates, Bloodshot took on two Specialists, defeated them, then chased down Oreck.

Bloodshot caught Oreck just as the former PRS director was about to escape. Oreck offered Bloodshot a deal: if Bloodshot let him go, he'd give Bloodshot a batch of brand new nanites that would reprogram the original nanites and abolish the flaw that prevented them from working properly. Bloodshot accepted the deal, releasing Oreck in exchange for the nanites.

ETERNAL WARRIOR

TAGS/CUES

- immortal ● Sumerian ● Sword of the Earth ● Geomancers
- war against the gods ● House of the Earth ● House of the Dead

THE FIST AND STEEL OF THE EARTH

Millennia ago, the Anni-Padda brothers—Ivar, Aram, and Gilad—were three of the leading citizens of the Sumerian city of Ur. The king, resentful of their popularity among Ur's populace, dispatched them on what he thought was a foolish quest: to find the fabled land of Faraway. But the brothers did find the Faraway, where they found the Boon, a device that sustained life. Gilad died during the Boon's retrieval, and Ivar, mad with grief, triggered the device in hopes of resurrecting his lost brother, despite Aram's protests. The Boon's energies infused Aram with immortality, but at the cost of nearly every other life in Ur except Ivar's.

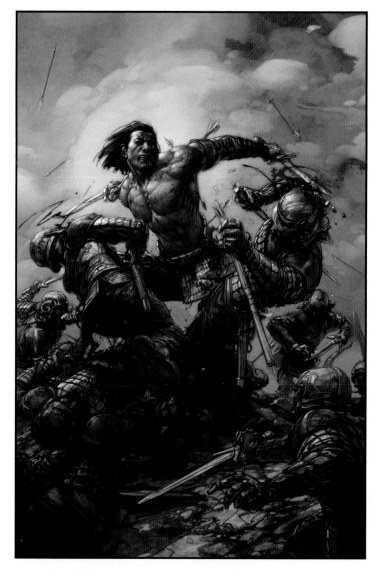

The Earth claimed Gilad for itself, and he was restored to life to serve the House of the Earth as its Eternal Warrior. His duty was to protect the Geomancer, a lineage of individuals known as the Speaker for the Earth. Gilad loyally served the House of the Earth as the Eternal Warrior, and six thousand years ago, he had a son and a daughter—Mitu and Xaran.

After Gilad's children had reached adulthood, an army from the House of the Dead threatened Gilad's tribe. He led his warriors to confront the enemy, taking Mitu along but ordering Xaran to help evacuate the tribe's noncombatants. Despite all of Gilad's skills, the House of the Dead was winning the battle. Disobeying her father's orders to stay behind, Xaran led a herd of elephants through the enemy army and turned the tide of battle. Xaran forged onward into the enemies' camp and began slaughtering the cult's women and children. Gilad and Mitu tried to stop her, but Xaran grievously wounded both of them in her bloodlust, leaving Gilad with a spear embedded in his torso. In front of Gilad, Xaran cut her brother's throat and disappeared into the countryside before Gilad could recover.

Unable to locate his daughter, Gilad continued serving the Earth, but constant warfare wore him down and made him question his role. Late in the nineteenth century, when the Geomancer instructed him to kill a woman and some children, Gilad walked away from the responsibility he had devoted a thousand lifetimes to and hung up the mantle of the Eternal Warrior for good. Or so he thought.

Living on the African savannah and killing only to eat, Gilad lived in relative peace until, after six thousand years of silence, Xaran showed up on his doorstep. Until recently, she had served as the Sword of the House of the Wild before she betrayed the Wild's inner circle and slaughtered them on the Geomancer's orders. Gilad's retirement had upset the delicate balances between the Houses, and Xaran came to ask Gilad to return to his duties as the Earth's Eternal Warrior. Gilad refused, but when members of the House of the Wild showed up in pursuit of Xaran, Gilad killed them all.

Reluctantly brought back into the war, Gilad and his daughter tracked down the current Geomancer Buck McHenry, who was held captive by the House of the Wheel. After rescuing McHenry, Gilad demanded the Geomancer tell him where to find the Earth Mother, the deity the House of the Earth served. McHenry said the Earth Mother could be found at the Methuselah Tree, in the White Mountains. Gilad announced that he intended to kill the gods, starting with the Earth Mother herself.

When Gilad and Xaran reached the Methuselah Tree, they found Rangers of the Earth waiting for them. In the ensuing fight, Gilad and Xaran defeated the Rangers. The Earth Mother warned Gilad that destroying the Methuselah Tree would open the hidden door buried beneath the Tree's roots. Behind that door lay the place where Nergal, the House of the Dead's god, was imprisoned, and if the Tree died, Nergal would be released in two thousand years. Gilad, determined to break free of the gods' influence, destroyed the Methuselah Tree regardless.

THE FUTURE: THE WAR NEVER ENDS

In the forty-first century, an older Gilad was the leader of a small community in the ruins of Little Rock, Arkansas. Known as the Eternal Emperor and Godkiller, Gilad's campaign to rid the world of the gods was successful. But civilization had regressed to a pre-industrial level, and Gilad concentrated his efforts on protecting his people.

When a large mechanical creature attacked the settlement, Gilad killed the creature. Upon examining the remains, he discovered the creature was powered by an unstable nuclear reactor that was about to go critical. He managed to get most of the community into a bomb shelter before the device exploded, but Gilad realized his people had developed radiation poisoning from the fallout. Taking only his young granddaughter Caroline, Gilad set out to find the creature's origin and an antidote for the radiation poisoning.

A meeting with a slaver caravan revealed that a city had been building the creatures. When a slaver offered to buy Caroline, Gilad killed him and gained enough respect from the rest of the caravan to gain safe passage to the city, called Big Town.

Claiming to be looking for work as a warrior, Gilad was allowed into Big Town. Once inside the city, a slaver tried to take Caroline. Gilad killed him and instigated an uprising, and when he killed the slaver boss, the slavers declared Gilad the new boss. While a slave named Namir gave him a tour of the city, Gilad discovered, to his horror, that the city had an unshielded nuclear reactor that was poisoning everyone in the area. He was ready to leave the city to its fate when he learned Caroline had already received a deadly dose of radiation.

Along with a band of former slaves and guards, Gilad traveled to the king who had built the mechanical monsters, reasoning that this king would have a supply of anti-radiation medicine. After traveling through rough territory and defeating both natural and robotic creatures, the party reached the town run by King Samuel.

The king had enough medicine on hand to cure Caroline and Namir, but he claimed the reason he was building robots was to defend against a death cult rampaging across the land. The lab that manufactured the medicine was surrounded by this cult, and Samuel had only a few guards and robots to defend the city. He proposed that Gilad lead his forces to rescue the lab, and in return he would give Gilad enough medicine for his people. Gilad agreed.

Using a store of old weapons, Gilad drew the death cult away from the bunker and wiped them out. He also destroyed all the old weapons and returned to his people with enough anti-radiation medicine to cure them all. But Gilad saw that Caroline, a bright and gifted child, had begun making machines on her own. He feared she would one day destroy the world.

HARBINGER

TAGS/CUES

- psiots ● the Renegades ● Harbinger Foundation ● Bleeding Monk
- mind squall ● Harbinger Wars ● activation ● Omega ● mental construct

Why is it considered heroic when a person with great power decides what's right for the rest of us?
—Kris Hathaway

Across the world, a new breed of man has awoken. Among the teeming billions of human beings on Earth, only a handful display psionic potential. Only two known living pisots were born with their powers already unlocked and thus were spared the perilous process of activation, which claims one in four of potential candidates who would walk among gods. Gifted with a kaleidoscope of mental abilities, these few bright souls wield incredible power.

Even among these extraordinary specimens, one man commands raw, sprawling ability which eclipses all others. Blessed with a depth of psionic capabilities that defy description and cloaked in the largest corporation the world has ever known, Toyo Harada has begun organizing his fellow psiots in a quest to remake the world and save humanity. Whether out of fear, hope, or a simple desire to be near such power, many have fallen in with this would-be savior.

Harada was the Omega, the first man of the nuclear age, the mightiest living being to ever walk the Earth.

Until now.

OMEGA RISING

Toyo Harada grew up outside Hiroshima, Japan, living a simple life in a small village with his family. That peaceful life was erased by the first atomic bomb. The explosion destroyed everything the youth had ever known but somehow activated his latent abilities. Harada drifted from a refugee camp to a life alone in the wilds, all the while receiving visions of a mysterious bleeding man in monk's robes. After traveling to the Flying Nest Hermitage in Tibet shortly after his eighteenth birthday, Harada located the Bleeding Monk, whose vast precognitive powers would guide the young psiot.

Those visions of the future also revealed that Harada would not remain alone: another Omega-level psiot, Peter Stanchek, was born in the last years of the twentieth century. Unlike Harada, Peter's powers were active from birth, a nearly-unique circumstance that left the boy unable to control his vast powers. Peter tried to activate his own father's latent psiot abilities, but the attempt left him in a coma, and Peter's mother checked him into a psychiatric ward. The youth would spend the next few years enduring a brutal regimen of so-called treatments until he escaped as a teenager with his only friend, Joe Irons.

Peter was still unable to control his powers, especially his telepathic abilities, and while living on the streets, he became addicted to the pharmaceuticals he used to drown out the minds around him. Peter was also trying to stay one step ahead of agents from Project Rising Spirit, an organization actively abducting and experimenting on psiots, but Harada intervened and offered Peter sanctuary and training with the Harbinger Foundation.

Peter proved a poor fit for the institution. Though he finally learned a measure of control over his powers, he rejected the Foundation's structure and demands, and he often clashed with his fellow students, who were both jealous and fearful of his powers. Also, the Bleeding Monk prophesied that Peter would be the "Great Destroyer," so Harada was eager to keep Peter in check to prevent this from happening. To that end, Harada ordered Joe's murder, expecting Peter to blame himself for his friend's death.

Instead, Peter saw through the ruse and confronted Harada in a violent altercation in the penthouse of the Foundation's Pittsburgh offices. Peter tore through the Foundation's senior staff, but Harada himself defeated Peter easily. Peter escaped only with the assistance from Harada's psiot attendant, Livewire, and a daring rescue by Faith Herbert, an eager young girl and psiot flyer Peter had activated during Harada's experiments.

RENEGADE'S CHALLENGE

Recovering from the disastrous battle, Peter contacted Kris Hathaway, a childhood friend. Though furious with him for briefly mind-controlling her into loving him, Kris wanted to oppose dominating organizations like Harada's Harbinger Foundation, and she saw Peter as her best chance to fight back. She, Peter, and Faith staged a brief clash between Harada and Project Rising Spirit and attacked a Foundation recruiter to retrieve the names of several latent psiots.

In Louisiana, Peter activated pyrokinetic Charlene Dupre before moving onto Georgia, where he activated John "Torque" Torkelson, a psiot capable of projecting a burly physical shell around his infirm body. Moments after Torque's activation, a PRS strike force apprehended Peter and most of his team. Only Faith remained free, and she succeeded in rescuing the rest of the group.

In search of direction, Peter received his own vision from the Bleeding Monk, who had departed Harada's service for parts unknown. The monk showed Peter a group of psiot children who escaped PRS custody and were in a standoff with their forces in Las Vegas. Slipping past the military blockade awaiting the arrival of the cybernetic assassin Bloodshot, Peter and his newly christened Renegades joined forces with the psiot children, who called themselves Generation Zero.

The plan Kris developed quickly crumbled before Bloodshot's tenacity. PRS's H.A.R.D. Corps strike team gained the upper hand until the arrival of Harada himself, who succeeded in claiming both Generation Zero and the Renegades.

GATHERING STORM

Harada's victory, though decisive, was not total. Peter and his Renegades survived, and Peter himself remained both too valuable to kill outright and too volatile to fully control. Instead, Harada and his top telepaths constructed a mental prison for the unconscious Renegades, a representation of a perfect day for each member.

But even Harada's powers were tested, both by his own physical exhaustion and the more willful Renegades' unwillingness to accept their new reality. As cracks formed in the false reality, Harada's extreme exhaustion pushed him to finally succumb to a mind squall, a violent, volcanic psychic blast that destroyed the minds of nearby Foundation members. The Renegades once again escaped, vowing that the time had come to stop running and take the fight to Harada.

The Renegades' opening move was to contact young Octavio Gonzalez, an adept hacker known online as @x, who had leaked a massive stolen database of PRS secrets. Gonzalez was determined to drag both the Harbinger Foundation and Project Rising Spirit into the light. Though damaging to the Foundation, the leak may have made the Renegades' plight even worse, as Harada now stands poised to simultaneously reveal his true nature to the world and finally reject its laws and morality.

The Harbinger Foundation possesses nearly unlimited resources and a cadre of highly trained psiots led by the most powerful of their kind. But the young Renegades have not backed down, and Peter may yet hold the power to change the world…

HARBINGER WARS

TAGS/CUES

- control of psiots ● the Harbinger Foundation ● Project Rising Spirit
- Bloodshot ● the Renegades ● Generation Zero ● Las Vegas

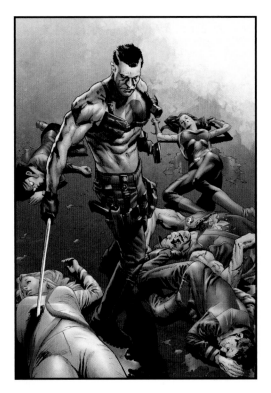

THE GAME

Across the globe, organizations that know about the existence of psiots, individuals that exhibit psionic abilities, harbor different views toward them. Some fear psiots in general, believing them threats to national security, so they seek to either contain or destroy psiots at all cost. Others see psionic powers as necessary evils that must be understood and, if possible, employed as weapons. Still other groups believe psiots should be protected and treated as human beings with free will.

When theses opposing philosophies collided, the Harbinger Wars resulted. Due to various attempts to suppress public knowledge of psionic abilities, most struggles regarding psiots took place out of the public eye. Under normal circumstances, the Harbinger Wars would have changed that, but all concerned parties went to considerable lengths to cover up what really happened during the Las Vegas incident.

THE PLAYERS

Several organizations and groups had important roles in shaping the events of the Harbinger Wars.

The Harbinger Foundation: Toyo Harada, founder and CEO of Harada Global Conglomerates and the most powerful known psiot on Earth, established the Harbinger Foundation as a secret haven for psiots. The Foundation trains psiots to use their powers in ways that they will not be a danger to themselves or others, and the most promising students graduate into Harada's elite cadre known as Eggbreakers. Harada believes that, for the betterment of society, psiots alone should decide the course of the future. Others view the Foundation as a prison that holds psiots against their will, for the purpose of being troops in Harada's personal army.

Prominent Harbinger Foundation representatives during the Harbinger Wars include Toyo Harada; the Bleeding Monk; Eggbreakers Ion and Stronghold; and Foundation student Saturn.

Project Rising Spirit and H.A.R.D. Corps: Project Rising Spirit is a secret US government-funded firm whose primary mission is the application of non-traditional weapons platforms, such as nanites and psionics. H.A.R.D. Corps— Harbinger Active Resistance Division—represents a department of PRS dedicated to the containment and eradication of psiot threats. PRS's Project Bloodshot rendered H.A.R.D. Corps obsolete years before, but the Harbinger Wars prompted Acting Director Kozol to reactivate the team.

Notable PRS personnel include Director Simon Oreck (MIA); Acting Director Morris Kozol; former researcher Dr. Emmanuel Kuretich (deceased); and H.A.R.D. Corps operatives Major Charlie Palmer, Hammerhead (KIA), Lifeline (KIA), Maniac, and Shakespeare (KIA).

Bloodshot and PRS Escapees: The man known only as Bloodshot was originally a PRS project involving the weaponization of nanites. PRS wiped his brain countless times, so he has no memory of who he truly is. PRS defector Dr. Kuretich agreed to help Bloodshot find his identity. Bloodshot infiltrated PRS Research Facility Theta in Nevada, but instead of finding the servers that housed his personal records, he found the Nursery, a laboratory that experimented on children with psionic powers. Bloodshot rescued as many of these children from PRS as he could.

The freed children accompanying Bloodshot at the beginning of the Wars include Clem (Headspace), Kalea (Cloud), Nora (Serenade), Ian (Ramsey), Graham, Baxter (Titan), Katherine Zygos, and Maggie.

The Renegades: Before the Harbinger Foundation recruited Peter Stanchek, he was a powerful psiot on the run from PRS. When Peter learned that Harada had lied to him and killed his best friend Joe, he escaped the Foundation. With the help of childhood friend Kris Hathaway, he began searching for latent psiots and activating their powers with the intent of someday toppling Harada's tyranny and freeing the psiots the Harbinger Foundation keeps prisoner.

During the Harbinger Wars, the Renegades' roster comprised Peter "Sting" Stanchek, Kris Hathaway, Faith "Zephyr" Herbert, Charlene "Flamingo" Dupre, and John "Torque" Torkelson.

Generation Zero: Among the psiot children at Research Facility Theta was PRS's A-team, a small group of older children and young adults used as a strike force for sensitive missions. PRS controlled the A-team by implanting micro-shrapnel bundles in their brains: these bundles would detonate if a child ever refused to follow orders. After the A-team and a few of the other children escaped on a helicopter and crash-landed in Las Vegas, the team's leader, a young healer named Cronus, announced his group to the world as Generation Zero.

Generation Zero comprises the following psiots: Christian (Cronus), Tara (The Telic), Wee Mad Mac (Traveler), Isiah (Little Castle), Pier (Hive), Jessica (Lady Astral), Simon (Atomus), James Zygos, Monica Jim (Animalia), and Jillian (Shadow).

THE WARS

The foundations for the conflict between these factions had been laid long before the so-called Harbinger Wars started. Bloodshot's assault on Research Facility Theta in Nevada was merely the match that lit the powder keg. The attack freed nearly two dozen psiot children of varying ages, powers, and threat levels. A full half of the psiots accompanied Bloodshot out into the desert; the remainder escaped in a helicopter that crashed into the penthouse of the Bellagio hotel and casino on the Las Vegas Strip. The crash prompted the US to place a military cordon around Las Vegas to prevent the psiots from escaping the city.

Though Peter Stanchek had escaped the Harbinger Foundation, PRS had never stopped pursuing him or his Renegades. After the Renegades eluded the pursuing PRS operatives, Peter received a vision from the Bleeding Monk. The vision showed Generation Zero at the Bellagio, and Bloodshot—the so-called "psiot killer"—on his way to kill or capture the rest of Generation Zero. Determined to help these kids, the Renegades slipped past the blockade and linked up with Cronus and his fellow psiots. Together, the two groups prepared for Bloodshot's arrival.

On his way to Vegas to reunite the two groups of psiot children, Bloodshot encountered Toyo Harada. Harada revealed that Dr. Kuretich, who led Bloodshot to the children, had been working for the Harbinger Foundation, and the Foundation aimed to take Bloodshot's psiots into custody. During the confrontation, a deep-seated PRS program triggered in Bloodshot's brain: the Harada Protocol. This protocol, which not even Dr. Kuretich had known about, almost resulted in Harada's death at Bloodshot's hands. Shortly thereafter, Bloodshot confronted Kuretich and killed him for betraying him to Harada.

Believing the Renegades in Las Vegas to be Harbinger Foundation students, Bloodshot pulled no punches when he and the psiots accompanying him fought with the Renegades on the Vegas Strip. The resulting struggle saw the Renegades limp away from the Vegas Strip only to end up imprisoned by Harada, and Bloodshot also suffered disastrous injuries.

At the beginning of the Vegas incident, PRS went into damage control mode. PRS reactivated its long-defunct Harbinger Active Resistance Division. Four H.A.R.D. Corps field operatives were dispatched to Vegas and given simple instructions regarding the Generation Zero psiots: "shoot to kill." During the Renegades' battle with Bloodshot, H.A.R.D. Corps landed on the Bellagio rooftop and killed some of Generation Zero's members before the psiots fought back. Harada, still hoping to absorb some of the psiots into the Harbinger Foundation, led an attack on Research Facility Theta, which cut off H.A.R.D. Corps from their support system. Without access to their powers, only two H.A.R.D. Corps members survived.

With the Renegades on the run, H.A.R.D. Corps defeated, and Bloodshot near death, Harada and his psiots arrived in Las Vegas. By manipulating Bloodshot into gathering all the children into one place and capturing Peter Stanchek's Renegades, Harada came out on top. He swept in and claimed all of the psiot children—and even Bloodshot's mangled body—for the Harbinger Foundation, further enlarging his psionic army.

QUANTUM AND WOODY

TAGS/CUES

● odd couple ● world's worst superhero team ● mysterious energy ● offensive and defensive powers ● Edison's Radical Acquisitions ● mad science ● the goat ● *KLANG!*

WARNING!!!

If you haven't yet read *Quantum and Woody*, you're doing the entire world a terrible disservice. (Plus, you've missed out on all the good jokes.) No, seriously. Good jokes make you laugh, and laughter makes the world a better place—which means reading *Quantum and Woody* sorta makes you like an honest-to-goodness superhero. So go save the world a little and have some fun doing it (because the jokes are *really* funny).

This has been a public service announcement.

WORST. SUPERHEROES. EVER.

You probably think someone that calls himself a "superhero" would be a shining paragon of selflessness, responsibility, courage, and heroism—a skilled fighter capable of handling just about any situation thrown his way. For most superheroes, that'd be a safe bet. For the duo known as Quantum and Woody, though, you'd might as well just douse your cash in gasoline and set it on fire. Quantum and Woody are hands down, bar none, the absolute *worst* superheroes on this planet. (I mean, what super duo has a *goat* for a sidekick? Granted, said goat shoots *laser beams* from its eyes, but that's beside the point.) Sadly, Quantum and Woody pose more of a danger to innocent people than they do the weird-science psychopaths they somehow keep (accidentally) running into, and they crack more jokes than they do skulls.

To make sure you don't let these inept "heroes" needlessly endanger your own life with their recklessness, here is a look at how all of these shenanigans started, so you can learn to recognize and avoid this clueless pair before it's too late.

THE SEEDS OF MISCHIEF

Quantum and Woody have been at the job of making the world a less safe place since long before they acquired their superhuman abilities. Eric and Woody Henderson have always gotten themselves in trouble. The Hendersons were an African-American family hoping to adopt a foster child, but when Eric was young, his mother passed away. Eric's father Derek decided it would be a good idea to go through with adopting a foster child because that's what Eric's mother wanted. Enter Woody—a young Caucasian boy and Eric's complete polar opposite.

Though Eric strived toward good grades, Woody aimed at being the class clown. Woody's big mouth and devil-may-care attitude was always getting him in fights at school, and Eric often got dragged along for the ride. (Some school records claim some of the fights started when Woody defended Eric from a classmate's racist comments, but this doesn't excuse such bad behavior.) It doesn't end there. At a Dallas Science Convention, the boys and two goats were involved in the destruction of expensive, high-tech equipment that their father was working on.

Now, many are quick to blame Woody's irresponsible nature for all of this duo's problems, but Eric is far from innocent. For example, to get dear old Dad's attention, this otherwise well-meaning kid blew up his school's chemistry lab (which Woody took the blame for and then disappeared), and after three years of service in the Army, he got himself dishonorably discharged for taking revenge on a soldier that ruined their commander's military career.

To top everything off, these estranged brothers got into a fistfight *at their own father's funeral* and knocked the casket into the grave. Of course, this only increased D.C. Detective Alejandra Cejudo's suspicions that these two had murdered their father to get an early inheritance.

EXPLOSIONS!

Eric and Woody's father worked on experimental technology for Quantum Laboratories, so they assumed someone had probably killed him to get their hands on it. These two decided to do some gumshoeing of their own, by —you guessed it—gaining unlawful entry into their father's lab. (They probably figured when you're already under suspicion for *murder*, a little B&E isn't such a big deal.) While looking for clues in the lab, the two got into another altercation, which resulted in Eric (accidentally) triggering the machinery in the room. As the energy began collecting, Eric and Woody realized the lab had only one containment suit—which they (naturally) fought over and ended up destroying just before the lab blew sky high.

Miraculously, Eric and Woody survived, and each was wearing one of the two control bracelets from the containment suit; however, their bodies were slowly dissipating into energy. The lab's explosion brought the D.C. police, and when Eric tried to surrender amid swirling energy from the explosion, Woody (accidentally) blew up a police cruiser with energy from his fingertips. The cops opened fire. The moment Woody and Eric (accidentally) touched their control bracelets together—*klang!*—their bodies re-stabilized, and a force field sprang up in front of Eric to deflect the gunfire. The pair escaped, further implicating themselves in their father's murder.

KLANG OF THE TITANS

To continue their search for evidence, Woody suggested he and Eric adopt secret superhero identities. They now had superpowers, after all, and the police were actively looking for them. Eric, who'd always wanted to be a superhero, adopted the name Quantum, and thus the duo "Quantum and Woody" was born.

Together, the masked avenger Quantum and the noticeably un-costumed Woody arrived at the Quantum Labs offices to demand information about their father's project. Little did they know that representatives from Edison's Radical Acquisitions— their father's killers—were in that office conducting a hostile takeover. After a fight with the Nightmare Brigade—mad-science monsters made by splicing clowns, needles, and spiders—destroyed all the evidence, the duo had a huge fight and went their separate ways.

By himself, Quantum tracked down the ERA members while Woody got abducted by Detective Cejudo—a clone of ERA's mysterious leader, a geneticist known as the Crone. The Crone was desperate to get her hands on Derek Henderson's research, so she planned to dissect Woody to learn how his powers worked. Unfortunately, both brothers were slowly dissolving into unstable atoms.

At ERA's secret island base, Quantum released the "breakthroughs"—countless experimental horrors, including the aforementioned goat that fires laser beams from its eyes. These experiments wreaked havoc on the ERA while Quantum freed Woody. Before the pair could destabilize into atoms, they *klang*ed their control bracelets together, which re-stabilized their bodies for another twenty-four hours. During the base's evacuation and self-destruct countdown, the duo (accidentally) killed the Crone and escaped with Detective Cejudo and Clone #69 (another Crone-clone) and the diabolical goat. (Woody later named his new pet "Vincent van Goat.")

FURTHER MISSTEPS

Quantum and Woody's misadventures don't end there. Since the destruction of ERA's island, this duo has been responsible for assaulting innocent nightclubs, giving cars and dangerous military equipment to homeless people, knocking down entire buildings, joyriding in (or running away from) mad-science robots, getting unwittingly involved in secessionist plots, and other ridiculous stunts.

No one is safe around these individuals. If you see one or both of these so-called superheroes: *run*. Turn and run as fast as you can. They'll probably (accidentally) get you killed.

SHADOWMAN

TAGS/CUES

- loa spirit ● Deadside ● Jack Boniface ● Master Darque
- New Orleans ● supernatural ● magic ● necromancy ● spirits

THE LOA SPIRIT

More than two centuries ago, a plantation owner from New Orleans named Darque had albino twins, a boy and a girl as pale as a fresh snowfall. As these children grew, their father taught them "the art," the secret of manipulating the indestructible energy that dwells within all living things. Throughout the years, the father tattooed arcane symbols called "grand veves" on his children to make them reservoirs of this necromantic energy.

Their father's dream was to reach a plane of existence called Lyceum, a beautiful realm where "all that was knowable was known," and his grown children would be the key that opened Lyceum's door. Only, the sole path to Lyceum lay through "the place between," a state of existence known as the Deadside; thus the toll to reach Lyceum was the death of his daughter Sandria. In a fit of rage, Sandria's brother Nicodemo killed their father with magic during the ritual and renewed his beloved sister's life force.

Together, the twins wandered the country, using their magic to fleece the locals. But Nicodemo also used his magic for darker purposes, and soon Sandria grew afraid of her brother's steadily growing necromantic power.

In 1864, Sandria fled from her brother and stumbled across the aftermath of a Union and Confederate battle. One of the Union soldiers, Marius Boniface, was still alive, and Sandria healed him. The two grew close, and when Nicodemo rampaged through the Union camp to rescue his sister, Marius attacked him and fled with Sandria.

The pair always kept one step ahead of Nicodemo, until they took refuge with magic practitioners in New Orleans. Nicodemo arrived shortly after Sandria had given birth to a stillborn child, and he raged upon Marius with jealousy and anger. Sandria knew she could not save her child, but she could use the child's indestructible energy to save Marius. Thus, she channeled her child's life force to bind to Marius a powerful loa named Umbra, a spirit from the Voodun pantheon, which transformed him into the Shadowman and gave him the strength to fight back. But Nicodemo would not be undone, and he used his power to vanish in an explosion of necromantic energy.

THE COMING DARQUE

Over the years, the loa's mantle passed to Marius's descendants, who each used the Shadowman's power to fight back against the schemes of Nicodemo—now Master Darque—and any dark creatures that threatened the living in

New Orleans. About two decades ago, everything changed: Darque declared war on the living and attempted to break through to Earth. The Shadowman—Josiah Boniface—and his Abettors fought back Darque's army. The cost of winning was Josiah's life, however, which sealed Darque in the Deadside but left the Abettors without a Shadowman for nearly twenty years.

Josiah's son Jack grew up in foster care, a strange amulet around his neck being his only connection to his dead parents. When Jack reached adulthood and learned about his parents' checkered history, he tore the amulet's chain from his neck and tossed it into Lake Pontchartrain. Without the amulet hiding him, Jack became a target for the Brethren, a secretive group of wealthy elite striving to see Master Darque return to the land of the living. The Brethren's sacrificial ritual created a flesh golem that called itself Mr. Twist, and two of Twists's monstrous parasitic creations abducted Jack. Just before they tried to kill him, the loa of Jack's ancestors bonded with him, creating the Shadowman once more and bestowing the power to defend himself. With the help of the Abettors Dox and Alyssa, Jack destroyed his assailants.

Mr. Twist later located the Abettors' safe house and abducted Dox, for the Abettor's body was covered in grand veves, making him the perfect battery of necromantic power for Twist to begin opening a bridge through which Master Darque could return to Earth.

To escape Twist, Jack used the Shadowman's powers to physically travel into the Deadside, where he met Jaunty, a spirit in the shape of a small, top-hat-wearing monkey. Jaunty taught Jack that the Deadside is a "house of many doors," a place of neither good nor evil. Then Jack met his father's spirit, who claimed Jack could give up the loa or embrace it and remain the Shadowman. Jack chose the latter, and upon returning to New Orleans, he shoved Twist through the Deadside portal to be eaten by hungry spirits, ending Twist's spell and closing Darque's portal to Earth.

THE TREE OF THORNS

In pursuit of another means to reach the living, Master Darque sought out Baron Samedi, the forgotten and weakened king of the Deadside, to form an alliance. Darque offered Samedi enough power to possess one of his living worshipers and help pave the way for Darque's return. Instead, Samedi joined forces with the Shadowman once he walked the Earth again, for he knew that Darque's return would destroy the world and its pleasures.

Samedi and Jack then brought the fight to the Brethren's stronghold, as weakening them would weaken Darque's power base. However, in the Deadside, Darque was busy impaling souls upon a twisted, towering thorn tree and reshaping them into an army of ravenous Eaters—warped, unfeeling souls that destroy other souls by devouring them.

Dox, angry with Jack for allying with the lord of the dead, took matters into his own hands and used a Devilheart to send his spirit to the Deadside. The plan backfired: Darque captured Dox's soul and pinned him to the thorn tree to begin draining the energy from his veves, for Darque planned to use the tree to break free of the Deadside, drain necromantic energy from every living being, and use that power to challenge and defeat God.

To rescue Dox and save Samedi's tortured subjects, Jack and Samedi returned to the Deadside, but they were too late. Darque infected Dox, slowly turning him into an Eater, forcing Jack to destroy Dox's soul. Then Jack impaled Darque on the thorn tree, creating a feedback loop that caused the tree to explode with necromantic energy, destroying Darque in the process.

THE RABID DOG

Soon after, Jack began waking up from blackouts and finding himself in alleys with people he'd nearly beaten to death. The senior Abettors Earlene and Henry believed Jack was unable to control the loa's wild power and had become too dangerous, like a dog that had become rabid. Alyssa told Jack the only way to rid himself of the loa would be to visit a swamp witch named Punk Mambo; otherwise, the other Abettors would kill Jack to keep the city safe.

According to Punk Mambo, Umbra had been exiled from the Voodun pantheon, and it wanted to hunt and kill other loa; Umbra had evolved since it first bonded with Marius Boniface, and not even she could separate it from him. Since past Shadowmen had loves to support them, Jack wondered if having his own love might help him control his blackout rages.

But this realization came far too late. Earlene and Henry decided to remove Jack from the equation and let the mantle of the loa fall to one of Jack's distant cousins. Earlene attacked the Shadowman with the Screaming Whip, a horrid artifact descended from European slavers. Moments from Jack's death, another loa named Tremble took advantage of the situation and infested the whole of New Orleans with crippling fear.

Earlene and Henry realized the mistake they had made and spared Jack's life, and Alyssa declared her love for him. With this newfound knowledge, Jack confronted Tremble, whisked him to the Deadside, and forced Tremble to look upon his own fears. The frightened loa then left his host, and New Orleans fell silent once more.

UNITY

TAGS/CUES

- international crisis ● Vine battleship ● Toyo Harada ● Eternal Warrior
- Livewire ● Ninjak ● Aric of Dacia ● betrayal ● X-O Manowar armor

OPENING MOVES

The sudden appearance of an alien battleship carrying the Visigoth Aric of Dacia, his freed people, and the X-O Manowar armor sent shockwaves across the world. The ship landed in Bucharest, Romania, and Aric claimed the country as his kingdom. Having found the remnant of his tortured Visigoth people on the homeworld of an alien race called the Vine, Aric wanted to do right by them and bring them home. However, as a time-displaced leader lacking knowledge on the workings of modern society, he could not anticipate the world's reaction. Many world powers viewed Aric's arrival as a hostile action and responded accordingly. When Aric destroyed a Russian tank battalion sent to drive out him and his people, the entire world was thrown into panic. Surrounding countries, especially Russia, prepared to invade and drive out the intruder.

Some saw opportunity in the chaos. One man willing to take advantage of the situation was Toyo Harada, founder of the Harbinger Foundation. Harada used his political connections to secure the backing to go after the X-O Manowar armor.

Harada first recruited the Eternal Warrior, Gilad Anni-Padda, to speak with Aric. Gilad had been Aric's mentor 1,600 years before, and Harada hoped the immortal could talk the hot-headed Visigoth into surrendering the armor.

The talk did not go well. Aric was still the stubborn, persistent warrior Gilad remembered, and the talk rapidly descended into arguing then fighting. Gilad's experience gave him the upper hand until Aric summoned the X-O Manowar armor and turned the tables. Aric shattered Gilad's arm and told him to leave. Aric's people were home and intended to stay.

Harada then hired the spy and assassin Ninjak to disable the Vine battleship Aric and his people had arrived in, to clear a path for a Harbinger Foundation team to capture Aric and the armor. The team, code name Unity, was the best team the Harbinger Foundation had produced, but they were woefully inexperienced.

Aric killed all four team members in seconds.

In the aftermath, Aric captured Ninjak. Harada's time to head off the impending crisis was running out.

FORGING A NEW UNITY

With Ninjak out of contact, Gilad hobbled by a shattered arm, and the Unity advance team out of commission, Harada was forced to ask for help from an unlikely source: the teletechnopath Amanda McKee, code name Livewire. Livewire had been one of the Harbinger Foundation's strongest psiots—humans with neurologically based preternatural abilities—but while she agreed with most of Harada's vision, she balked at his methods. After suffering a period of exile, she agreed to help Harada defuse the crisis.

Harada planned to seize the alien ship and use Aric's people aboard as a bargaining chip. Together, Harada, Gilad, and Livewire managed to reach the ship and enter it, where they ran into Aric's royal guards. Elsewhere on the ship, Ninjak used his skills to escape his bonds and fight his way to the ship's bridge. But just as Harada's team thought they had the upper hand, the ship suddenly launched itself into the sky and headed for orbit.

Aric had laid a trap. Only his Visigoth warriors were on the ship, and using the Manowar armor to interface with the ship, Aric sent the team into space so he could fight without his people getting caught in the crossfire.

A SHIFT IN FORTUNES

After another clash with Aric's royal guards, Harada sent Livewire and Gilad to the engine room to take control of the ship's power systems while he would reach the control room to join Ninjak. Using her psionic ability to control machines, Livewire found she could communicate with the ship without having to physically touch the system. She used this ability to lead Gilad to the ship's engine room. With Gilad guarding her back, Livewire interfaced with the ship and found herself in a virtual world—where she ran into a virtual representation of Aric.

She told Harada that Aric had interfaced with the ship and someone needed to break Aric's concentration. Gilad left Livewire, and on the bridge he found Aric physically attached to the ship through the X-O Manowar armor.

The fight raged both in the real world and the virtual one. Aric managed to hold his own against both Livewire and Gilad, but Harada and Ninjak's arrival altered the balance. Now fighting four opponents, Aric's inexperience with technology took a toll on his concentration. Livewire, who had been exploring the ship's system during her fight with Aric, injected a computer virus into the ship's systems and thus into Aric's armor.

The result was unexpected. The X-O Manowar armor ripped away from Aric and sought out Livewire. The sudden shift knocked Livewire unconscious. With no one at the controls, the battleship plummeted to Earth, crashing into the Atlantic Ocean and sinking into its depths.

A WATERY GRAVE

A mile under the ocean, the team fought to stay alive as the ship was rapidly taking on water. Inside the X-O Manowar armor, Livewire found herself fighting the armor, as Aric still had control over it. She remained helpless as the armor nearly killed the rest of the team and blew a hole in the ship's hull. Aric escaped, leaving the team to drown. Harada used his abilities to seal the hole long enough for the team to escape the compartment. Livewire gained full control of the armor, but not before being forced to relive Aric's troubled past though the armor.

On the surface, fleets from three different countries closed in on the area where the ship crashed. The Russians launched a nuclear missile, intending to destroy the ship .

The team pursued Aric and his people, who were in the middle of trying to escape the doomed vessel. After a fight with the Visigoths, Aric and his people boarded the last escape pod. Harada, unwilling to watch them escape, punched a hole through the pod's side, leaving the Visigoths to drown.

Through the X-O Manowar armor, Livewire learned of the nuclear missile and left the ship. She stopped the missile from exploding, but when she saw that the rest of the team was on the surface and the Visigoths weren't, she descended into the ocean to rescue them. Her efforts brought the crippled escape pod to the surface.

Harada met with the leaders of the three fleets and brokered an agreement with them: the Harbinger Foundation would keep the armor safe, and Aric and his people would be taken into custody.

A CHANGE OF HEART

Though Livewire no longer wore the X-O Manowar armor, she discovered her time in the armor had increased her abilities: she could access data without having to physically touch the equipment. Some of the data she intercepted were Harada's private files, and in those files she found evidence that Harada was a cold-blooded killer pursuing an agenda she refused to support. Armed with this knowledge, she convinced Ninjak and Gilad that the X-O Manowar armor couldn't remain in Harada's hands.

While Livewire and Gilad kept Harada busy, Ninjak infiltrated the Foundation's headquarters and ran afoul of Anchor, a psiot Harada had tasked with guarding the armor. Despite Gilad and Livewire's best efforts, Harada detected the security breach and tried to stop the theft. Ninjak managed to defeat Anchor, but Harada arrived and tried to take the X-O Manowar armor, only to have Livewire don it once more. Livewire ended the fight by flying Harada into the upper atmosphere, where she renounced any loyalty she had left for her former master. She dropped Harada, and only his psionic force field protected him from an otherwise lethal fall.

Now that the armor was out of Harada's hands, Livewire decided only one person deserved to wear it—Aric. The team went to the detainment camp where the Visigoths were being held, and Livewire returned the X-O Manowar armor to Aric.

X-O MANOWAR

TAGS/CUES

- Visigoth ● man out of time ● the Vine ● aliens
- Sacred Armor of Shanhara ● time dilation ● Loam ● MERO

THE CHOSEN OF SHANHARA

In 402 AD, the Visigoths planned to sack Rome, but the Roman Empire preemptively attacked King Alaric's men at Pollentia. After a disastrous defeat at the hands of the Romans, Alaric's nephew Aric used the cover of night to attack what he believed to be a detachment of Roman soldiers. The battle was quickly lost, for Aric's foes were not Romans: they were scouts from the Vine, an alien race that left "plantings"—aliens genetically modified to appear human—on each world they visited. Aric and several of his most trusted warriors were taken captive and brought to the Vine colony ship as slaves.

The Vine meant for Aric and his Visigoths to work themselves to death tending the colony ship's sacred gardens. Aric had other plans, and not even the Vine cutting off his left hand could stifle his resolve. The prison break he orchestrated led his men to the ship's temple, where Aric found a single suit of armor—the Armor of Shanhara. Unaware of the sacred relic's history of suffocating and killing each Vine warrior that attempted to don the suit, Aric allowed the armor to cover himself.

To the Vine High Priest's astonishment, the Armor of Shanhara did not kill Aric. Instead, Aric became a one-man army seemingly impervious to the Vine's most advanced weaponry. He fought through countless waves of Vine warriors until an explosion in the colony ship's hull forced him into space.

When Aric envisioned himself back on Earth, the armor responded to his desire and flew him back home. When he arrived, he found himself hurtled into the twenty-first century Roman Colosseum back on Earth. Confronted with

Italian SWAT teams on the ground and fighter jets in the skies, Aric knew he was out of his element. To confirm his belief, the armor showed him flashes of everything he had missed in the last sixteen centuries due to the time dilation caused by space travel.

Everything and everyone Aric knew from the fifth century—his uncle Alaric, his wife Deirdre, and his home country of Dacia—had been dead for nearly 1,600 years.

ARIC ON EARTH

After fleeing Italy in confusion and despair, Aric flew to the middle of the Peruvian rainforest, where he rested and wrestled with his future in this strange new world. The Vine, having learned through their plantings that the Armor of Shanhara had arrived on Earth, tasked the planting Alexander Dorian, a wealthy business mogul, to retrieve Aric's armor. Dorian's strike team proved no match for Shanhara's might, and Aric spared only Dorian for questioning.

Desperate, the Vine used their contacts in MI-6 to send superspy-assassin Ninjak after the armor. Ninjak caught Aric unarmored and unawares, and he took possession of both armor and wearer—but not for long. Dorian learned that his Vine masters intended to annihilate the population of Earth: the humans had witnessed the power of Shanhara and thus could not be allowed to live. Instead of helping the Vine destroy the planet he had grown to love, Dorian helped Aric escape with the armor and later convinced Ninjak that he was collaborating with Vine agents inside MI-6, and further involvement would ultimately help the Vine destroy Earth's population.

Together, the trio mounted an assault on MI-6. The attack cleansed the Vine plantings infesting the intelligence organization.

X-O VS. THE VINE

When the Vine fleet arrived in Earth orbit, a specially trained squad of X-O Commando armor attacked Aric in Manhattan with the express purpose of destroying the X-O Manowar armor. Aric defeated the Vine Commandos, but their leader, Commander Trill, came prepared. The Vine had been torturing Aric's friend Gafti, long thought dead during the prison break on the Vine colony ship, and Trill threatened to kill Gafti if Aric did not stand down. Gafti was injured in the fight, but Aric lent him the X-O Manowar armor to heal his wounds. Instead of waiting to recover, Gafti flew into orbit and used the suit to drain power from the Vine fleet, knocking all the ships out of commission. He then expelled incredible amounts of energy through Shanhara, destroying the entire fleet in one fell swoop. However, the action was too much for Gafti's wounded body, and the armor returned to Aric on Earth.

Saddened at his friend's death, Aric took Trill's strike ship to Loam, the Vine's homeworld. He arrived angry and killed every Vine he encountered until he came across the High Priest, who claimed Aric was the Chosen of Shanhara. The High Council refused to believe such heresy and sent a massive army to destroy Shanhara once and for all.

With the help of the High Priest, some Vine loyal to Shanhara, and Visigoth descendants still living on Loam, Aric rallied an army composed of all the slave races the Vine had gathered from across the galaxy. The Vine army crumbled beneath Aric's resolve. His victory forced the High Council to surrender to Aric's demands and acknowledge him as Shanhara's Chosen. Aric placed Loam under the High Priest's stewardship, loaded the descendants of his Visigoth kin onto a Vine battleship, and returned them to Earth.

X-O VS. UNITY

Under the scrutiny of MERO, a US military organization tasked with tracking extraterrestrial threats, Aric landed his ship in the middle of Bucharest, Romania, and claimed himself king of Dacia. Though his people began farming the land rather than conquering the city, the world leadership was not happy with these primitive people taking up residence in a sovereign nation. Russia, concerned about this potential threat, sent submarine-launched missiles and a tank battalion against the Visigoths. Aric sank the sub and destroyed the Russian ground forces, which brought his actions to the attention of psiot and business mogul Toyo Harada.

Harada sent a handpicked team of psiots, code name Unity, to capture the armor and make Aric stand down. During the attack, Aric launched the Vine ship into space, but the battle aboard the bridge sent the vessel plummeting into the ocean. Before the ship could sink, one of Harada's teammates gained control of the armor, and Unity delivered Aric and his Visigoths into MERO custody.

A short time later, the armor was returned to Aric, and Dorian convinced MERO to strike a deal with Aric and offer the Visigoths asylum in western Nebraska. However, in exchange for his people's new homeland, Aric would become a MERO agent, and should he ever get out of line, his own people would pay the price.

ORGANIZATIONS

ABETTORS

● Shadowman ● protectors ● magic ● necromancy ● New Orleans ● war against darkness

A CALL TO ARMS

Think supernatural creatures are something from horror movies or from sensational televangelist broadcasts? Think again. There are plenty of dark threats lurking in the unseen places, just waiting to prey on the living—you, your loved ones, anyone. And on the worst days, the only force capable of walking into the belly of the beast and coming through the other side is the Shadowman, a defender of the living, a mortal man clothed in the powers of a loa spirit.

As Abettors, our goal is to help whoever wears the mantle of the Shadowman in any way we can, sometimes even in ways that feel counterintuitive to those outside our organization.

THE PAST

The first members of our little group organized back in the mists of Louisiana at the tail end of the Civil War. In the bayous and plantations of New Orleans, the original Abettors were all practitioners of necromancy—magic, to all the uninitiated. When Sandria, the sister of the powerful and twisted necromancer Master Darque, showed up seeking sanctuary and protection from her jealous and dangerous brother, the swamp witches and backwoods magicians of New Orleans came together to hide her and her lover, a Union soldier named Marius Boniface. Darque came calling, and though the first Abettors did everything in their power to conceal his sister, all of the Abettors' efforts were for naught in the end. He and his sister's disagreement led to a powerful loa spirit

bonding to Marius, and the resultant Shadowman proved to be Darque's undoing.

After the necromancer's disappearance, many of the witches and houngans and mambos of New Orleans took on the sacred duty of keeping the Shadowman safe so he could protect the world from threats like Master Darque. Over more than 150 years, these Abettors trained Marius's descendants to take up the mantle of the loa on the event that a Shadowman met an untimely death.

A few times we were forced to carry on our mission *without* a Shadowman to abet. In those dismal times, our mission remained unchanged: while waiting for a new Host to appear, we still fought against the denizens of darkness that sought to prey upon the living; we abetted even in the loa's absence. And on even rarer occasions, Abettors were forced to put down a Shadowman due to a Host being unable to control the mantle of power the loa bestows upon him. The mission of protecting the Shadowman and the loa always came first at any cost, even if that cost was destroying the Shadowman himself.

THE FUTURE

These days, the Abettors of New Orleans aren't as plentiful as they once were. Among our current members are two senior Abettors (Earlene and Henry) and myself (Alyssa). My old mentor, Dox isn't around anymore, but sometimes I like to think he's still out there looking out for us somehow. Doesn't sound like much, I know, but I'd like to think we get the job done.

We aren't a deeply organized and regimented group because we need to be flexible. Our mission is to serve the living no matter the time or place, be it by magic or more mundane methods. We must be ready to abet any potential Host by locating, training, and protecting him wherever and whenever he may surface.

The creatures of darkness we fight see the living as pets, toys, food—or all three—but the Shadowman is the candle that stands against that darkness, and we are the wick that keeps him burning.

Are you brave enough to be that wick? Then come. The Shadowman needs all the help he can get.

THE BRETHREN

● secret society ● New Orleans ● Master Darque ● occultic ● controlling ● modern ● sacrifices

THE SUIT

Welcome to Mr. Sabatine's estate. Let me guess: you're probably down on your luck. Can't even rub two pennies together. Or maybe you're suffering from something: you've got a dying relative or you're battling suicidal depression and you have nowhere else to turn. Well, you've come to the right place. Help us, and we'll fix you right up, no matter what ails you.

You see, we've found exactly what this world needs: a panacea that cures all ailments. And we're trying to make it happen. With your help, there's a good possibility we might see this in our own lifetimes.

Are you interested? Then come on in and follow me. Pretty soon you'll be wearing nice three-piece suits just like mine.

THE DRUG

See this little vial here, this fluorescent pink liquid? This is what we call soma. You've probably never heard of it before, and that's because you likely can't afford it: our clients are super-rich. This wonder drug is made by—ah, I won't bore you with the details—but it comes from distilled dreams, and those dreams make you feel like you are the ruler of the world—no, of *heaven*. This is as close to God as you'll probably get in this lifetime.

We control the supply, you see? You want some soma, you have to come through us. The movers and shakers of New Orleans, the politicians and lawmakers—they *all* buy from us, and it's one of the ways we can control what goes on in this town. One word from Mr. Devereaux or one of the other Brethren leaders, and the offender's supply dries up, and soon the whole city forgets about them.

This little vial makes people do exactly what we want them to. If you join us, I might give you a sample—just so you can see what it's like—but that's it. And only if you can follow orders. Got it?

THE ELITE

You've probably seen—or at least heard of—most of the people in this room here. That there is Gloria Vega, who is in charge of all shipbuilding in New Orleans. Next to her is Leland Paige, who controls politics here in the Big Easy. Martin Swaim is over petrochemicals, and our illustrious leader in the wheelchair, Thomas Sabatine, oversees all the city's oil refineries. We did have someone in charge of commercial fishing—Mr. Gregoire Rosso—but some gun-toting lunatic killed him not long ago, and we're still trying to find his replacement.

So we already control this city; the common folk just don't see it. We have people at the top of every single major industry in New Orleans. Nothing in this city gets done without their express approval. And if you cross one of them … well, I wouldn't suggest you try.

THE SACRIFICE

Now, pay no attention to the corpses in that corner of this room. They're for a ritual you needn't concern yourself with, and we'll clean them up when we're done.

What I want to show you is this. See the pattern drawn on the floor, these geometric lines? This is for a spell, a form of necromantic energy we used to contact Master Darque while he was trapped in Lyceum. Master Darque has devised a way to end all suffering in this world. That ailing relative or that too-small paycheck—Darque will make such petty concerns no longer matter. We need only help him break free of his prison so he can remake the world and place us—the Brethren—on top.

So, what do you say? Whether you deal soma for us or end up as a blood sacrifice like the rest of those bodies in the corner, you're going to help us one way or another.

EDISON'S RADICAL ACQUISITIONS

● Thomas Edison ● mad science ● secret society ● experimentations ● unethical ● greedy ● the Crone

NOTE: A recruitment film for this secret society is available on request. Analog film projector required. Please note that this film may be hazardous to your health: to maintain secrecy, ERA reserves the right to murder viewers who are not immediately inducted into ERA after the film's conclusion.

PURPOSE

All secret societies the world around have a concrete mission statement. Some, like the Freemasons, seek to better human society. Others, like the Sect, strive to rule the world by pulling unseen strings, while Yale's Skull and Bones fosters a sense of fraternity among its members. Edison's Radical Acquisitions, however, may *claim* its goal is to follow famous inventor and opportunist Thomas Alva Edison, but superhero duo Quantum and Woody have come to the conclusion that ERA's ultimate goal is to make the world *weirder*—as weird as scientifically possible.

Edison was best known for inventing light bulbs, phonographs, and motion pictures, but he stole and registered the ideas for most of the many patents he owned. (This explains Edison's famous, oft-misunderstood quote "genius is one percent inspiration and ninety-nine percent perspiration." Edison let others provide the "inspiration" while he did all the "perspiration" to claim that idea as his own.) Edison soon realized that some of these discoveries, such as Nikola Tesla's advocacy of wireless electricity, were too profitable to just give away for free. Instead of sharing these scientific discoveries, Edison locked them away so that he and his associates could control them and eventually profit handsomely from revealing these technologies to the world. This secret group of associates began calling themselves Edison's Radical Acquisitions.

ERA concentrates on stealing any technology its members can get their hands on and either recruiting or silencing the original discoverer. Through subterfuge, sabotage, murder, and other creative methods, ERA collects new technology and has purposely stunted the world's scientific growth. At certain times throughout history, ERA allows "new" technology to be made public. Each time this has occurred, ERA pocketed at least $3 trillion in pure profit.

NOTABLE MEMBERS

The Crone: Leader of ERA. A geneticist who invented human cloning in 1945. Maintains an army of her own clones, which she uses to replace various body parts. Believed to be more than a century old. Presumed dead at the hands of Quantum and Woody.

Johnny 2: A diminutive, sickly man with twisted, genius-level intelligence. Requires medical equipment to remain alive and uses a special mechanized chair for mobility. Twin brother Johnny 1 was killed when Quantum and Woody blew up ERA.'s island headquarters. Current whereabouts unknown.

The Soviet: Female Russian agent altered to look male. Stone-cold killer. Current whereabouts unknown.

Haz-Matt: A scientist whose bio-energy experiments required his disfigured head be sealed in a glass helmet. Current whereabouts unknown.

Beta-Max: First successful fusion of man and machine. Overdue for an upgrade. Incorporated technology includes film projector (which overheats), fax machine (which needs a landline connection), and a pager.

"Carl": An ERA member who bears an uncanny resemblance to a certain famed astrophysicist and science communicator who reportedly died in 1996. Current whereabouts unknown.

Omaha Jack: Creator of Septapussy, a genetically altered white cat with tail-like tentacles instead of legs. Current whereabouts unknown.

FORMER MEMBERS

Alejandra Cejudo: A Crone-clone posing as a D.C. Metro Police Detective. Left the organization due to being undervalued by the Crone. Watches out for her "sister," Sixty-Nine and (unsuccessfully) tries to keep Quantum and Woody out of trouble. Location: Washington, D.C.

Sixty-Nine: A naïve nineteen-year-old Crone-clone, designation #69 (AKA "the foxy one"). Liberated by Woody Henderson before the destruction of ERA.'s island base. Woody's current fling. Location: Washington, D.C.

GEOMANCERS

● Voice of the Earth ● Book of the Geomancer ● The House of the Earth ● Earth's key ● controls elements and nature

Geomancers are the voice of the Earth, able to feel and understand the Earth's needs and wants. Selected by the Earth itself, these men and women are the conduit the Earth uses to speak to her current Fist and Steel, Gilad Anni-Padda. Only one Geomancer exists at any time. Most of the time, the Geomancer selects and trains a successor, but when a Geomancer dies without one, the Earth chooses another to assume the mantle. In those rare cases, a powerful artifact known as the Book of the Geomancer allows Gilad to find the next Geomancer.

In return for being the Earth's speaker, the Geomancer can see the universe's "source code" and rewrite this code as needed. This ability lets the Geomancer control the elements and nature to accomplish feats such as creating openings in walls or rock faces, using air currents to lift him or her into the air, or detecting hidden objects by listening to the different tones the Earth makes. In addition, a Geomancer can convince objects to accede to requests, allowing them to do things like unlock any door.

An increased lifespan is another benefit, but the constant difficulty and sacrifice of deciding who lives and who dies takes a toll on the Geomancer. Each Geomancer hears the Earth's will and follows it without question and no matter the cost.

The Geomancer's power attracts enemies looking to take the power for their own or kill the Geomancer to weaken the Earth. The House of the Wild, the Dead, and the Wheel pose a constant threat, as do members of the secret, world-dominating organization known as the Sect, especially the Null. The Null wants the universe to be unmade and spent centuries developing a doomsday code to destroy it. Gilad and the Geomancers have clashed with the Null numerous times over the centuries.

For thousands of years, Gilad has been the Geomancers' protector, rescuer, and occasionally their avenger. However, Gilad had a falling out with Geomancer Buck McHenry, resulting in Gilad walking away from his duties for more than a hundred years.

When Buck was killed, the Earth passed the Geomancer's mantle to Kay McHenry, a distant relative of Buck's. Kay was a media spokesperson for Elliot Zorn's company, Zorn Capital. When she discovered Zorn was the leader of the Null, Zorn ordered her death. With the help of Gilad, former Sect assassin Obadiah Archer, and Gilad's immortal brother Armstrong, Kay used her newly acquired Geomancer powers to escape from a watery grave.

The four traveled to Greenland to stop Zorn from carrying out his plan to project a cosmic computer virus into space to destroy the universe. During the fighting, Kay discovered she could use the Book of the Geomancer to consult with the spirits of her predecessors. Acting on their advice, she neutralized the computer virus by rewriting the planet's default language settings so the doomsday code would be unwritten.

Now Kay is learning the ways of the Geomancer, serving the Earth as so many others before her have done.

THE HARBINGER FOUNDATION

● vision ● Toyo Harada ● psiots ● Harada Global Conglomerates ● private army ● New World Order

All you see here at the Harbinger Foundation began with a vision and a man. The vision offered a better future, one in which all human potential was realized, and the man offered us a better way, his way. Here at the Harbinger Foundation, you will help make Toyo Harada's vision a reality.

Founded by Harada-*sama* in 1965, the Foundation lies at the innermost circles of the sprawling Harada Global Conglomerates business structure. The Foundation doubles as a school for training psiots like you, as well as the special security force for all Harada holdings. But we're not just a corporation, we're a culture.

The Foundation has no single home; instead, we use an innovative distributed-headquarters model. Each of Harada Global's primary offices has the resources needed for our operation, ready to be activated on short notice. The Foundation's special abilities shield our facilities from hostile outsiders, and the organization and its students move as Harada-*sama* directs, to best fulfill his vision.

Each prospective student undergoes long-term observation in his or her natural environment to ensure they meet rigorous standards. After the process of observation and recruitment, the recruit's gifts are activated. This is an imperfect process, and setbacks occasionally occur. Once activated, a recruit begins a three-year program, progressing through the ranks from *ichinensei* to *nensei* to *shinia* and eventually standing alongside the Foundation's elite.

The intensive training you'll receive will help fully develop your abilities and prepare you to contribute to the Foundation's work. Through means beyond our ability to understand, Harada-*sama* knows the path stretching before us all, and he foresaw a great evil that will descend on humanity unless it unites.

Once, we worked in secret, gently guiding humanity onto a more enlightened path with an unseen hand, but with our leader's vision threatened by rebels, usurpers, and anarchists, Harada-*sama* decided the time had come to make clear our intentions for the world. He announced our existence to the world's leaders, revealed our power, and declared our intention to oppose those who stand in the way of a better world. Some fear the upcoming battles and whisper that our master has lost his way, but many more know that Harada-*sama* is the Omega and will lead us all to a glorious rebirth.

The human race must come together, achieve cohesion as a species, and work together to forge a brighter tomorrow.

The future has a place for you. Come with us.

H.A.R.D. CORPS

● Project Rising Spirit ● cybernetic implants ● psiot abilities ● recommissioned ● Director Kozol ● Major Palmer

HISTORY

The Harbinger Active Resistance Division was Project Rising Spirit's answer to Toyo Harada and his growing army of psiots. PRS fast-tracked H.A.R.D Corps into existence after Harada raided Rising Spirit's primary psiot research facility in North Carolina. The death of Director Leopold Carter showed that a new approach to management was needed and that PRS's activated psiot programs was not yet a viable solution to countering Harada's psiot army.

While PRS's psiot program killed nearly all test subjects, Rising Spirit's research did discover a way to download latent and active psiot abilities. Combined with cybernetic implant technology, normal humans could replicate psiot abilities, though at a severe cost to their longevity and well-being.

First tested during the Vietnam War, H.A.R.D. Corps saw extensive use throughout the 1980s and early 1990s. While H.A.R.D. Corps proved highly effective, the technology's compatibility limitations and the life expectancy of an agent made the program very costly to maintain. By the mid-1990s, PRS decommissioned H.A.R.D. Corps in favor of Project Bloodshot and other more aggressive psiot programs.

H.A.R.D CORPS TODAY

Recently reactivated by Director Kozol during the Harbinger Wars crisis in Las Vegas, H.A.R.D Corps quickly reestablished itself as an effective asset. Partnering with the self-aware cybernetic soldier known as Bloodshot, the current team has proven that the program continues to have significant value to PRS.

Traditionally, H.A.R.D. Corps recruits had been drawn from trained and decorated soldiers, but since the reactivated H.A.R.D. Corps program had to hit the ground running, the current crop of recruits consists of implant-compatible individuals, each harboring personal reasons to accept such a dangerous but rewarding job.

Major Palmer, H.A.R.D. Corps' field commander until Bloodshot was brought on board, has since whipped these non-soldier recruits into shape, and the new blood shows great promise for the missions to come.

PSIOT ABILITIES

H.A.R.D. Corps' main advantage over traditional PRS assets is the agent's ability to simulate psiot abilities in the field.

H.A.R.D. Corps' remote-support system, code name Lifeline, currently has seventeen psiot abilities ready for instant download. Other powers, known as

"bee stings," are available, but they must be prepared prior to a mission for an agent to have access to them. The use of a bee sting is a last-ditch option, as normal human physiology cannot survive the power's activation.

To align with Major Palmer's "guns for offense, powers for defense" maxim, all H.A.R.D Corps agents are trained in the use of Shield and Flight, then they typically train with two to three other abilities to form their primary tactical abilities. They can call on any of the other active download powers if needed.

CURRENT LIFELINE DOWNLOADS

Arc Charge: Projects lethal levels of electrical energy, which can affect machinery and living organisms.

Breakdown: Accelerates molecular decay on contact.

Detonation Mode: Directs explosive energy into objects on contact.

Fire: Generates and projects fire from the hands.

Flight: Confers the ability to fly at subsonic speeds.

Invisibility: Bends ambient light around the agent, making them invisible. Ineffective against infrared.

Ghost: Renders agent completely intangible and able to pass through physical objects. Agent cannot breathe while in Ghost mode.

Muscle: Enhances the agent's natural strength to superhuman levels. The stronger the agent, the greater the increase.

Neural Spike: Generates intense neural stimuli which will completely incapacitate normal humans. Has limited effectiveness against psiots with telepathic or empathic abilities.

True Sight: Confers the ability to see through psiot projections.

Shield Mode: Forms an energy shield, either a localized projection in a specific direction or a weaker spherical shield around the agent.

Sleep: Induces sleep on contact. A focused form of Stun Ram.

Stun Ram: Projects nonlethal pulses of concussive force.

Suggestion: Makes a target more receptive to the user's suggestions.

THE HOUSES

● continuous war ● gods ● the Earth ● the Wild ● the Dead ● the Wheel ● minor Houses

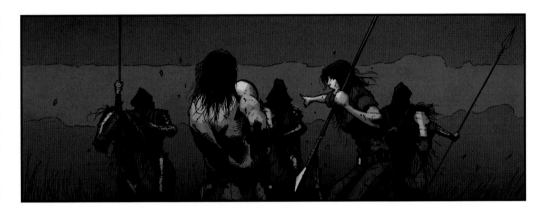

The four major Houses are locked in continual war with each other to preserve and expand their dominion. Directed by gods, the wars between the Houses are ancient, never-ending, and rarely glimpsed by most of humanity. Humans chosen to become part of the war serve willingly and, for the most part, faithfully.

Each House has several classes of members. Rangers are the House's foot soldiers, which protect the House's holdings or attack another House's assets. Priests serve as conduits between the House's deity and the rest of the House. Some, like the House of the Wheel, have a large Technician class that works on the Wheel's machinery.

Each House has champions known as Swords, who act as that god's commanders and agents. Warriors all, each Sword has been chosen by their respective god and given extra abilities to aid in the war. Gilad Anni-Padda has been the Sword for the House of the Earth for many lifetimes. His daughter Xaran served as a Sword of the Wild for two thousand years before massacring the Wild's inner circle on orders from the House of the Earth through the Geomancer Buck McHenry. Mitu, Gilad's deceased and resurrected son, served the House of the Dead as their Sword.

The four most active groups are the Houses of the Earth, the Wild, the Wheel, and the Dead. Other Houses either ally themselves with one of these four or avoid them altogether.

THE HOUSE OF THE EARTH

● Fist and Steel ● life endures ● balance to all Houses ● the old ways ● Mother Earth

The House of the Earth keeps all the other Houses in balance. Whether by culling the House of the Wild or stopping the latest House of the Dead surge, the House of the Earth's sole purpose is to make sure life on the planet endures. If that means people have to die, it's for the greater good.

THE HOUSE OF THE WILD

● Swords ● Rangers ● protectors of animals ● aggressive ● uncontrolled ● ecoterrorists

This House's domain is nature and wildlife. The Swords and Rangers of the Wild defend against hunters and anyone else who despoils nature. Aggressive and feral, this House is culled by Mother Earth every few generations to keep them in check.

THE HOUSE OF THE DEAD

● Berserkers ● monsters ● indiscriminate killers ● worshipers of death ● Nergal

The House of the Dead stands in direct opposition to all life and seeks to destroy it all. Known for their Berserkers, men infused with a potion that turns them into massive killing machines, this House is Mother Earth's main foe and the one Gilad has fought the most. Nergal, the god of the Dead, is trapped in a vault buried beneath the now-destroyed Methuselah Tree, and the tree's roots will keep the vault's doors closed for another two thousand years.

THE HOUSE OF THE WHEEL

● technology ● Technicians ● Lady Ara

Unlike the other houses, the Wheel uses technology in all facets of its operations, including the battlefield.

MERO

● US military ● covert agency ● extraterrestrial threats ● Monument Valley ● Satellite Defense System

OVERVIEW

The Military Extraterrestrial Reconnaissance Outpost is a covert agency of the United States Armed Forces, and its goal is to locate, track, evaluate, contain, and repel any threats potentially of extraterrestrial origin. MERO carries out its mission by maintaining several dedicated assets and utilizing Cabinet leadership.

ASSETS

MERO's equipment and personnel fall into two categories: ground and space operations.

The main MERO facility, constructed in the 1960s, is located in an undisclosed area of Monument Valley, Utah, and it comprises several acres of chambers and tunnels. From this installation, a general advisor and staff can monitor and respond to any spaceborne or ground-based situation.

Six dedicated troop battalions remain on standby at undisclosed locations around the globe. Each battalion is capable of deploying anywhere in its operational region in less than eight hours. These troops are intended to be first on the scene of any extraterrestrial landing and contain the situation until more troops can arrive. In addition to land forces, several US Navy ships also have secret orders to

mobilize against potentially hazardous objects landing in the seas. Lastly, MERO has access to aerial drones that can be used for pinpoint surveillance.

Perhaps MERO's most important space-based system is the Satellite Defense System. A trio of classified satellites in low Earth orbit are capable of monitoring nearby space and the Earth's surface with incredible accuracy, and each platform can launch space-to-ground missiles with pinpoint accuracy.

MERO's newest asset is Aric of Dacia, a man claiming to be from 400 AD wearing an armored suit of alien provenance.

LEADERSHIP

Though a department of the US Armed Forces, MERO does not report to the Joint Chiefs or the head of a specific service branch. The director of MERO answers directly to the Secretary of Defense, and the Monument Valley base has a direct line to the Secretary's "Champagne Room" in Washington.

The current director is Colonel Jamie Capshaw, who has shown resilience even when faced with alien threats. Since her period of service began, she has dealt with several high-profile incidents, including the Manhattan attack, the Vine ship landing in Bucharest, and the imprisonment and recruitment of Aric of Dacia.

MI-6

● United Kingdom ● Secret Intelligence Service ● deep-cover operatives ● disguise experts ● compromised

Leader: Neville Alcott
Affiliation: United Kingdom
Secret Affiliation: The Vine (formerly)
Headquarters: Vauxhall Cross, London

BACKGROUND

Military Intelligence, Section 6 (MI-6), also known as the Secret Intelligence Service (SIS), collects and interprets foreign intelligence for the British government. For over a century, MI-6, under various names, has protected Crown and Country from external threats. Phrases like "save the world" or "save humanity" are meaningless if the cost is the Crown or the nation.

MI-6 is not ubiquitous, but it's close. The intelligence service has operatives everywhere, even among the UK's allies. At all times, MI-6's operational orders are to safeguard the kingdom. That encompasses operations such as conducting assassinations, fomenting uprisings, stealing military deployment data, sabotaging enemy installations, and so on. At present, the organization's high-priority missions are intended to prevent technology of alien origin from falling into the wrong hands.

In defense of the Crown, MI-6 employs a large variety of agents, some of whom possess extraordinary or even superhuman abilities. The two most prominent such individuals are Ninjak, unparalleled assassin and sword-for-hire, and Livewire, teletechnopath and former protégé of the powerful psiot Toyo Harada. Gilad Anni-Padda, the immortal known as the Eternal Warrior, has also worked alongside MI-6 operatives, but he is not considered an official asset. Agents with abilities such as these are routinely sent on missions that could decide the fate of national security or even the world at large.

Whenever mutual benefit can be gained by sharing information or assets, MI-6 routinely cooperates with the intelligence agencies of the UK's allies. Director Neville Alcott often coordinates with MERO, a US-based covert organization, and when circumstances warrant, MERO in turn has lent MI-6 the support of Aric of Dacia, wearer of the X-O Manowar armor.

RECENT EVENTS

MI-6, like most other major organizations of any influence, was compromised by the alien race known as the Vine, and the contamination went all the way to the top. Patrick Clement, MI-6's Chief of Operations, was a Vine planting, an alien modified to look human. He secretly guided the intelligence apparatus to support the Vine's ultimate goals. When Aric of Dacia returned to Earth wearing a suit of armor sacred to the Vine, Clement sent an MI-6 covert strike team to recover the armor. The team's complete failure forced Clement to acknowledge his organization's failings and call in an outside operative to carry out the mission. That operative was Ninjak.

When Ninjak learned the truth of the Vine infestation and the imminent plans to eliminate humanity, he turned on his employer. With Aric as an ally, Ninjak launched an onslaught on MI-6's headquarters at Vauxhall Cross. When the attack began, the Vine plantings first eliminated their human MI-6 comrades, facing the attack without human aid. Aric slaughtered the bulk of the defenders while Ninjak found Chief Clement and eliminated him.

With the Vine completely purged from MI-6, the organization's leadership was assumed by Neville Alcott, one of the few surviving non-Vine members of MI-6. Together, he and Ninjak now seek and destroy all other Vine plantings while rebuilding the gutted organization.

PROJECT RISING SPIRIT

● technology ● arms dealer ● H.A.R.D. Corps ● Bloodshot ● psiots ● nanites

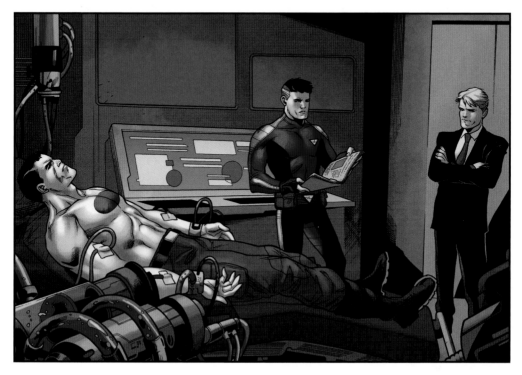

Officially, Rising Spirit Securities is a US-based security firm like Blackwater, Brinks, or Pinkerton, just with a decidedly technological flair. In reality, Rising Spirit is the public face of Project Rising Spirit, a multinational shadow organization boasting a client list that is a veritable who's who of the World Economic Forum. This organization runs facilities so black no one even knows they exist. With nearly unlimited resources and facilities on every continent, Rising Spirit is theoretically one of the most powerful non-government organizations in the world.

Project Rising Spirit has gone through many names in its history, too many to easily keep track of. Where you find cutting-edge weapons technology or extreme warfare, you will likely find agents of Rising Spirit. Where some Sect factions seek power through direct control, PRS has chosen to be the world's arms dealer.

The discovery of psiots coupled with techno-logical advancements showed PRS a path that no longer relied on ancient promises of immortality. In the early 1970s, PRS initiated the H.A.R.D. Corps program, which created a capable strike force and technological

advances in medicine and power generation. Project Bloodshot, a more recent program, employed regenerative nanite technology, and the results it produced could effectively change life sciences forever, were PRS to share it. However, PRS remains committed to developing weapon technologies..

Under Director Leopold Carter, PRS learned of the Omega-level psiot Toyo Harada, and they discovered Harada's ability to activate latent psiots via technological means. While PRS knew of the existence of psiots, the extreme rarity of psionic powers made psiots a minimal threat. The sheer power that Harada and his organization represented forced PRS to reprioritize its goals.

Since 1969, PRS's primary mission has been keeping the growing psiot menace in check and looking for a way to bring down Harada without revealing the existence of superpowered beings to the world. This shadow war has recently escalated to the edges of public awareness, first with Harada's attempt to subvert Project Bloodshot, which led to the battle in Las Vegas and the showdown in Harada's California headquarters.

THE RENEGADES

● psiots ● fugitives ● resistance ● wild cards ● freedom ● independence ● hot-headed ● hopeful

A better future, right? Human potential? Or maybe you just thought it'd be cool to shoot lightning bolts?

However the Harbinger Foundation roped you in, we're here to tell you they want to make a "better future" by using your "human potential" to shoot those lightning bolts where they tell you to. But we stand for something different, for choice. To them, we're dangerous, uncontrollable. We're Renegades.

We came together around Peter Stanchek, a former Foundation recruit and the only one who rivals Toyo Harada in raw power. Don't kid yourself, Peter's no hero. He grew up rough, barely able to control his powers, and he destroys everything and everyone he touches. I'm no exception: initially, Peter's idea of asking me out was to force himself into my mind and override my free will, an act I'll never forgive.

But Peter saw through the Foundation's lies and promises—especially when he discovered that Harada the "peaceful humanitarian" had ordered the death of Peter's best friend Joe as a ploy to keep Peter under control.

Peter had no grasp of tactics or subtlety at the time, so he tried to hit Harada head on and nearly got himself killed in the process. Clinging to life, Peter escaped with the help of Faith Herbert, who would become the first—and maybe the best—of us.

I wanted Peter dead after what he did to me, but I couldn't ignore the truth about Harada, about his foundation. I wanted to fight monsters, so I chose to walk beside one—for Joe, who was my friend too, and for anyone who'd struggled against authority.

To take on an army, we needed one of our own, and the first order of business was to "borrow" a list of latent psiots and start activating them. Faith eagerly join up as our aerial scout, but she's the true heart of this group: whether she's flying or not, nothing seems to burden her. We all look up to her when things seem

darkest, and she delights in taking to the skies, always finding a new way to soar.

Our first new addition was Charlene Dupre, a former exotic dancer who uses her stage name Flamingo and has a personality as fiery as her powers. She's been running from one bad situation to another for years, but I think she's finally starting to trust us. In the backwoods of Georgia, we met John Torkelson, who insists we call him Torque as part of the fantasy he-man reality in which he wraps himself. All of that is just compensation for the scared, crippled boy desperate to fight his way out of his own life.

Other recruits found their way to us. Monica Jim, a Generation Zero psiot known as Animalia, played a key role in freeing us from Harada's imprisonment. Her ability to cloak herself in cartoonish creatures belies even greater power. Then we have Octavio Gonzalez, the über-hacker known as @x. He's human like me, but he can break into any secure system; his theft of a top-secret Project Rising Spirit database put him on our radar.

I won't lie to you—the past year has been rough. We've been ambushed by PRS, who wanted to use us against Harada for their own ends. Our attempt to rescue a group of young psiots who'd escaped from PRS didn't go well, and our mental captivity inside Harada's virtual funhouse showed us what can happen when he's not in control.

That glimpse of a broken god changed our strategy. If Harada is coming apart, then the world has never seen a greater threat—and we've never had a better opportunity. Now is the time to take the fight to him. You might make the difference, if you're willing to join us, and if you're willing to stand with those who won't be told what to do.

—Kris Hathaway

THE SECT

● secret society ● He Who is Not to be Named ● secrets of immortality ● factious ● the Boon ● multifaction cabal

HISTORY

In ancient Egypt, the court poet and advisor Aram-Ho-Tep ("Aram is pleased") presented Amenhotep IV, tenth Pharaoh of Egypt's Eighteenth Dynasty, with the design of a supernatural reliquary able to transform the energy of worship into power. The pharaoh decreed Egypt would honor only the god Aten, and Amenhotep declared himself Akhenaten ("beloved of Aten") to be worshiped as Aten's presence on Earth. Akhenaten stripped the priests of their authority and appointed his own ministers to oversee public works, law enforcement, food production, and the treasury. His mistake was assuming men given such power would remain loyal. These ministers secretly promised the deposed priests that they would remove Akhenaten and restore them to public power; in exchange the priests would keep the citizenry complacent and leave managing the empire to the ministers. In 1336 BC the ministers assassinated Akhenaten and his court advisors. Resolved that true power was wasted on priests or kings, they swore loyalty to each other, creating the Sect, a group dedicated to controlling civilization from the shadows.

During the ministers' coup, the pharaoh's advisor Aram-Ho-Tep survived by killing his would-be assassins—after they had plunged a spear through his throat—and escaping. The Sect ordered his name and any record he existed destroyed, they wanted to hunt him down without any interference or competition. The Sect's goal was to torture "He Who is Not to be Named" to gain the secrets of the immortality-granting relic known as the Boon.

THE MODERN SECT

Since its inception, the Sect has evolved into a multifaction cabal of conspiratorial organizations, each with its own agendas and methods. Though some factions still seek the keys to immortality and revenge against "He Who is Not to be Named," most concentrate on completing their own goals and guiding the world from the shadows. This is not without risks, however. The now-defunct factions known as the Dominion, the Green Dragon Lamas, and the Null played their hands too early and lost.

Today the Sect comprises the following factions.

Black Bloc: A coalition of Sect henchmen fed up with being foot soldiers for other established factions. They're tactical Dadaists with no apparent agenda beyond disrupting their employers' plans by any ironic means necessary.

Church of Retrology: The church's members follow Symbolix, the philosophy of founder J. Douglas Morrison. Retrology fuses shamanism with science, and Retrologists actualize their ideal selves by retreating from modern distractions.

Gnomes of Zürich: Believing power lies in controlling the flow of resources, the Gnomes of Zürich are masters in the art of international commodities trading. Also, they are actual gnomes.

Hashish Eaters: Thieves, assassins, and spies, Hashish Eaters sharpen their senses with vaporized THC. Enemies learn too late it does not dull their minds as much as they pretend.

Master Builders: Known for their charities, the Master Builders have been part of America since before the nation's founding. They built the country and claim it as theirs, and they act like frat bros.

The One Percent: The One Percent control global finances and money markets. They move only to secure profit or prevent loss, and they worship Mammon.

Project Rising Spirit: PRS is the current incarnation of a clandestine research and development company supplying the world with cutting-edge weapons. Focused on developing psiot weaponry, PRS has drawn away from the Sect.

Sisters of Perpetual Darkness: Daughters of Lilith, mistresses of God, and guardians of forbidden knowledge, the nuns of the Dark Cloister find redemption in spilling the blood of their enemies.

The Vine: In 402 AD, an alien race known as the Vine left "plantings"—aliens genetically modified to appear human—to cultivate and perfect Earth for eventual occupation. The Sect dismisses the Vine's origin myth but respects their effectiveness.

THE VINE

● alien race ● Shanhara ● sacred armor ● Loam ● colony ship ● High Council ● High Priest ● the Sect

HISTORY

Millennia ago, an intelligent, nameless race lived on a paradisiacal extraterrestrial planet. One day a cruel race of energy beings arrived on the planet and terrorized the indigenous population, forcing them into slavery and hardship. The inhabitants named these invaders the Torment and watched helplessly as these insatiable, wanton creatures transformed the planet from a paradise into a wasteland. Most of the enslaved gave up hope of earning freedom and resigned themselves to watching the planet burn around them.

When nearly all hope was lost, a lone wanderer resolved to find some trace of the old world out in the scorched wilderness. Out of food and nearing death, the wanderer stumbled upon the mighty Hara vine, the last vestige of paradise left on the planet. As the wanderer settled beneath the towering vine and decided to remain beneath its branches until death claimed him, a single pod growing from the vine dropped to the ground. The shining orb enveloped the wanderer as a suit of unimaginable power. With this armor, the lone wanderer drove back the Torment and reclaimed his planet.

This victory united this warrior's people in common purpose. He named his race the Vine in honor of the sacred Hara vine, and the suit of armor became known as Shanhara, the X-O Manowar armor. Loam, as the warrior called his homeworld, flourished and transformed into the paradise it once was.

Before the warrior died many years later, he prophesied that the armor would one day reveal its gifts to another and usher in an age of prosperity. For centuries thereafter, thousands of the Vine's bravest warriors and tactical masterminds tried to don the X-O Manowar armor, but none survived the bonding process. And so Shanhara sat silent, waiting.

The prophecy's fulfillment would eventually come in a strange and altogether unexpected form.

LEADERSHIP

Before Aric of Dacia claimed the Armor of Shanhara, the Vine was ruled by a High Council comprising the three most important individuals on Loam. Each Council member represented the interests of a single branch of Vine society (the clergy, the military, and the citizenry), and together the Council would decide on the best course of action to steer their race toward its ultimate destiny. Due to the vastness of space, the Council relied on psychic meetings called gatherings to meet the needs of even the most far-flung Vine colonies and fleets.

However, the power structure on Loam turned upside down during Aric's assault on the planet. The resulting war between Aric's forces and those loyal to the High Council removed the Council from power. In its place Aric set the Vine High Priest as the ultimate authority on Loam. The High Priest and his associates have dedicated themselves to spreading the belief that Aric is the Chosen of Shanhara that the original wanderer once prophesied.

GOALS

The defeat of the Torment and the restoration of Loam led the Vine to undertake a divine mission to spread word of Shanhara to the farthest reaches of the galaxy. To this end, the Vine colony ship departed Loam with Shanhara aboard and began wandering the stars for countless millennia.

Whenever the ship discovers a planet bearing intelligent life, the Vine takes specimens from the inhabitants and adapts Vine physiology to accommodate the environment. Then the indigenous DNA is injected into Vine offspring so that they take on the physical appearance of the local life forms. These changelings are known as "plantings" and can access the gatherings.

GAME RULES

Gameplay in *Valiant Universe* revolves around two things: *Building the Story* and *Rolling Dice*. Once more detail is provided on what you need before your game begins, we'll dive into explaining both aspects.

Note: For ease of reference, the first time an important term is introduced, it will be bolded. Additionally, the rules may reference the "Cue System." This is a general name for this unique rules system, while "*Valiant Universe RPG*" or "*Valiant Universe*" represents this entire volume, meaning the Cue System rules paired with the Valiant Universe skin.

Dice

As noted in the *Introduction*, *Valiant Universe* uses polyhedral dice: D4, D6, D8, D10, D12, and D20 (the value representing how many faces each die has); anytime "D" is used, as in "D12," it's shorthand for "die."

Abbreviations

This section makes use of several different types of abbreviation. For example, if a term has an abbreviation in parentheses behind it, from that point forward the abbreviation will be used: e.g., **Lead Narrator (LN)**.

Another example is "**Might Stat Die**," "**Action Stat Die**," and so on. After they appear as written the first time, all future references will be abbreviated as "Might Die," "Action Die," and so on. Each time it is assumed the player will understand that all such instances are referring to a "**Stat Die**."

BEFORE THE GAME BEGINS

On page 6 of the *Introduction* is a list of the basics you need to start playing. The following information builds off of that list.

THE LEAD NARRATOR

Valiant Universe does not require a gamemaster for play. Instead, the responsibilities of the Lead Narrator (LN) rotate from player to player throughout the game. However, an appointed LN isn't prohibited either. Ultimately, it's up to the player group. If the group performs better with a dedicated LN, appoint one. But if the group doesn't require one, simply use the rules as presented.

CHOOSE A HERO

Each **Character Dossier** (starting on p. 74) consists of an illustration and all the pertinent information for a *Valiant Universe* character. To make sure you choose a character you'll like, you'll have to understand the different parts of a Dossier. Let's take a look at the Dossier for Peter Stanchek (see p. 124).

Illustration/Description

The first page of the Dossier includes an illustration of the character as well as an indicator of the Title Exposé where they primarily appear, along with Vital Factors, such as name, affiliation, **Character Level**, and a place to track **Event Points** (see *Character Advancement*, p. 70). This section also includes a set of one-word **Tags** that immediately provide a grasp of what defines this character at a glance.

This page also includes a history of the character, along with a short personality description. All of this, along with the Tags and the material on the second page, provide everything the player should need to quickly get inside the head of their hero or villain and leap into the action.

Stats and Stat Dice

Beginning at the top of the Dossier's second page, you'll see the different **stats** for Peter and the different dice that represent those stats (**Stat Dice**).

Might: This represents the physical build of the character, whether endurance, brute strength, sheer stamina, and so on.

SUPERHEROES: ACCEPTING THE PREMISE

From the moment the first superhero comic book stories began to unfold, writers had a conundrum. They had some characters seemingly as powerful as gods fighting alongside (or against) characters with extremely limited abilities, if not downright mundane attributes. How does the villain with only genius-level intelligence stand up to a being that can annihilate planets?

In the real world, it's simply not plausible, but as we step into a comics universe, we come upon the following: "X is only as powerful as the plot needs him to be." That is the basic premise a comic reader must accept, as this mechanism is used across the entire spectrum of comic books. Sure, some comics manage to pull that off with more panache than others, but it's a suspension of disbelief you must accept if you're going to enjoy the medium.

Superhero RPGs run into the same problem. What's more, it's exacerbated by rules mechanics that try to codify powers, such as laying down rules for what they can and can't do. Furthermore, most superhero RPGs lock those various powers into defined space, thus creating a framework of comparison that comic book authors can usually ignore with more aplomb. If it's not needed for the story, the writer can ignore it or explain a plausible way around it. When there's a hard-and-fast rule for how all of a superhero's powers work, however, that type of "just ignore it and the players will be okay" mentality doesn't always work very well.

In that regard, Valiant Universe is luckier than most superhero RPGs. The Powers within this rule set are all about enabling players to use their imaginations to figure out what they can do as opposed to limiting a given Power to an inflexible set of guidelines and stats. For example, rather than stating that Bloodshot can deadlift X tons, the Cue System allows him to lift as much as the story needs. The nature of the Cue System lends itself wonderfully to the "come up with a cool superhero reason and get back into the action" mindset comic book authors enjoy.

From inception, the Valiant Universe has kept such obvious ploys within more plausible boundaries by maintaining an internally consistent universe where powers have more of a sci-fi explanation and don't vary wildly according to the vicissitudes of the plot. The Cue System, working within the well-defined boundaries of the Valiant Universe's more real-world style, helps ameliorate such issues.

That being said, the nature of an RPG—despite the Valiant Universe's ability to avoid such things—means there will still likely come moments when players are reviewing character stats and may come away shaking their heads. For example, in the Valiant Universe, the psiot Toyo Harada is almost godlike. And in that reality, if we created a "true" system for defining his Powers in direct comparison with, say, a run-of-the-mill PRS soldier, Harada would likely be rolling a D100 as opposed to simply his D8 Action Die vs. the soldier's D8.

Since the system would break down under such circumstances, the ultimate definition of a character's Powers is left up to the players. Always remember: Harada is only as strong as the plot needs him to be. That means, even with the game stats showing that the PRS soldier might be able to harm Harada, as the players develop the story at the gaming table, Harada is almost always going to win (even if that takes some Plot Point nudging by the Lead Narrator). However, remember that the Valiant Universe is grounded in realism wherever possible, so "lucky shots" against an incredibly powerful character like Harada can still have a plausible, plot-related explanation. For example, despite his incredible power, Harada is not invincible: his hubris means he can underestimate what even one committed person can do with even a little bit of power. Thus, a "lucky shot" against a powerful character like Harada would make a more convincing story when it is portrayed as a character exploiting that overconfidence rather than simply "getting a good roll" or "being in the right place at the right time."

Intellect: This corresponds to the mental faculties of the character, whether street smarts, learned science, or just plain inherent brilliance.

Charisma: The ability of a character to lead or to talk his way out of a situation is based on charisma; a character's presence as he walks into a room.

Action: How good a person is in combat—whether ranged, close quarters, hand-to-hand, or even vehicle-to-vehicle or ship-to-ship—is covered by this stat. Basically any action-oriented maneuver a character wants to try that doesn't use his or her **Powers**.

Luck: Luck is a very special number for each character. It's not a Stat Die but instead a static number that represents the capriciousness of fate. If any Stat, Action, or Power Die result on any roll should ever match the character's Luck Stat, the roll is a success, no matter what. When rolling multiple dice for a Power, check the Luck Stat against both dice before discarding any dice, if necessary.

Powers

Each character has a unique set of Powers, each with a corresponding Power Die. Whenever a player uses that particular Power to accomplish an action, the exact manner of how the player rolls dice is determined by the Power on the Character Dossier (see *Powers*, under *Rolling Dice*, p. 51, for more information).

Powers are not just superhuman in nature. Instead, powers represent the unique capabilities of a given hero (or villain) and what he or she excels at, whether that's Livewire's psionic ability to talk to machines or the endless years of training and drive that let Ninjak move silently through the shadows or Faith's Pop Culture Knowledge that weaves with her Optimism to act as the glue keeping the Renegades together no matter how dark it gets. During the game, players may quickly find that some of the most memorable moments come when using "non-Power" Powers to save the day.

If a Power has a direct translation as armor, a weapon, or some other aspect that applies to the rest of the character sheet, either the Power or that portion of the sheet will include a name in parentheses. In other words, review your sheet to ensure you know where all the elements that make up a Power are located. The various sections provide all the details a player needs to appropriately explore what he or she can accomplish with their abilities during a game.

The name of each Power provides a guideline for what the power does, but ultimately it'll be up to the player, the Lead Narrator (LN), and the roleplaying group to determine what a character can and can't do with each Power. For example, a player may want a given Power to do two relatively different things in a given gaming session. The LN may allow both, or he may allow the second only after the use of a **Plot Point** or after lowering the Power Die value. In the end, as with all great comic books, a character is as strong—or as weak—as the plot needs him or her to be, and your stories will need the same flexibility.

Chris is playing Livewire as the characters are trying to exfiltrate from a PRS facility with crucial stolen data. Time for Livewire to step up, especially as Ninjak just finished taking care of some security personnel at their station.

One of her Powers is "Manipulate Electronic Devices." Obviously this is wide open, and so Chris knows he's got a lot of latitude. Chris provides the following Narration: "Livewire sprints to the station and touches the computer screen. 'This will only take a moment!' She then taps into the building's security feeds to find out where the bad guys are and devises a path out."

The LN doesn't have any issues with this use of her Power, so Chris makes a standard Challenge dice roll (see p. 51).

In a subsequent turn, Livewire's team is nearing the outer wall of the facility, but they're out of explosives and the door access is crawling with ever-increasing numbers of PRS security.

The LN sets the stage of the current turn: "The characters find themselves in a small, fully-automated assembly hub. A myriad of loud sounds, blurring wheels and rotating robotic arms doesn't mask the shouting of guards as they seal the two doors and begin sweeping into the cluttered space searching for you with deadly intent. Chris, you're up."

Chris thinks for a moment, then snaps his fingers and smiles at a new idea and begins: "Livewire notices a large flywheel spinning at high RPM near the outer wall. 'Cover me.'" She crabs over to a terminal, plugs into the machine with a touch, overrides the safety protocols, revs the RPM as high as the machine will go, and then drops the brake. The machine vibrates wildly as the howl spikes up to a screeching pitch, then the flywheel breaks free and slams into the wall, shattering open a hole."

The LN slowly closes his mouth as he thinks it over then determines that seems a bit much for the Power as is. As such the LN tells Chris that it can happen like this, but instead of Livewire's usual D10 Power Die, she must use a D8—rolling it with the Intellect Die—for the Challenge and Chris needs to spend a Plot Point to show the flywheel casing had a hairline crack from the lack of proper maintenance to allow the catastrophic event.

Chris happily tosses in the Plot Point and grabs dice to make the roll!

Cues

In the center of the Dossier are the character's **Cues**. Cues are statements or quotes that help define the character—whether it's attitude, capabilities or personality. Each Cue helps form the basis of a **Narration** (see p. 47). Additionally, they are split into Cues and **Action Cues.** While they are interchangeable as the situation dictates, generally Action Cues are for when characters are storming the heavily secured facility in all their superhero majesty.

Disposition

Below the Cues are a few quick lines that help convey the Disposition of a given character and provide additional hooks that help a player understand how they might roleplay that character. In other words, Dispositions define how a character will react in various circumstances, whereas Tags define what your character is.

Armor

The **Armor** track gives the number of Armor pips the character has. Armor is a generic term that covers everything from a Kevlar jacket, military-grade body armor, superhuman thick skin, to extreme agility that keeps a person from being hit, and beyond. For example, Peter Stanchek is a young man that doesn't think about wearing body armor; if he's surprised, he's got very little protection, but he's almost never caught unaware, and his Psionic Shield Power acts as Armor. Note the "(Armor)" next to Psionic Shield in the Power's section pointing toward the Armor portion of the character Dossier. Armor helps deflect damage during **Combat** (see p. 52).

Health

The **Health** track defines the character's Health status. Once a character's Armor (or any Power acting as Armor) has been depleted from damage, he begins to take damage to his Health track. As injuries pile up, a character will start to suffer negative performance effects (see p. 55).

Weapons

In a dangerous universe, most characters carry one or two weapons. The weapons column lists those weapons, the damage they inflict on a successful hit, and their range. In some instances, additional rules might be included for the effects of the weapon.

Remember that Powers that act as weapons can have additional stats here. Let's take a look at Flamingo's Dossier (see pp. 96-97). Her Pyrokinesis Power is a weapon and so it has "(Weapon)" next to the name in the Powers portion of the character Dossier, which directs the player to both the Fireblast and Immolate stats in the Weapon section. These two sections combine to provide all the details a player needs to use this attack. In this case specifically the player rolls a D8 (alongside the appropriate Stat Die as determined by the LN) when attacking with either "weapon" (as noted in the Powers section), with the range of the Power determined by which the player chooses to use. If an attack is successful the player rolls either a D4 or D6 to determine damage (as noted in the Weapons section).

Don't forget, though, that even while the Power is noted as primarily a weapon, the Power can be used in a variety of ways only limited by the imagination. For example on the Dossier you already have Vectored Thrust (Pseudo-Flight) and Micro-Combustions (Armor) Powers—all abilities connected to her primary pyrokinetics. But what if a player wants to simply heat up a gun at 100 meters without a big fireball giving away their location? Make the Narration and see if your LN likes where you're taking it!

Equipment

While Peter trusts his abilities, he also carries some tools and supplies, as shown in the Equipment column of his Dossier. Unlike weapons, equipment in *Valiant Universe* has no set stats. The Bottle of Painkillers … sure, they could just be painkillers. But what if right in the middle of an escape the LN drops a Plot Point to say that Peter pops a pill thinking to overcome a migraine from extensive use of his powers. Yet they're not his usual painkillers but actually drugs gene-tailored to Peter's system that the Harbinger Foundation managed to get into Peter's bottle…What might happen?!

Or take a look at Flamingo's Dossier again, under Equipment, where it says: "Copy of *Heat, Thermodynamics, and Statistical Physics*." Did she pick that up herself or did someone give it to her? Is there a secret character in her life the others aren't aware of? Is he a mundane or is he a psiot? What if during a game the LN decides the time is perfect for dropping the bombshell that Flamingo's been "hiding" a psiot…What might happen?

In all such instances, the player may have to answer those questions during gameplay with a clever Narration (see p. 47).

NPC Dossiers

Finally, there are two types of Dossiers—those for fleshed-out characters like the heroes (or villains) players will become, and those for less-important individuals like henchmen or supporting characters. These **non-player character** (**NPC**) Dossiers take up a third of a page and contain much less information than player character Dossiers. Lead Narrators can also modify the NPCs in the NPCs section (see p. 146) to expand the number of enemies for a given Event, and each NPC Dossier includes blank spaces to add Powers, if desired. LNs can also visit **www.catalyst.com/valiant** to download a blank NPC Dossier (it's also found at the back of this book).

Note

Players can easily grab a Dossier and leap into action based on the name of a character, his Tags and Cues, or even just the artwork. However, some players may feel the need to fully understand how the core dice-rolling mechanics work before making such a decision. In such an instance, the players should thoroughly review the *Rolling Dice* portion of this section before selecting their Dossier (see p. 51).

SELECT AN EVENT BRIEF

The stories in the Valiant Universe comics are myriad and endless, and so are the Event Briefs. Flipping through that section (see p. 162) will showcase a huge variety of action, from cities to small towns, from action-oriented combat to stealthy intrigue, and more. Pick the poison, and there's a vial ready to drink down at the gaming table.

Event Briefs supply all the information you'll need to start a gameplay session with little effort required on the part of the players. Each Brief includes many points that players can use to play the Event or string together multiple Events into a Campaign (see p. 48).

Exposé Title: For ease of finding specific Events, each includes the corresponding Title Exposé at the top, meaning the source material used to create that Event was drawn from the comics within that Title. When two or more Events are designed to directly follow each other as part of a connected story, these Events are numbered sequentially (1, 2, 3, and so on) to form part of a Campaign (see p. 48). Connected Events like these can provide many evenings of play as players move through each Event and ultimately reach the climax of the story arc.

Suggested Characters: The Events in this book weave through existing comics material. As such, in front of each is a suggested list of characters to play for a given Event. However, they are just suggestions. If all players agree, you can bring in any existing characters—or those created from scratch—into any Event. Just provide a quick Narration for why your character is participating in the Event, and into the gaming you go!

Context: A short overview of what the Event will be about, what the objectives will be, and what opposition the characters can expect to find. This will be presented as "sourcebook fiction," as though the reader was a character transplanted into the game universe, reading military documents, historical texts, security briefs, intercepted personal communications, local newspapers, and so on.

Objectives: The Objectives list a set of goals or accomplishments that characters are expected to do, though they aren't mandatory.

Cues: The Event's Cues function the same as the Cues on a Character Dossier. Each Cue can be the basis for a Narration as well as a description of the Event itself.

Tags: Tags give short descriptions of the Event in order to give players the gist of the adventure—for example, when trying to skim and find a specific flavor for an Event to run—or to aid the creation of a campaign.

The Setting: Below that is the Setting, a description of the area where the characters find themselves at the beginning of the Event.

Enemies/Obstacles: Finally, an Enemies/Obstacles list gives the opponents and obstacles that the characters may have to defeat or overcome to successfully complete the Event, with each considered a Scene, or section, of the overall Event Brief. As with the Event as a whole, for ease of use each Scene includes suggested NPCs to use from the book. However, once more, those are just suggestions. Use whatever NPCs your groups think will make the most enjoyable roleplaying experience! Each Scene may also offer some special-case rules or LN advice for ways the players can tackle that particular Scene.

As with almost every aspect of *Valiant Universe*, much of the information given in an Event Brief is up to the discretion of the players. Want to add your own Cues? Go for it! Want to change parts of the Scene? No problem! Want to change the Objectives? No one's stopping you! Always remember to keep the fun factor high.

BUILDING THE STORY: PLAYING VALIANT UNIVERSE

Once each player has a set of dice, the appropriate Character Dossier at hand, an Event Brief selected, and an LN chosen, your group is ready to get started.

Valiant Universe play is divided into a series of segments that build on each other: *Turns and Narrations*, *Scenes*, *Event Briefs*, and *Campaigns*.

TURNS AND NARRATIONS

Valiant Universe gameplay is divided into a series of turns. Each turn, every player will have a chance to play out and describe his character's actions. These descriptions are called Narrations, and as the game progresses these Narrations will build on each other and form the story of the game.

Lead Narrator

Each turn begins with the LN and continues with the player on the LN's left until all players have had a turn at Narration.

The LN begins the turn by giving a narrative of the current situation and advancing the plot, as described under Event Briefs (see p. 162). The LN also makes any actions or die rolls for enemies the characters may encounter. Though the LN begins the turn, he is the last to act with his character.

Once all players have had a chance to narrate their character's actions, the turn ends and a new turn begins.

SCENES

A Scene is defined as the start and finish of a given section of time within an Event Brief. A Scene will contain a number of turns, which will vary depending upon what's occurring within a given Scene.

For example, take a look at *X-O Manowar: Her Majesty's Alien Service* (see pp. 186-187). Each of the three descriptions of the Enemies/Obstacles found in that Event Brief is a Scene. There is no hard and fast rule on how many turns are in a Scene. Instead, that will be based on how many players are involved, their style of play and their Narrations, which ultimately leads to how quickly (or slowly) they're able to accomplish the goals of a given Scene.

Scenes and the LN

The LN starts a Scene and is the LN for every turn until a Scene is accomplished. Once a Scene is finished, the player to the right of the current LN becomes the new LN. The new LN starts the first turn of the new Scene by providing a narrative of the current situation, and so on, as described above.

EVENT BRIEF

An Event Brief usually constitutes a single game session, and the session ends when all of the Scenes within an Event Brief are completed. The number of Scenes required to finish an Event Brief is detailed in each Event Brief, but this can be modified by the player group.

For example, one player group may decide after accomplishing the three Scenes laid out in *X-O Manowar: Her Majesty's Alien Service* that the

Event Brief is done, and their *Valiant Universe* gaming is over for the day. However, another group playing the same Event Brief might decide to add in a new fourth Scene that helps close up some of the plot threads that grew through players' Narrations, so they keep playing. A third group might not have as long to play as the other groups, so they actually split the Event Brief up into two different days of gaming sessions. Whatever works for each playing group is just fine.

CAMPAIGN

The four-part *A Hunt For The Ages* Event Briefs (see pp. 191-199) are designed to stitch together a larger story that will span many gaming sessions.

This can be done intentionally if the group decides what larger stories they'd like to participate in. Or the group can assign a dedicated LN to devise some plots that will bridge multiple Events. A campaign can also occur unexpectedly if players finish an Event Brief and realize that some excellent unfinished plots threads developed, and they want to see what new and exciting plot twists might occur in a longer campaign.

BUILDING THE STORY: NARRATION AND FLOW

Giving a Narration is quite easy. All a player has to do is describe what his or her character is doing, whether it's engaging in combat, exploring a room, using a Power, or repairing a device.

If any action has a chance of failure, then a die roll is made to determine whether the action succeeds.

Many Narrations are based on Cues provided on Character Dossiers or Event Briefs.

CUES

Cues are building blocks players can use as a basis for Narrations. Cues are both suggestions and descriptions. Cues can be positive and negative and never have to be narrated the same way twice. If a player draws a blank or wants to make sure he's staying on topic, he can take a look at a list of Cues and choose an appropriate one to base a Narration around.

> *Phil—playing as Toyo Harada—finds himself in perilous circumstances. He's the first player to make a Narration this turn, and the situation isn't good: the players are trapped in an alien spaceship that's crashed and is heading toward the bottom of the ocean. Phil takes a quick look at Harada's Dossier and sees the Cue "We have very little time." That couldn't possibly fit the situation more perfectly. What's more, from the character's bio, Phil knows that Harada is a dominant leader. He also knows that with such a charismatic character there needs to be some gravitas, even as death looms immediate and large.*
>
> *"Attend!" Harada commands. He forcefully sweeps his arms to include his team. 'We have very little time. Give me status updates immediately and your recommendations for action!'"*

MOVING THE STORY FORWARD

Collaborative Narration is about creating a story and moving it forward. *Valiant Universe* is about making impossible choices, facing terrifying challenges, and overcoming them in fantastic and fun ways. It is all about saying "yes" to fun, not "no" to something unexpected.

So when you are faced with the impossible, you smile and say, "Yes, and …" Then you make it up! There is no wrong way in *Valiant Universe*. Want to have the characters swallowed by a timearc into the Faraway that just appeared in San Francisco's Chinatown and took half a building and a taxi with you? Then do it!

But be ready for the LN to have a Generation Zero psiot step out of that taxi for some butt-kicking on you. After all, the rule is "Yes, and..."

For example, the players are all gathered around the table for the night's adventure (Event Brief) and are already in the thick of the action. In the previous turn, Brandie, the current LN, revealed that after the group was swept into the Faraway by a timearc and a large war band of what appears to be Mesoamericans started hunting them, one of the walls of the cave the group has been backed into suddenly appears to be acting funny...

After the rest of the players make their Narrations in an effort to determine what's going on, Brandie's character (as the LN, her character is the last to act in a turn) says, "I use my scanner to see if the wall's becoming unstable at a macro- or micro-atomic level," hoping that'll provide some data on the strange-acting wall.

It is now the beginning of the next turn, and Brandie, still the LN, sets the stage for the start of this turn's events. She takes a moment to gather her thoughts, based upon what's just transpired from the previous turn, and says, "Unfortunately, that didn't bring up any data as whatever is occurring appears to be beyond the scanner's abilities. A new round of loud but unintelligible shouting comes from the Mesoamericans outside, and another fusillade of arrows arcs into the partially blockaded cave, narrowly missing one of you. Additionally, the cave wall now appears to be going transparent in a beating rhythm. And each time it goes transparent, you appear to see someone shouting at you from within, or without—you can't tell." The LN, wanting to have a little fun, then places a Plot Point into the pool and says, "Ninjak, you recognize the man from your young school days. Despite his exotic uniform, built from what appears to be crystal pellets, it's Colonel Percy Fawcett, the explorer who disappeared close to a hundred years ago in South America. Ninjak, you're up."

Joshua—playing as Ninjak—gapes at the surprise twist but quickly smiles and says, "Yes, and on seeing Percy Fawcett during one of the wall's phasing moments, I say, 'Harada, I think a timearc is tunneling between parts of the Faraway. This might be an escape that doesn't involve several hundred warriors. Use your AI and see if she can't establish a quantum field that'll stabilize the singularity enough for us to escape. I'll keep the warriors at bay!' Ninjak moves carefully back to the cave mouth, preparing to unleash

a storm of knives and throwing stars should the warriors try and rush the cave."

Collin, Harada's player, mouths to himself, "Quantum field?" With a shrug and a smile he picks up the thread of the adventure. With his best serious impression of a man like Harada, he says, "You confirm my own suspicions, Ninjak!" Collin drops one of his Plot Point tokens on the table. "I'll inverse my Psionic Shield to act as a conduit for Cassandra to infiltrate the singularity and stabilize it with the introduction of a quantum field!" Out of character, Collin then says to the LN, "I'll use the Plot Point to support this." Collin reviews his Character's Dossier quickly to ensure he knows how his Power is used and rolls a D12 for the Challenge (see p. 51) with a result of 2. Then he rolls a D10 for his Power Die and a D10 for his Intellect, getting a result of 5 and 7 (neither of which match his Luck Stat), which add to 12 due to the Power's Type; the LN decides there are no modifiers, so the total rolled is 14. Brandie, as the LN, rolls the opposing D20—their gaming group decided the LN would roll the D20—rolling a 17 (no modifiers are added). Looking at the result, Brandie shakes her head. "It appears your AI did its job too well. Yes, the cave wall is holding and now you can also hear Percy Fawcett yelling, 'Hurry it up, chaps, or those natives will be chopping you but quick.' However, the instability of the timearc tunneling has breached Cassandra's quantum field and is starting to consume the rest of the cave. If the instability reaches critical, it'll bring the whole mountain down on you." Brandie turns to Bo, nodding to him that it is his turn now.

Staying in character, Bo pantomimes sheathing a blade and affects his best Gilad Anni-Padda voice, saying, "Even the Eternal Warrior knows when it is time for a strategic withdrawal, especially as we appear to have unexpected allies.' Gilad quickly leaps through the opening."

PLOT POINTS

Plots create twists you never saw coming—a HALO drop of H.A.R.D. Corps troopers right in the middle of your firefight, that hidden button that does something, or an alien beast suddenly rampaging out of a timearc. Plot Points can make all these happen!

In gameplay, Plot Points may be used in many ways. They are used to interrupt or alter another player's Narration—a method of adding a twist to the game. They can also be used to change player turn order, alter a die roll, or gain back a point of Health. The ways players utilize Plot Points are only limited by how creative they want to be.

Players will be earning and spending Plot Points throughout the game, and using some type of tokens (such as poker chips) is the best method to track them. However, players are free to use whatever system works best, whether it's chips, dice, noting them down on a piece of paper/tablet/smartphone, and so on.

Earning Plot Points: Players

Players begin the game with three Plot Points each and may be awarded more points by the LN for particularly good Narrations. Players may have a maximum of five Plot Points at any time and only one point may be awarded to a player at a time.

Players with no Plot Points are automatically given one at the beginning of their turn.

The LN is the only person who may award Plot Points.

Earning Plot Points: Lead Narrator

The LN also receives Plot Points into a Plot Pool. The LN starts an Event Brief with one Plot Point and every time a player spends a Plot Point (see below), the LN receives a Plot Point.

Unlike the players, the LN's Plot Pool has no size limit.

The Plot Pool transfers between LNs in between Scenes. If the Plot Pool is empty at the start of a new Scene, the new LN receives 1 Plot Point.

Spending Plot Points: Players

No matter what effect you want to cause, the cost is one Plot Point and the change is immediately made to the game. Players may not spend more than one point at a time in an attempt to maximize the twist, though they can spend multiple Plot Points during any player's Narration (whether their own, or another player's).

Example things to do with Plot Points:
- Change turn order
- Give a modifier to a dice roll (positive or negative)
- Unseen PRS soldiers attack!

- Regain a Health point
- The character's Powers suddenly fail for a short period of time
- The sky's the limit!

> A new turn of Valiant Universe has started and Jason's character is injured. At the beginning of his turn, Jason spends one Plot Point to regain a point of Health beyond what he's recovered with the character's Accelerated Healing Power.
>
> He deposits his Plot Point token into the Plot Pool and restores one of the Health pips on his character's Dossier. He then makes a quick Narration:
>
> "Gilad Anni-Padda, still bleeding after he tangled with X-O Manowar, focuses his millennia of accumulated willpower into moderately healing his injury."

Just remember, Plot Point use doesn't always mean a positive change. Often plot twists are a negative event—something goes wrong that must be fixed or adapted to by the characters.

Spending Plot Points: Lead Narrator

Like players, the LN can spend Plot Points in any fashion he chooses, with the following caveats:
- Plot Points can only be spent to aid NPCs or create plot twists; they cannot be spent to directly aid or hinder a player.
- The LN can only spend one Plot Point per turn, unlike the players who can spend more than one per turn.

TROUBLESHOOTING

In an improv-style game such as *Valiant Universe*, the single greatest issue that can suck the life and energy out of a gaming session is if players start spending too much time deliberating over their actions and Narrations. If you've ever watched an improv play, when a character pauses too long trying to follow up with what's just been said, you're thrown out of the action and the energy is gone.

If this starts to occur, players should work together as a group to help a player feel more at ease with this style of play. This could be practice sessions outside of a game, or could be something as simple as finding an enjoyable improv play to watch that can provide an example of how this style can unfold. Finally, at www.catalystgamelabs.com/valiant find videos showing Valiant Universe game play in action.

ROLLING DICE

No matter how well your storytelling is unfolding, there will come a time when the dice need to come out to help resolve a given situation.

THE CORE MECHANIC

As a story-driven roleplaying game, *Valiant Universe* uses a simple, cinematic dice-rolling mechanic to resolve **Challenges**, **Tests**, and **Combat**.

The Basic Mechanic for Challenges and Tests

A D12 is the **Base Die**, and forms the foundation that all players' rolls are based upon. The result of this roll is modified by the appropriate Stat Die and any additional **Modifiers**. The basic dice rolling mechanic for all Challenges and Tests is:

D12 + Stat Die (D4, D6, D8, D10, D12) + **Modifiers** vs. **D20**

A Challenge is any action taken against an inanimate object, while a Test is any action taken against another character or any NPC that is non-combat related.

Which Stat Die To Use: The appropriate Stat Die to use will usually be very easy to determine: trying to lift something heavy? Might. Trying to outsmart an opponent? Intellect, and so on. Ultimately, however, if the situation is too muddy, the LN makes the decision on which Stat Die to use (see p. 42).

Modifiers: Modifiers represent good or bad situational circumstances that take an ordinary situation and make it extraordinary. For example, while trying to work on X, the player is: being attacked (a negative modifier); he's wounded (a negative modifier); there's no gravity (depending upon what he is trying to accomplish, it could be a positive or negative modifier); the player is getting additional help (this also could be a positive or negative modifier depending upon the Stat Die of the player trying to help); the device he's working on is extra difficult (a negative modifier) or extra easy (a positive modifier)—the sky's the limit on what might happen.

The decision on what modifiers are applied to any die roll, if any, and whether they are positive or negative, is always made by the LN.

Powers: If the character is attempting a Challenge or Test covered by a Power, the way in which the player rolls that Test/Challenge will be determined by the Power on the Character Dossier. Here are a few of the most common ways in which a player will roll dice when using a Power (in all instances, the "appropriate Stat Die" is determined by the LN):

- **Replace:** Roll the Power Die in place of the appropriate Stat Die.
- **Discard Lowest:** Roll the Power Die with the appropriate Stat Die and discard the lowest value result.
- **Keep Both:** Roll the Power Die with the appropriate Stat Die and keep both results.
- **Add + X:** Roll the Power Die in place of the appropriate Stat Die and add X value.
- And so on…

Each Character Dossier will indicate the manner of rolling dice to determine the outcome of the Challenge or Test.

As a final example, below are two formulas written out to describe the first two bullet points above for clarity:

D12 + Power Die (D4, D6, D8, D10, D12) + **Modifiers** vs. **D20**

D12 + (Power Die [D4, D6, D8, D10, D12] + **Power Die** [D4, D6, D8, D10, D12], discard lowest result) + **Modifiers** vs. **D20**

Luck Stat

Always remember that regardless of the overall result, if the Base Die and/or Stat Die (and/or Power Die, if used; check dice rolled before discarding any) result equals the character's Luck Stat, that character automatically succeeds at his action (see p. 43).

Who Rolls the D20?

When a player makes a Challenge or Test roll, whether the LN or the player rolls the D20 is completely up to each gaming group. Since a character will never be rolling a D20 for a Stat/Power Die, there will never be confusion on which dice stack against the D20 if the player rolls the Base Die, Stat/Power Dice, and the D20 all at once. It will certainly speed up play and accentuate that the Cue System doesn't have an "us vs. the gamemaster" mentality that can often crop up in other roleplaying games. However, some groups may enjoy the vibe of two players rolling dice to determine the outcome of an action. Before playing the first *Valiant Universe* game, simply decide which style the players prefer and stick with it.

On a mission for MI-6 to infiltrate a potential Harbinger Foundation facility in Africa, Ninjak comes up against a locked door, and he needs to get past it. Charlie, playing as Ninjak, knows this is what Ninjak is famous for, so he has an excellent chance of bypassing the door's security to gain access.

Breaking a complicated lock is definitely a Challenge, as it's against an inanimate object. Charlie decides this is an Intellect Challenge (and the LN agrees), which again is perfect for Ninjak, who has a D10 in that category. Charlie rolls for the Challenge, rolling a D12 (Base Die) and a D10 (Intellect Die) along with the D20 (their group has decided the players will roll it). The LN decides there are no special circumstances requiring any additional modifiers. The result is:

4 (D12) + 9 (D10) + 0 (no modifiers) = 13 vs. 6 (D20)

A big success! With little effort, Ninjak bypasses the security. However, the whole thing leaves Charlie nervous. It looked like a much more difficult door to bypass, regardless of Ninjak's specialty. Charlie knows this is either a trap, or something else strange is going on...Time to find out.

COMBAT

Combat is a variation on the basic dice-rolling mechanic for Challenges and Tests. The Action Die forms the foundation of all combat rolls instead of the usual D12 Base Die. The result of this roll is altered by any applicable modifiers. The basic dice rolling mechanic for all combat is:

Action Die + Modifiers vs. **Action Die + Modifiers**

As shown, combat is a straightforward contest between combatants' Action Dice, plus any applicable modifiers.

Modifiers

As with Challenge and Test rolls, combat can have a variety of situational modifiers added, all of which are decided upon by the LN.

Ranges

All weapons (and any Powers that act as weapons) fall into three range brackets for combat (the range of each weapon/Power is noted on the Character Dossier).
- **Close** (Melee)
- **Near** (Pistols)
- **Far** (Rifles)

If a weapon (or Power) is used in a range bracket one higher than its noted "OK" bracket(s), apply a −2 modifier. A weapon cannot be used in a range bracket two higher than its listed bracket, though it can always be used in a closer bracket. For example, Shadowman's Shadow Scythe is a Close (Melee) weapon: if it's used at Near range the player would apply a −2 modifier; it cannot be used at Far range. Any rifle, however, which all have Far range, can be used at Near or Close without any issues.

It's important to note, though, that a specific Dossier may change these values based upon a specific weapon. So if you see different values than the norm, those are not in addition to the standard above but instead fully replace the above modifiers.

Power Die

As with non-combat situations, if the character has a Power Die that is combat-related and appropriate to the current situation (as determined by the LN), the way the player rolls the dice in that combat situation will be determined by the Power on the Character Dossier.

Once more, here are a few of the most common ways in which a player will roll dice when using a Power for combat:

- **Replace:** Roll the Power Die in place of the Action Die.
- **Discard Lowest:** Roll the Power Die with the Action Die and discard the lowest value result.
- **Keep Both:** Roll the Power Die with the Action Die and keep both results.
- **Add + X:** Roll the Power Die in place of the Action Die and add X value.
- And so on…

Below are two formulas written out to describe the first two bullet points above for clarity:

Power Die + **Modifiers** vs. **Action Die** + **Modifiers**

(**Action Die** + **Power Die** [discard lowest result]) + **Modifiers** vs. **Action Die** + **Modifiers**

Or, if two characters are fighting Power vs. Power, the dice might look like the following:

Rolling for a "Keep Both" Power vs. Rolling for a "Replace" Power Die:
Action Die + **Power Die** + **Modifiers** vs. **Power Die** + **Modifiers**

Rolling for a "Discard Lowest" Power vs. Rolling for an "Add + 5" Power:
(**Action Die** + **Power Die** [discard lowest result]) + **Modifiers** vs. **Power Die** + **5** + **Modifiers**

And so on…

Luck Stat

Always remember that regardless of the overall result, if an Action Die (and/or Power Die, if used; check dice rolled before discarding any) result equals the character's Luck Stat, that character automatically wins (see p. 43).

Unusual Circumstances

Any time an unusual circumstance arises not directly covered by the rules, the LN modifies the situation on the fly. For example, if two combatants are at a significant range from one another and the LN decides the "winner" of a combat roll couldn't possibly damage the "loser," he simply doesn't apply damage and moves on; in this instance "winning" was simply an avoidance of damage on the winner's part.

Jordan—playing as Monica Jim (Animalia), a Generation Zero psiot—is hunting along the slopes of Mount Kilimanjaro for a secret PRS facility. She's part of a Renegades team that heard there's another facility with a "Nursery" that's experimenting on young, captured psiots, and the team will do anything to find it and free those inside. Though she's been told her animal forms don't look like real animals, she still doesn't quite get it and feels her Lion Form Power will allow her to blend right in: there's lions all through the area, after all! As soon as she sees an enemy, she'll let the others know. But for now…lion!

She doesn't get far before a rogue psiot on patrol instantly knows what Animalia is and attacks with a psionic blast.

Before making the die roll, however, the LN—along with Jordan—makes a few decisions. First, the LN decides the rogue psiot surprised Monica Jim, so she'll apply a −1 modifier to her attack. Additionally, as indicated on her Dossier, Monica Jim's Lion Form Power only attacks at a Close range, while the LN determines that the rogue psiot starts the current turn at Near range, which means that as the first turn will stand, Animalia cannot damage her attacker.

The LN rolls for the rogue psiot, with the following results:

3 (Action Die) + 4 (Psionic Attack Power Die) = 7 (the rogue psiot's Power keeps both rolled dice)

Jordan then rolls for Monica Jim, with the following results:

9 (Lion Form; this replaces the Action Die so it's not rolled) −1 (surprised) = 8

Even with fewer dice to roll and a surprised modifier, Monica Jim manages to win the attack! However, because of the range difference, there's no way Jordan's character could strike back at the rogue psiot.

Additionally, the LN explains—as Jordan starts reaching for a Plot Point—unlike a situation where perhaps someone is attacking with a knife at a difference in range, there's no way Jordan could "throw" Monica Jim's Lion Form attack. So even if a Plot Point is spent, the LN isn't going to allow it—unless Jordan can give one amazing Narration!

She decides against it and knows she simply needs to close the range next turn!

Aaron's character, Bloodshot, is facing off with a Harada Global Conglomerates security agent. Bloodshot is using a rifle he secured earlier in the game. Unfortunately the security agent was previously disarmed—though he managed to escape—and so he only has a crowbar and is on the other side of a large open area.

Aaron rolls a D8 (Bloodshot's Action Die) and the LN rolls a D6 (the security agent's Action Die). Because Bloodshot can attack from a distance and the security agent can't, the LN awards a +1 modifier to Bloodshot's roll. Aaron rolls a 7 and adds the +1 bonus for a final result of 8. The security agent rolls a 2; with the −2 modifier for trying to attack with a weapon into a larger range bracket, the result is 0. The security agent loses and gets shot.

Of course, there are many ways this could have played out.

Aaron loses the roll:

Aaron rolls badly with the D8 resulting in a 1. With the +1 modifier, the result is only 2. The security agents rolls high and gets a 5; with the −2 modifier it becomes 3. While the rules allow the LN to say that the security agent could've won that round and thrown the crowbar to hit Bloodshot, the LN decides this security agent isn't that good, so Bloodshot's shot simply misses the target.

Aaron loses the roll
and a Plot Point is used:

Aaron loses the roll again, but this time another player spends a Plot Point to have Bloodshot win the fight, and she immediately tosses out a Narration: "The shot misses but strikes a support column that collapses, dropping most of the roof between Bloodshot and the security guard, effectively cutting him off!"

Aaron loses the roll
and a Plot Point is used
for the security agent:

Aaron loses the roll and another player is feeling meddlesome. Karla spends a Plot Point in favor of the security agent! Rolling with the punches, Aaron narrates the scene: "The security agent dodges the shot and chucks his crowbar at Bloodshot. As luck would have it, the crowbar finds its mark, giving Bloodshot's arm a pounding." In this instance, although the LN would not have given the security agent the ability to hit out of his range bracket, he rolls with the flow because a Plot Point was used.

There are numerous ways the encounter could play out. Just remember to roll with the dice and the Plot Points. Anything can happen!

Vehicle Combat

There is no separate system for combat between vehicles, whether they be Vine space ships, F-15s, or Russian tanks the players have seized. Instead, the focus is kept where it should be, on the action of the characters, with the LN deciding what Challenges/Tests/Action should occur under any given situation.

For example, if a player group's car is trying to outrun a chasing vehicle, then the LN could decide it's a straight-up Intellect Test of the driver, as he tries to use his innate knowledge of the car and the city streets to lose his pursuer (though it could require multiple rolls if he's weaving through traffic, then taking a shortcut down pedestrian stairs, and then trying to lose the tail in a large parking lot).

However, if the players find themselves in a straight up vehicle-to-vehicle gunfight, the LN may decide it's Action. Or, depending upon the size of the vehicle (say, a Vine battlecruiser) the players are on, the LN may require one person to make an Intellect Test (the piloting of the ship), while another character makes the Action roll (actually firing the weapons).

Finally, how much damage a vehicle can take and how that damage affects its movement, weapons fire, and so on is absolutely up to the plot and how the storyline is developing: just remember the superhero premise that any vehicle is as strong—or not—as the plot needs it to be (though some Event Briefs will provide specifics to help things alone). Instead of tracking the nitty-gritty details of damage to a vehicle, the LN should weave that type of information into the narrative: engine sputtering and billowing smoke; tires shredding; explosive decompressions (if in space), or flooding with water (if underwater); ammo exploding (if in a military vehicle); abrupt 1000-meter drops in altitude (if flying); power system fluctuations and failures— your imagination is absolutely the limit for the fun and challenging scenarios you can throw at your players to overcome during such a conflict.

Damage, Armor, and Health

Whenever a fight occurs, or a dangerous situation is encountered, there's a chance a character could take damage.

Damage: On every Character Dossier, there's a Weapons column that lists the weapon (or Powers) the character started the game with and its **Damage Value**. Whenever a character takes damage, the damage is first applied to the Armor column of the Dossier. Once all Armor pips are marked off, damage then begins to apply to the Health column. If that happens, it's time for some serious heroics!

Health Flow Chart: The Health column of the character Dossier takes the form of a flowchart. Players start at the top, left-hand pip and move to the right until the first row is marked off, then move to the left-hand pip of the second row and move to the right until the second row is marked off, and so on.

- **First X:** When the first "X" (on the second row) is reached, the character immediately applies a –1 penalty to all future Might Die rolls.
- **Second X:** When the second "X" (on the third row) is reached, a –1 to all future Might and Action rolls is immediately applied.
- **Staggered:** When the first "Staggered" pip is crossed out, the character simply cannot give anymore and may take no actions (he does not give any more Narrations until he's healed; he cannot spend any Plot Points either). However, there are instances in which a Power could still work even if the character is Staggered, such as Bloodshot's Nanite Regeneration Power; the final call on whether a Power is still active while a character is Staggered is up to the LN.
- **Knocked Out:** The character is wounded so badly he or she is fully unconscious and completely out of action for the rest of the Event. (This is NOT the same as a dead character; the character will fully heal before the next Event. Really "killing off" a character should be reserved for truly epic moments of storytelling where the players will be recounting stories about the game for years to come. For more details, see *Character Death*, p. 58.)

Secondary Effects: Generally speaking, *Valiant Universe* doesn't assume weapons have any other effects beyond straight-up damage as noted on the various Dossiers. Those weapons with additional effects are specifically noted, of course. However, like the equipment also noted on the Dossiers, players and LNs are free to come up with additional effects from a weapon, provided they can make a good Narration for it.

For example, Gunslinger has an "NEMO Omen Rifle" on his Dossier (see p. 105). The player choosing Gunslinger could pitch to the group that this is a custom mod of that gun. The modification would allow the weapon to knock the target out after dealing its damage. The starting LN feels that's too powerful and decides that first, the weapon can't be used at Near range, and second, if the weapon scores a hit, the target will make a Might Test with a modifier determined by the LN. If the target succeeds, he or she withstood the extra effects of getting hit with such a powerful rifle; if the target fails, he or she is immediately in dreamland for D6 turns.

Meanwhile another LN may decide when a Berserker of the Dead (see p. 153) hits a target with a Mace that the weapon's mystical power partially numbs the target, so the target applies a –1 to any actions for the next D4 turns. The LN could also step this up by declaring that if the same Berserker strikes the numbed target with his Fist, that D4 becomes a D8 (but the Fist's damage is dropped to just 1 to provide some balance)!

And so on. As usual, unleash your imaginations at the table!

Regaining Armor/Health: Fortunately, there are many ways to regain Health or repair Armor. A player could spend a Plot Point to regain a pip of Health or Armor. Some characters carry first aid kits as equipment, which can restore Health. Additionally, some characters are doctors or engineers or even have a healing Power and can use a Narration to fix Armor or heal a teammate; in this instance how much they repair the Armor and/or the Health of a character could largely depend upon the quality/uniqueness of the player's Narration, with the LN fixing two or even more pips for a particularly superb recitation.

Weapons

Weapons come in all shapes, types, and sizes. You name it…and it probably comes in a variety of colors and styles as well.

Most *Valiant Universe* characters start each Event with a default set of weapons. These are listed on the Dossier along with the amount of damage they do when used successfully against a target, and their range bracket.

Carry Limits: A character can carry no more than two weapons at a time. If the player already has two and wants the character to acquire a new weapon, a current weapon must be discarded.

If a character has a Power that requires use of their hands, then the character can't use that Power if they are holding a weapon (or equipment) in that hand. If there is the slightest doubt about how the character uses said Powers, before gameplay begins, the players and LN will need to determine for their games whether a particular character's Power(s) requires a free hand to use it.

Changing Out Weapons: A character could end up using a weapon that he didn't start the game with. In those cases, when a weapon is found that's not previously been used in a game, use this rule of thumb:

- Normal weapons do 2 points of damage
- Larger, heavier weapons may do 4 points of damage
- Rare, extremely dangerous, or special weapons may do 6
- In place of a static Damage Value, a die can be assigned, which is rolled every time the weapon strikes a target to determine damage: only use D4 or D6. Weapons with higher variable damage are extremely rare or unpredictable.
- Melee Weapons are "OK" at Close range, "–2" at Near range, and cannot be used at Far range.
- Pistols are "OK" at Close and Near range, and "–2" at Far range
- Rifles are "OK" at all three ranges
- Tweaking the values above will create weapons with their own flavor

And the Rest: *Valiant Universe* doesn't require players to track mundane things like ammunition or shots fired per turn, or how long a Power can last, or how quickly a player can move in combat, or change clips, and so on. If there's a good reason for that psionic shield to survive the endless blasts trying to penetrate it, go for it!

Making the Game More or Less Lethal: The weapons on the Dossiers are geared towards a good mix of speed of play and fun combat action that'll span multiple turns of dice rolling to resolve a given situation. However, some groups may decide they want to switch things up to suit their style of play.

Less Lethal: If a player group decides they want more dice rolling and heavier combat-oriented play, simply lower all Damage Values by 1, or even cut Damage Values in half. If weapons have a die in place of a static Damage Value, only use a D4.

More Lethal: If another group wants quicker combat and more cinematic style where the good guys can take out the bad guys in a single swipe, increase all weapon Damage Values by 1 or even 2 points. If weapons have a die in place of a static Damage Value, a D8 can be used in addition to a D4 and D6.

Equipment

Besides weapons, many character also carry a variety of equipment to use during Events. The uses of many of the different items may be obvious: a first aid kit would help treat a character who's been injured, or a tool kit could be used to repair Armor or other devices. The intended application of other equipment may be obscure or even totally unknown. In many cases, this is intentional and gives the players a chance to decide exactly what that equipment does, based on the name.

ADDITIONAL RULES

The Cue System is not rules heavy. Instead, it's about creating a framework off of which players simply spin up their imaginations through improv play to work through whatever characters, environments, and terrain they may come across. However, the very nature of superhero powers—not to mention exotic places like prehistoric terrains, alien planets, the amazingly strange Faraway, or any other unusual locales populating the Valiant Universe— means players might stumble a bit here and there.

For those that would like a few more guidelines when dealing with extreme situations, use the following rules. Of course, these can be used to craft further rules that will cover a variety of other circumstances and locales a player group may encounter.

BREATHING

Various situation and environments, such as toxic areas and being underwater or outside a space ship, may threaten a character's ability to breathe.

A character can hold his breath for a number of Narrations equal to his Might stat divided by 3, rounded up. Once this period expires, he will suffer 1 point of Health damage (ignoring Armor pips) until he can safely take another breath. Once a character has been reduced to Staggered status, he will take no further damage.

ENVIRONMENTAL CONDITIONS

The following rules for environmental conditions are optional and should be agreed upon before gameplay. In all instances, as usual, final adjudication for what does or doesn't work under these circumstances falls under the LN's purview.

- **Darkness:** A dim room or fighting at night inflicts a –1 modifier to all die rolls; complete darkness conveys a –3 modifier. There are numerous NPCs/characters that might ignore this, from a robot to a player with a Power to see in the dark, to supernatural creatures that live in the dark and are fully adapted. For example, Shadowman has the Power Deadside Sight. In a given Narration, a player may determine—if the LN agrees—that to Shadowman, even the blackest room or a moonless night is just dim lighting, so no matter the condition, only a –1 modifier ever applies.

- **Acid, toxic waste, alien substance, and so on:** Coming in contact with acid, toxic waste, or other corrosive substances will cause a lasting damage effect. Any such substance (whether naturally occurring, manmade, alien, and so forth) initially inflicts 2 points of damage to Armor or 1 point to Health if Armor is depleted. Unless the substance can be immediately washed off or treated with a repair kit (for Armor damage) or a first aid kit or healing Power (for Health damage), the substance will inflict the same amount of damage for another two Narrations (or turns for NPCs without Narrations) before rendering itself inert.

- **Liquid Metals/Rocks:** There are numerous comic-book situations where Powers or military equipment are so powerful they liquefy metals and rocks. Coming in contact with such a substance causes 3 points of Armor damage and 1 point of Health damage as the character starts to cook. Incidental splashes of such substances only cause 1 damage.

- **Hot/noxious gas:** Hot/noxious gas affects visibility by imposing a –2 modifier when a character or NPC is trying to attack into or through a cloud of gas. Moving through a jet of gas causes 2 points of Health damage, regardless of how many Armor pips the character has remaining (i.e., no Armor pips are reduced).

- **Underwater:** Due to the difficulty with moving while submerged in water, ranged weapons suffer a –1 modifier, and melee weapons incur a –3 modifier.

- **Airless vacuum:** Treat any airless situation as forcing characters to hold their breath (see *Breathing*, p. 56).

MIND CONTROL

Various enemies and characters may have the ability to take over a character and control her actions. When this occurs, the following rules are in effect.

When a character is under mind control, the controlling NPC (i.e., the LN) dictates that character's actions during her Narrations rather than the controlling player. Successful mind control will remain in effect until the affected character resists the control or the controlling enemy is Staggered or Knocked Out.

The mind control will last a minimum of one of the affected character's Narrations. Every subsequent Narration the character must make an Intellect Test; succeeding in the Test ends the mind control.

An NPC controlling a character may not make the character perform any actions that would result in her character (or her companions) being Knocked Out; she will disbelieve those actions so strongly that the enemy cannot force her to take them. In other words, a mind-controlled character cannot shoot herself in the temple, shove a character out a window, and so on.

THE COMIC BOOK STORY ARC AT YOUR TABLE

The best stories usually follow a try-fail-try-fail-try-succeed cycle. This means the protagonists often get their heads handed to them on a silver platter several times over before they find a solution to the story's primary problem and finally achieve victory. And depending upon the author in question, the victory might be very Pyrrhic in nature: the word *victory* applies in name only, and that victory costs the protagonist far more than that success is worth. Comic books in particular embrace this style of story arc, handing their superheroes defeat after defeat before allowing for a slim yet fantastic victory.

A lot of RPGs, whether computer-based or tabletop, don't follow this format, however. Instead, the players run into a lot of low-level minions, boosting their stats from the experience they gain, but then they run into a boss that might defeat them. More often than not, tabletop RPGs will try to set things up so the players can defeat the boss the first time, whereas computer games might require you to replay the boss fight numerous times to pull off a win.

The primary reason for this flip is that players sink a lot more time into playing an RPG (especially at the table) than simply reading a novel, comic book, or even watching TV. As such, the idea of going through several evenings of gaming to only be handed defeat after defeat isn't always that appealing.

STANDARD RPG STORY ARC

If players wish to maintain the standard RPG story arc in their gaming, that's completely understandable. That means the first NPCs the players run into should be below the characters' median stats. The middle batch of NPCs should be equal to if not still slightly under the character's median stats. Then, the final NPCs (the boss fight) should be above the players' but generally not so high the players can't pull off a win, even if they need to spend a fair bit of Plot Points to make it happen.

THE COMIC BOOK STORY ARC

However, if you want to fully embrace the comic book story arc and are willing to put up with some epic losses early in the gaming session (or even across several gaming sessions), use the following guidelines:

- In the first Scene, the NPCs should be obviously superior in their stat averages.
- In the middle Scenes, the NPCs should either stay flat in their median stats, or even increase in ability to ensure the possibility of an even worse defeat.
- The NPCs in the final Scene should have median stats equal to or even slightly lower than the characters' to ensure the likelihood of a final victory.

While this should bring comic-book storytelling to life, striving to maintain the try-fail-try-fail-try-succeed cycle at your gaming table could run into some issues. Here's some ideas on how to resolve various problems players may encounter.

Character Death

As noted under *Damage, Armor, and Health* (see p. 55), the standard rules for the game do not allow a character to die. This was done for two reasons.

First, this is a roleplaying game about superheroes, and superheroes get kicked often and hard and still drag themselves up to beat down the bad guy for a last, heroic victory. Additionally, as discussed in *Superheroes: Accepting the Premise* (see p. 43), a character is only as strong as the plot needs him or her to be, and the same applies here: "Death is only as strong as the plot needs it to be." In other words, death shouldn't just occur due to bad die rolls but instead should be reserved for epic storytelling moments when the death of a much-loved character will save not only his teammates or the city but perhaps even the whole world and beyond. *That's* how superheroes go out.

Second, this is the Valiant Universe. And here, when a character dies, he or she stays dead. As such, having a mechanism for easily dying isn't appropriate.

That being said, some players may agree that although the Knocked Out character isn't dead, there should still be some consequences for a character running through his or her whole Health track. Or maybe the player was Knocked Out of an evening's gaming session too early, and he or she doesn't want to sit out for the rest of the session. For these situations, here are a few options players can use to provide more depth of play:

Unlike most things in *Valiant Universe*, the players should decide as a group which of these options are allowed and which option a player will use if a character is Knocked Out during a game.

Knocked Out: The player controlling a character whose Health track reaches Knocked Out status should choose one of the following options:

- **Don't count me out just yet:** The character spends all but 1 of his available Plot Points to avoid being Knocked Out and suffers no further effects. Heal the Knocked Out Heath pip, and leave the character Staggered. If the character has no available Plot Points to spend, this option cannot be chosen and another option must be chosen instead.

DEATH AND THE VALIANT UNIVERSE

Death in the Valiant Universe is both permanent and often senseless and tragic. While this makes for wonderfully bittersweet reading, most roleplayers don't like spending a lot of time developing a character only to experience that character being taken out by say a stray bullet not even meant for him or her. That's simply not enjoyable.

That's why the Character Death section describes permanent death as a plot device that is reserved for a most heroic end, a style of play most roleplayers will recognize and appreciate. However, players that have long admired Valiant's adherence to a more realistic take on death may decide that they want to emulate that in their games. Death should still be a rare event, but instead of an epic stand, it could be that at a moment a player least expects it, death takes his character. And in a very different way, a whole new set of unforgettable roleplaying memories will be born.

The device for managing this could be something as simple as whenever a character is Knocked Out, the current LN rolls a D20, and on a 1 the character dies. Period. Or it could be something more convoluted that the players determine themselves.

Whatever direction the players decide concerning character death—the more true-to-Valiant standards or the usual RPG-style heroics—all players should agree on that direction up front and stick with it throughout.

- **Just give me a minute:** Heal the character's Knocked Out pip, and leave the character Staggered. In addition to the standard Might and Action modifiers for damage on the Health track, the character will suffer an additional −1 modifier on all Challenge, Test, Action and Power rolls for his next 2 Narrations once the character is healed out of the Staggered condition.

- **I'll never be the same:** Permanently reduce the character's total Health pips by 1 (the Might Die remains unaffected). Heal both the Knocked Out and Staggered pips; i.e. all 3 pips on the bottom two rows are healed.

- **I've had better days:** Permanently lower one random Stat Die to the next value (e.g., a D8 would be reduced to a D6); a Power die cannot be lowered. If Might is the affected Stat Die, adjust the character's total Health pips as per standard rules (see *Damage, Armor and Health*, p. 55). Heal both the Knocked Out and Staggered pips; i.e. all 3 pips on the bottom two rows are healed..

Fall Back!

If the players are on the verge of having multiple characters Knocked Out and they've already spent their allotment of Plot Points to keep themselves up and fighting, the best solution may be the hated retreat.

At the end of a round of Narrations, if all players agree, they can end the Scene. Any Plot Points remaining are forfeit (except the LN who receives an additional Plot Point). Additionally, the players do not receive a Plot Point on their first two Narrations in the next Scene.

If the players failed to achieve any objectives in that Scene, then in addition to the restriction above, players will have a temporary maximum of 3 Plot Points (instead of the usual 5) for the duration of the next Scene.

Just Need a Breather

When using this style of storytelling, the characters are likely to see their fair share of scrapes and bruises. Because of this, the characters charging from one Scene to the next against tough NPCs without stopping to take stock of their condition is liable to get them killed pretty quickly.

In order to keep the game moving along at a brisk pace—even if the characters had to fall back because they were almost Knocked Out—after each Scene, characters automatically repair or heal half of their current Armor or Health damage for free, rounding up. All remaining damage must be recovered by normal methods, such as spending Plot Points or using medical, repair or Power abilities.

They're Just Mooks!

There are many instances in comic stories where the superheroes lay down the hurt on a slew of mooks or henchmen that are all taken out in one fell swoop. While this shouldn't be embraced very often in an RPG setting, as that approach would most likely make an evening's gaming a tad too boring, the LN should be willing to accept this type of scenario every now and then. Perhaps a character rolls the highest value on multiple dice, or maybe the player provides a fantastic Narration that is wonderfully creative and causes the whole group to explode into laughter. What ever the instance, don't be afraid to let the "wall of mooks" go down when it feels right and makes that game all the more memorable, but this option should be used sparingly.

THAT Was The Boss Fight?

Right out of the gate, some players may run into a significant problem with this style of storytelling. It's one thing to play out the comic-book story arc at the table; it's another for a boss NPC actually having stats that leave some players feeling like the Event's grand finale was a let down.

To prevent this problem, if the LN realizes the boss fight is going a little too easily, he or she can use Plot Points to abruptly toughen up the last NPC or even drop in some other NPCs to ensure the fight is heroic and difficult but hopefully results in an ultimate victory for the players.

THE GAMING GROUP

Due to the loose nature of the Cue System, it's highly recommended that players create new characters as part of a group process. This is particularly true when generating Powers. It's all too easy for a single player to get caught up in a desire to craft a cool character and end up with Powers (even under the guidelines provided) that might be excessively powerful. To forestall any arguments that might occur at the table as a new character is introduced, involving the player group during the process can ensure the best experience for everyone.

Of course if a player group loves powergaming and doesn't have a problem with freakishly powerful characters, then go with it! Just make sure your group knows which style of playing everyone prefers and stick to that process from the get go.

CHARACTER CREATION

As previously noted, this book contains a slew of sample Character Dossiers that allow players to snag a character and leap into the fray. However, some players prefer to craft their own characters to take into the action.

The following rules provide a framework for character creation. As with all aspects of *Valiant Universe*, the framework is light and fast and designed for players to playfully and enjoyably create a Character Dossier that reflects the style they want to embrace in a game. If you don't like where your character is going at any time during the process, feel free to back up and start down the path that'll make it the most fun!

Note that the sample Character Dossiers might not follow these rules.

Superheroes: Accepting the Premise: As noted in this sidebar (see p. 43), superheroes and RPGs don't always make a lot of sense. That's particularly true with the Cue System, as it is very limited in its application of hard rules and instead empowers players to determine how a character evolves at the gaming table. When creating new characters, then, try not to think in terms of "I want a character that's stronger or faster or smarter than X character." The rules don't lend themselves to that type of direct comparison very well. Instead, it's all about asking yourself, "What will I enjoy playing the most?" and creating a character based on that answer.

FOLLOW THE STEPS

Download and print out the blank Dossier from **www.catalystgamelabs.com/valiant** (they are also found at the back of this book) and proceed through the following steps to create your character:

1. Create A Character Theme (Character Name)
2. Assign Stat Dice
3. Create Powers
4. Assign Armor
5. Select Weapons
6. Select Equipment
7. Create Cues and Action Cues
8. Create Dispositions
9. Final Tweaking

1. CREATE A CHARACTER THEME

Imagine you're a casting director for your favorite TV show and you've got a selection of walk-on characters you've got to fill for a new episode, characters that need to be cool and vibrant, even if they're only on-screen for a few minutes.

As you review the script you run into a list of short character descriptions: male, late thirties, stoic and very tough, doesn't talk much; woman, early twenties, always smiling, with a devil-may-care attitude; male, teen, a brooding anger that he fails to leash more often than not; and so on. In the role of casting director, you'll use those descriptions to find the right actor to convincingly fill that role in the episode.

In a similar fashion, as you work to create a *Valiant Universe* character, you need to find a short and flavorful description of the theme of your character. Do you want to play the white knight, with your thousand-watt smile and pectorals that can deflect a psionic blast? Or do you want to be the brainy nerd who feels he's stuck in a world of imbeciles and can hack any computer system on the planet without a single ounce of superhero juice?

Anything's possible, with only your imagination to hold you back. Just remember as you pick a theme that the more wild and crazy you make it, the more you'll have to figure out how to convey that during gameplay.

With that in mind, jot down a few descriptive words that outline your theme. Don't hesitate to fill a page if you're still trying to feel your way to what you want, knowing you're going to toss most of the concepts by the wayside as you zero in on your mark. Additionally, if you're still floundering a little, feel free to find out what everyone else in the group is playing and find a niche to fill: no sarcastic, brooding, older doctor as a mentor-type for an up-and-coming superhero on your team? Jump in and see if that role fits you.

Once you've got your theme, you'll use that as the framework to help you make the decisions involved in the rest of the process.

Character Name

While this step appears at the start of character creation, it can actually happen anytime during the process.

Some players will find they've already got a character name they've been hanging on to for just such an adventure; the name itself drips with theme and will immediately lend itself to a certain flavor. If I say Blue Flame, most people will likely have a preconceived notion of where the character creation process is going to take them: flame-oriented powers, flamboyant (no attempts at subtlety here), enough brains to know that flames turn blue when they get real hot, and so on.

Other players, however, may find they don't have a good name in mind and instead, even with a theme, may have to travel most, if not all, of the creation process before a great name presents itself. And of course don't forget to trawl through the sample characters for a myriad of names that might spark your imagination to craft your own unique take on a given theme.

Tags

While not a requirement for character creation, every sample Dossier includes a short list of one-word Tags, and these Tags are carried throughout most of the sections of the book. They're designed to give a very quick look at the theme/style of what you're looking at. In the case of characters, Tags define what a character *is*, as opposed to how a character would react in a given situation (see *Create Dispositions*, p. 67).

2. ASSIGNING STAT DICE

Use the following rules when assigning Stat Dice (see p. 42). After assigning a Stat Die, simply write in the value and draw in the die shape, mimicking the style shown on the sample Dossiers.

Might, Intellect, Charisma, Action

Each player has a D6, two D8s, and a D10 to assign to the Might, Intellect, Charisma, and Action Stats (see p. 42). It is up to every player how they assign these values, but they should use the theme of their character, as determined in Step 1, when making such assignments.

For example, a Blue Flame character, as described above, would perhaps assign the D8s to Might and

Neil recently discovered Valiant comics and has since devoured dozens of issues. As a long-time roleplayer, he knows it'll be an absolute blast gaming within such a fantastic setting. Always one to tinker, though, he decides he wants to create a brand new character.

While he's enjoying all of the titles, something about Shadowman has really grabbed him, and he knows he wants to create a new character in that setting. Additionally, while he has gamed in a huge variety of settings, something about Shadowman invokes a 1910s–1920s noir vibe for him (too much Cthulhu reading/gaming perhaps). Since his gaming group is up for a series of "historical" Events—made all the easier by the fact that the Valiant Universe has a continuity of storytelling spanning thousands of years—Neil decides he's going to create one of Jack Boniface's ancestors.

Shadowman #10 shows the interaction of Sandria and Nicodemo Darque during the Civil War—a weaving of supernatural occurrences with a real-world event to create epic storytelling. Neil, being a World War I buff, decides to create a character—one Damien Boniface—who was drafted into the Great War and finds himself fighting not just soldiers but undead entities across a war-torn Europe.

Additionally, after reading Shadowman: End Times #1, Neil knows the comment from Jack's father Josiah—"It's what drove my great-grandfather to hard liquor"—most likely makes Damien the character in question. It gives Neil another hook to play with: a man struggling with the loa, as all Shadowmen do, but unbeknownst to any of his progeny, he's also struggling to master the Art and thus falling into hard liquor. Yeah...this is gonna be great roleplaying.

Action, a D6 to Charisma (a little too arrogant for his own good), while the D10 would be assigned to Intellect (we just mentioned that arrogance, right?).

D4 & D12: If a player chooses, he can change the D10 Stat Die to a D12, but he must then change the D6 Stat Die to a D4. For example, to really go over the top with our Blue Flame character, the D10 Intellect could become a D12, but the Charisma would need to be changed from D6 to a D4 (he's *really* not a people person).

Health

The Stat Die assigned to Might has a direct correlation to the Health track of the Character Dossier. Use the following rules for determining the character's Health track:

- If a D12 or D10, do not mark off any pips.
- If a D8, mark off one pip from the first row.
- If a D6, mark off one pip from the first row and one pip from the second row.
- If D4, mark off two pips from the first row and one pip from the second row.

Luck

Luck is not a die, but instead a fixed value that'll remain constant once it's determined. Roll a D12 and assign that value to the Luck Stat. Or simply pick your favorite number from 1–12—whichever way works best for you.

> *A new character gets a D10, two D8s and a D6 to assign to stats. Additionally, Neil wants to make sure Damien isn't too similar to the Shadowman character in this book, while accentuating a "bookworm" angle...at least as far as one can go while still having a character that can kick Deadside butt. With that in mind he assigns the following stats:*
>
> *Might: D8*
> *Intellect: D10*
> *Charisma: D6*
> *Action: D8*
>
> *Finally, he's fond of the number 7, so he chooses that for the Luck Stat.*

POWERS: THE BEST & WORST

For most, Powers will be the real reason to play. Whether in a movie, a comic book, or just imagination, the ability to accomplish the unthinkable within a game is what drives the excitement. After all, it's called superheroes for a reason.

However, Powers can also be the bane of a game. While the rules try to convey as thoroughly as possible that the Cue System is about coming up with how Powers work on the fly and having fun, there will be times when Powers get in the way. One player might not understand why his Speed ability doesn't allow him to mop up the floor every time, or another player might not understand why her Telepathy can't just control the villain. After all, these players saw that in a comic!

Now a quick-thinking LN should be able to adjust things rapidly to meet such situations. Perhaps he might decide that, now and then, a really good Narration and a Plot Point allows a character with a Speed Power to actually multiply the results of two dice together! However, other LNs may not feel comfortable flirting that much outside of the rules of the game. And at that moment, it's the LN's decision to keep within established limits.

That being said, keep two things in mind: First and foremost, talk about this as a group and decide what best fits your style of play. If you want to allow for a more fast-and-loose changing of rules that Powers can sometimes create, embrace it. If you feel more comfortable always sticking to the rules, that works great too. Second, never let these arguments bog down the game: nothing sucks the life out of a game—especially an improv-style game—like arguments over rules. If no solution can be found quickly, roll a die to determine the outcome and address it as a group after your session.

3. CREATE POWERS

Powers can be one of the most enjoyable aspects of character creation. More so than any other element, this is where you can unleash the superhero geek to come up with that one cool-sounding Power you've had stuck in the back of your head for ages.

When creating your Powers, use the following rules:

A. Determine Character Level

During Powers creation, players need to determine what level of characters they wish to play, which will determine the points they can spend on Powers. If you review the Character Powers Table (see below), it includes four levels of superheroes: Sidekick, Hero, Super, and Legend. The majority of the characters within this book fall into the Supers category. Though some of them fall into the Sidekick and Hero character, while a very few, such as Harada, actually fit the Legend category.

If players want to experience the full breadth of character growth and challenge themselves from the first roll of the dice, by all means create a Sidekick. If you're looking to knock it with the big boys right out of the gate, then a Hero or Super is your ticket. Finally, if you want to powergame and have over-the-top Powers, then strap in for what you can accomplish as a Legend.

Note, however, that the NPCs you face will need to be adjusted to take into consideration the level of the characters.

Once you've determined the Character Level, as shown on the table, that will provide the maximum Power Points the character can spend and the maximum number of Powers the character can start with.

Note that even when creating a Legend character, the Dossier will have an empty Power slot. This is done on purpose so players have a chance to create, discover, earn, or be afflicted with a new Power during gameplay.

> *Neil decides that he'd better make Damien a "Super"-level character if he's going to survive the brutality of the World War I setting he'll be experiencing.*

CHARACTER POWERS TABLE

Character Level	Maximum Power Points	Maximum # of Powers*
Sidekick	15	2
Hero	30	3
Super	45	4
Legend	60	5

*At the end of character creation (characters can acquire more Powers during game play).

Determine Power Points: Die Point Cost x Power Type Point Cost

Die	Point Cost
D4	2
D6	3
D8	4
D10	5
D12	6

Power Type	Point Cost
Replace: Roll the Power Die in place of the Stat Die	1
Discard Lowest: Roll the Power Die with the Stat Die and discard the lowest value result	2
Keep Both: Roll the Power Die with the Stat Die and keep both results	3
Add + X: Roll the Power Die in place of the Stat Die and add X value	1 + X**

**Where X is the value added to the die.

B. Determine Powers

When creating your Powers, remember that this is the Cue System, which means you're not locking down exactly what a given Power can do, necessarily. Instead, the goal is providing an evocative name that can be explored more fully during gameplay.

Now that doesn't mean some minor specifics can't be provided. Take a look at Peter Stanchek's Dossier (see pp. 124-125), for example. Psionic Shield and Mind Wipe both have very specific details, i.e. reducing damage and taking away a character's next action. However, what about Telepathy or Levitation (Flight)? Sure, we know the broad meaning of those terms, but can he read just one person's mind? Can he read a hundred? A *thousand*? Can he fish across the globe for a single thought? And as for Flight, how fast are we talking about? Can he outrace an airplane? Can he put himself into orbit (provided he has a way to breathe)? What about a cool combination of flying super fast and then using the Psionic Shield as a battering ram to break through a heavily fortified wall? Let gameplay, some Plot Points, and some fantastic Narrations win over the LN.

"Non-Power" Powers: Don't forget that some of the best comic book heroes (and villains) of all types haven't had Powers, necessarily. Instead, through wealth, luck, or simply a savage drive for vengeance or justice, these characters can hold their own in any circle of superhuman heroes. These skills and assets can be just as much a Power as the superhuman abilities of Flight, Telepathy, or Pyrokinesis. For example, take a look at Faith (see pp. 94-95). She's got Optimism and Pop Culture Knowledge as Powers. Those are just as important to her character as her other Powers. What's more, during a game a player is likely going to find the most enjoyment—and craft the most memorable moments—when those Powers help save the day.

Once more, Neil wants to ensure his version of an ancestral Shadowman feels different from the one in this book. That said, he knows that he has to keep the Deadside Sight and Transit to/from Deadside Powers as those are too intrinsically linked to the character to leave out.

Now, to really throw in some unique angles, he decides he wants to create some Powers based on the Art (i.e., magic). While ultimately a horrifying situation, Neil finds the story unfolding in Shadowman #0 very compelling: the forbidden knowledge of the Art that can be gained if you're willing to pay the price. So he decides to emulate some of that in two different Powers: Illusions and Physical Manipulation. (He also loves this angle as he can see some brilliant storytelling hooks layered into the idea: Damien has to keep these new, burgeoning Powers a secret, for fear the Abettors will believe he's becoming too powerful—too close to following in Master Darque's footsteps—and will place him six feet under at the first discovery.)

Because of this unique angle on the Powers, Neil also discusses this with his gaming group to ensure there won't be discord if he suddenly shows up at the table with abilities that some feel are too potent. They're fine leaving the Illusion Power open ended, giving him lots of freedom to play with that ability during the game. However, they've all read Shadowman and know that something like Physical Manipulation—even if the Power Die is kept low—could be incredibly powerful. Exploding heads, anyone?! As such, they agree that if Neil really wants to keep that Power, it needs to be changed to "Liquid Manipulation" (the ability to force liquids into various forms, move them around, and so on) and have a Touch stipulation. That way Damien can still touch a human and get that exploding head if he wanted, but he wouldn't be able to tear out a chunk of a steel foundation at a distance to drop a whole bridge. Neil accepts the limitations as appropriate and continues building his character.

C. Assign Power Dice

Once you've determined the general scope and a name for a Power, you need to assign a Power die, which can be a D4, D6, D8, D10, or D12. The only limitation here is to keep in mind the Determine Power Points formula from the Character Powers Table. The larger the die, the more points it will cost.

Also, as with all aspects of the Cue System, more powerful does not always mean better. Coming up with a lower die value for a Power might spark a great set of Cues and ultimately lead to some great roleplaying as you figure out the "why."

> *Keeping that bookworm angle in mind, Neil assigns Deadside Sight a D12, and Transit to/from Deadside a D8 (more thinking, a little direct action). Normally he'd contemplate assigning a D6 to the latter Power for balance purposes, but he's planning to keep the new Power levels low, so he feels okay about it at this stage. He may need to tweak later in the process, which is just fine as that's how it works.*
>
> *For the new Powers, he wants to keep them low, so he gives Illusion a D6 and Liquid Manipulation a D4.*

D. Assign Power Type

As discussed under *The Core Mechanic* (see p. 51), the way in which a Power interacts with standard dice rolling mechanic is left up to the player. The most common forms are the following:

- **Replace:** Roll the Power Die in place of the appropriate Stat Die.
- **Discard Lowest:** Roll the Power Die with the appropriate Stat Die and discard the lowest value result.
- **Keep Both:** Roll the Power Die with the appropriate Stat Die and keep both results.
- **Add + X:** Roll the Power Die in place of the appropriate Stat Die and add X value.

And those specific examples are provided as multipliers on the Character Powers Table (see p. 63) to determine the final point value of a Power.

If the player creates a new mechanic not covered on the table, simply use the table as a guide to determine the best multiplier applicable. In all such instances the group should agree on the values applied.

> *Since two of the Powers are relatively low, Neil decides he can go a little more powerful on the two original Powers, giving him the following:*
>
> *   **Deadside Sight: D12 (Add + 1)**
> *   **Transit to/from Deadside: D8 (Keep Both)**
>
> *He decides since the group approved Illusion that he'll keep that moderately powered, but even with the limitation on Liquid Manipulation, he wants to ensure it remains appropriately low, providing the following:*
>
> *   **Illusion: D6 (Discard Lowest)**
> *   **Liquid Manipulation: D4 (Replace) [Touch]**
>
> *Because he sufficiently nerfed that last Power, there's little chance of a player raising an objection. Also, while slightly disappointed at that need, he quickly realizes there's plenty of opportunity to roleplay his character digging deeper into that knowledge and slowly increasing that Power during gameplay.*

E. Sum Up Points And Final Tweaking

Once you've assigned dice values and mechanics to all of your Powers, run through the Determining Power Points formula for each. Then add all the points together and compare with the Maximum Power Points allowed by the choice of Character Level.

Players may find that they've run over their Maximum Power Points allowed. If this happens the player can simply decide (provided their group agrees) to run a slightly more powerful character. Or, she can simply take one or two Powers and tweak down either the Power Die or the Power Type until the points fall below the maximum threshold allowed.

The reverse might also be true, however. After adding up the points, a player may find he has leftover points. He can leave it as is if he's happy with his Powers, or he can tweak the Powers to maximize his allotted points.

Leftover Power Points: If a playing group agrees, characters that did not max out their points for a given level can carry those leftovers as Event Points. Simply divide the number of Power Points remaining by 2 (round down) and assign them as Event Points (see *Character Advancement*, p. 70). For example, if a player is creating a Hero Level character and only uses 25 Power Points, that would leave him with 2 Event Points [5 (leftover Power Points) ÷ 2 = 2.5, rounding down to 2].

Neil runs through the numbers and comes up with the following sums:

Deadside Sight: 12 [6 (D12) x 2 (Add + 1) = 12]

Transit to/from Deadside: 12 [4 (D8) x 3 (Keep Both) = 12]

Illusion: 6 [3 (D6) x 2 (Discard Lowest) = 6]

Liquid Manipulation: 2 (2 (D4) x 1 (Replace) = 1]

Summing those up gives him 31. Checking the Maximum Power Points, he sees that yes, he falls into the Super category...but just barely. He's got some wiggle room and decides he wants to take it. After a quick discussion with his gaming group, Neil changes the D4 on the Liquid Manipulation to a D6 while increasing Deadside Sight to "Add + 3" (he's got some cool storytelling thoughts on what he can do with that much ability to see such entities). This gives him final Powers of:

Deadside Sight: 24 [6 (D12) x 4 (Add + 3) = 24]

Transit to/from Deadside: 12 [4 (D8) x 3 (Keep Both) = 12]

Illusion: 6 [3 (D6) x 2 (Discard Lowest) = 6]

Liquid Manipulation: 3 (3 (D6) x 1 (Replace) = 3]

A total of 45 points, right at the max he can go for a Super. Since there's no Power Points left over, Neil doesn't need to confer with the group to decide if he can carry any leftover points as Event Points.

Note that Neil tried to make the argument that the "Touch" limitation on the Liquid Manipulation Power would siphon off points; however, the rest of the group decided that level of minutiae is beyond the Cue System's scope and overrules him ("Get your character done so we can play!").

4. ASSIGN ARMOR

All characters have at least ten Armor pips.

Following that rule, Armor is based on a combination of the Action and Might Stats; how much your body (or other personal defenses) can withstand, as well as how hard it is to hit you.

Use the following rules for determining the character's Armor track:

- Add the Might Die and Action Die values of your character together then divide by two (rounding up). That result equals the additional Armor pips applied to the character.

Remember that Powers can be related to Armor and additional pips and/or how the Armor works may be modified based upon the Powers created.

Adding the Might and Action Dice and dividing by 2 provides Damien Boniface with 8 Armor, for a total of 18 Armor pips.

5. SELECT WEAPONS

As with the Cues in a later step, selecting your weapons can be fun. You can simply copy the weapons from one of the sample Dossiers. However, unleashing the kid inside can be far more enjoyable: just make up whatever cool name you want! Have you always wanted to use a Quantum Hero Blade?

Write that down. Or have you seen a weapon in the pages of a comic and always wondered what name it might have? What about a Vine Phasic Displacer Rifle? Write that down too. When it comes to your weapons, look at the theme of your character and embrace it.

To determine the stats of a weapon, use the rules for Changing Out Weapons (see p. 56). Just remember that you can only ever use two weapons at one time.

Neil assumes the character will have a M1903 Springfield rifle as part of being a US soldier in World War I. He gives it an "OK" at Close and Near ranges, while giving it −2 at Far range and a Damage value of 3.

And of course a Shadowman isn't a Shadowman without his Scythe; he uses the exact same stats as that shown on the Shadowman Character Dossier (Damage of 4 [+3 damage against Master Darque], OK at Close range, −2 at Near range and N/A at Far range).

6. SELECT EQUIPMENT

As discussed under Equipment (see p. 56), equipment in *Valiant Universe* is not a set of hard rules. X is not required to do Y. Instead, they almost act as their own Cues, propelling the action forward without dropping into the minutiae of what exactly a piece of equipment weighs, what it does, and so on.

Use the few lines on the equipment list to accentuate the theme of your character, providing items you feel will be fun and enjoyable during game play. You don't even have to know what some of them do…one or two could just be crazy, fun-sounding names that you'll figure out on the fly!

It's important to make clear that due to the loose nature of these rules, it's all too easy for players to create wildly powerful/ludicrously small equipment; e.g., an "X-O Manowar-annihilator pinhead." After all, "the rules didn't say I couldn't!" If your player group decides such a thing is cool and fits with what you want to see in your games, by all means allow it. But most player groups will realize that even within these rules, a limit needs to be set on the power of equipment (going back to "X is only as powerful as the plot needs it to be" idea). Player groups may want to police equipment during character creation to ensure it's within the limits they're all comfortable with…or be stuck with the LN having to say, "Yup, sorry, that X-O Manowar-annihilator pin you just spent a dozen playing sessions obtaining fizzles, spurts, and goes silent…It's a dud. And now Aric of Dacia is *really* pissed."

> *Once again, the Utility Belt from the standard Shadowman character feels totally appropriate. Additionally, Neil loves the idea that the Gris-gris Amulet on Jack Boniface's Dossier actually is Damien's Amulet, providing a nice thread of story continuity between characters. The stories that amulet will tell…*
>
> *To provide some additional roleplaying opportunities that tie into Damien's burgeoning Art Powers, Neil also includes a Lyceum Scroll—a nice tie-in to the comics but one that can be as loose or as concrete as the gaming situation requires.*

7. CREATE CUES AND ACTION CUES

As noted under Cues (see p. 45), these are phrases that can be bold statements a character might make in a given situation, or can be used to spark an idea of which direction a character might leap.

Most of the Cues found on the sample Dossiers were drawn directly from the comics to ensure the flavor for each character is maintained from the comics to the gaming table.

Also note that each Character Dossier includes both Cues and Action Cues. While the general idea is that the Action Cues are more about when the character is suited up, so to speak, it's really up to the player to determine how to organize and ultimately use the Cues.

When creating Cues for your own character, use the same method you used when generating your character theme: jot down different phrases, sentences, or just saucy, juicy words that sound like something that would be fun to say during the action of the game. Then use the list to zero in on the best set of Cues.

You can also review the sample Character Dossiers (starting on p. 74) to spark your own ideas for Cues. If you're having a difficult time, feel free to use catchphrases taken from your favorite comic books, movies, TV shows, and novels, just tweaked slightly to make them unique to your character. For example "That was totally wicked!" could be tweaked to "I am totally speechless…"

If you're still struggling, feel free to make the generation of Cues into a party game for all those that'll be involved in an Event. Each player can write down two or three (or more) Cues based on your character theme, and then you can select some, none, or all of them. Even the craziest Cues could prove an interesting take on your character's personality under the right circumstances, so don't be so quick to toss the more wild concepts out.

> *Neil has a blast reading up on sayings from the 1910s to create some period-appropriate Cues that will set the mood of the game every time he uses one.*

8. CREATE DISPOSITIONS

Like Cues, your character's Dispositions should flow from how you're building your theme and the Cues. Even the description you used when generating your theme could be turned into Disposition statements.

As previous noted under Tags (see p. 61), Dispositions define how a character will react given various stimuli and circumstances (as opposed to Tags, which define what your character is).

Again, review the sample Dossiers, or ask for suggestions from your player group if you're struggling to define this aspect of your character.

It's hard to have a "loner" character that's very much within the template of a Shadowman without using some of the same material from the Jack Boniface Shadowman. As such, Neil decides he can use the "Utterly ruthless when the need arises" and "Brooding" Dispositions. However, since his character has been fighting alongside a squad of troopers—many of whom may be aware of his Powers and while somewhat terrified are also thankful he's saved their lives multiple times—"Always feels as though he's alone" doesn't apply. Additionally, "On the edge of holding it together" doesn't feel appropriate either. So to better reflect the Shadowman Neil's created, he goes with "Driven" and "Curious to a fault."

9. FINAL TWEAKING

Once you've written down all of your character details on the blank Character Dossier sheet, review the final superhero to ensure it's everything you want it to be. If you want to nip and tuck a little here and there, by all means, feel free.

Some of the places you can tweak characters are:

- Decreasing or increasing the pips on the Health track.
- Adjusting Armor up or down.
- Changing the way Powers work.

Such tweaking should be kept within reason. For example, you shouldn't rotate Stat Dice up or down as that has far too great an impact on the mechanics of gameplay. Any final tweaks should be reviewed by the player group to determine if anyone feels that any such tweaks are too much. Of course, the players in the group may decide one of your more extreme tweaks is just fine (especially if you give a really cool backstory for the tweak!), but be prepared to green-light their more extensive character tweaks in return.

Ultimately, however, these are just guidelines. Each player group is free to determine what works best for them and run with it…just have fun!

There's only one tweak Neil has in mind. Even for a more bookworm-oriented character, he feels 8 extra Armor (18 Armor total) is too low if he wants the character to survive, so he adds one more onto that for a total of 19.

He fills out a complete Character Dossier and is ready for some surreal, noir storytelling in Europe!

NON-PLAYER CHARACTER CREATION

To create non-player characters (NPCs), download the blank NPC Dossier from **www.catalystgamelabs.com/valiant** (it's also found at the back of this book) and use the following rules.

Note that the sample NPCs might not follow these rules.

1. CREATE A CHARACTER THEME

For most NPCs a theme is not really needed. However, for a "boss" NPC, or an NPC the LN thinks will be around for a while, a theme may be just the thing to bring such an important character to life.

2. ASSIGNING STAT DICE

Use the following rules when assigning Stats and Stat Dice (see p. 42). After assigning a Stat Die, simply write in the value and draw in the die shape, mimicking the style shown on the sample Dossiers.

Might, Intellect, Charisma, Action

Each NPC has two D6s and two D8s to assign to the Might, Intellect, Charisma, and Action Stats (see p. 42). It is completely up to the LN how they assign these values.

D4 & D10: If a player chooses, she can change one D8 Stat Die to a D10, but she must then change one D6 Stat Die to a D4.

D12: Most NPCs should never have a D12 Stat Die. Only the most significant NPCs should be assigned such a die. When making such a character, simply rotate the D10 to a D12; no other change is required.

Health

The Stat Die assigned to Might has a direct correlation to the Health track of the NPC Dossier. Use the following rules for determining the character's Health track:

- If a D12, do not mark off any pips.
- If a D10, mark off one pip from the first row.
- If a D8, mark off one pip from the first row and one pip from the second row.
- If a D6, mark off two pips from the first row and one pip from the second row.
- If a D4, mark off two pips from the first row and two pips from the second row.

3. CREATE POWERS (ASSIGN POWER DICE)

Powers on an NPC are all about what Power Type is needed and where or how it'll be used. If the NPC is just a run-of-the-mill soldier, then no Powers should be necessary. However, if the NPC is supposed to be a serious threat, then one Power should do the trick. Only NPCs that are meant to be the biggest threats or are intended for long-term use should include more than one Power. Also, coming up with a brand-new, unique Power or a cool twist on an existing Power will instantly turn a mundane NPC into a memorable one.

4. ASSIGN ARMOR

All NPCs have at least five Armor pips.

Following that rule, Armor is based on a combination of the Action and Might Stats. Use the following rule for determining the character's Armor track:

- Add the Might Die and Action Die values of your character together then divide by three (rounding up). That result equals the additional Armor pips applied to the NPC.

5. SELECT WEAPONS AND EQUIPMENT

Follow the rules for Select Weapons and Select Equipment as shown under Character Creation (see p. 66).

6. CREATE CUES AND DISPOSITIONS

As with the theme in Step One, the vast majority of NPCs will not need this step. However, the LN may decide that for the truly important bad guys, having some easy quips at hand will make any scene the NPC is in all that more dynamic and fun. The NPC Dossiers do not include room for Cues/Dispositions, so if they're created, player's will need to figure where to note them.

7. FINAL TWEAKING

As with character creation, the LN can heavily tweak an NPC to fit the bill, from a weak PRS soldier to a powerful Harbinger Foundation Eggbreaker. Just remember not to make the NPCs too powerful or too weak; either case may leave the players unsatisfied. Ultimately the ability of the LN to create characters that provide just the right amount of challenge for a player group in any given Scene simply takes practice and tossing some dice.

CHARACTER ADVANCEMENT

Players may advance their characters by accumulating Event Points earned during game play and translating those into improvements on their character Dossiers.

There are three ways to earn Event Points:

- **Game Play:** Every time a player finishes an Event, their character earns 1 Event Point.
- **Team Vote:** After each Event, all characters vote on a player they feel made the game the most fun. That player earns 1 Event Point.
- **Lead Narrator:** At any time, if a Lead Narrator feels that a player has truly created a memorable Narration and/or action, she may award 1 Event Point (this should be kept to a rare minimum).

In all cases, the players should remember to mark down their accumulated Event Points in the appropriate spot on their Character Dossier.

After noting accumulated Event Points after an Event—if enough is available—players can then turn accumulated points in (erasing them off the Dossier) in three ways:

- **Change a Die:** Rotate a Stat/Power Die to the next largest die (e.g., a D4 to a D6 or a D10 to a D12, and so on)
- **Change Power Type:** Change the Power Type of an existing Power (see p. 65).
- **Add New Power:** Add a brand new Power (if there is a slot available on the Dossier; if no slot is available, the player must remove a Power to add a new Power).

To make any of these changes, using the following rules (no other aspects of the Dossier change):

STAT OR POWER DICE

- D4 to D6 = 3 Event Points
- D6 to D8 = 5 Event Points
- D8 to D10 = 8 Event Points
- D10 to D12 = 12 Event Points

A player can rotate more than a single die value at one time but must pay the cumulative value. For example, a character that has a D4 Might and wishes to rotate it to a D10 would need to pay 16 Event Points.

A character can never have a Stat Die or Power Die higher than D12.

ADVANCING EXISTING POWERS TYPES

Event Points can be used to "upgrade" Power Types in the following manner (these points are IN ADDITION to any points spent above to rotate a Power Die):

- **Replace** to **Discard Lowest** = 3 Event Points
- **Discard Lowest** to **Keep Both** = 5 Event Points
- **Keep Both** to **Add +1** = 8 Event Points
- Every "+1" to **Add +X** above the original "+1" = 2 Event Points (these points are cumulative)

If players come up with a new mechanic for a Power that they wish to upgrade an existing Power to, they'll need to reach a consensus on how many Event Points are required to move up to that new Power Type.

Note: It's important to remember that these are guidelines. The Cue System is rules light and the character advancement is purposefully kept light as well, which means in some instances, the math isn't going to feel right. For example, the third bullet point above has 8 Event Points being spent to move from a "Keep Both" to an "Add +1" Type of Power. Except, depending upon the Dice involved, that could provide some real wackiness.

For example, if a Power is D8 (Keep Both) and the Stat Die it is rolled with is a D4, and the player changes that to, say, an Add +3, that would require 12 Event Points [8 (changing from Keep Both to Add +1) + 4 (an additional +2 to make it +3) = 12]. That's all fine as is. But if the Stat Die it is rolled with happens to be a D8, a D10, or a D12? Suddenly not only is Keep Both likely a better option, but the values of those two upgrades are not even close to each other.

In such instances, it will be up to the players to come to a consensus and modify the points appropriately.

ADDING BRAND NEW POWERS

The Character Dossiers include at least one empty slot for adding new Powers that evolve out of game sessions. Players use the exact same rules as those found on the Character Powers Table (see p. 63), translating the "Power Points" to "Event Points" requirements.

The one change to those rules is the point cost for the Power Die is lowered by one: i.e. D4 = 1, D6 = 2, D8 = 3, D10 = 4 and D12 = 5. Yes, this means new Powers can be acquired more easily, but a player has to put many hours into playing his character to reach this point and so has earned that easier take.

The Power Type Point Costs on that table remain the same when multiplying by the new Power Dice Point Costs above.

Maximum Powers: A player can only have a number of Powers equal to the slots available on a Character Dossier. If a player wishes to add a new Power and has no available slots, then she'll need to win over the LN (or the whole gaming group, depending upon how they play) by creating a cool Narration to explain how the new Power replaced the old.

After many gaming sessions, Neil has racked up an impressive 8 Event Points. While he could easily use those Event Points to rotate Stat or Power dice (or even advance existing Power Types), he instead likes the idea of Damien continuing to unlock additional Art-related Powers. To Neil's thinking, Damien's continued curiosity and drive is uncovering more knowledge, but not enough time has really passed for existing Art Powers to advance much.

Once again he's been delving into the Shadowman comics (man, he loves Shadowman #0) and decides he wants to create a Reanimate Power, an idea that fits well with some of the gaming sessions delving into the horrors of the battlefield. He assigns it a D6 and Keep Both, giving him the following:

Reanimate: 6 [2 (D6) x 3 (Keep Both) = 6]

Neil's gaming group reminds him that the comics state that anything reanimated isn't living again and is really just a bad copy that will have issues (not function properly, hard to control, and so on). Neil is well aware of the limitation and while their gaming group has bent comics-established "canon" now and then to fit their needs, he's got no qualms sticking to this one: he can't wait for the roleplaying such undead horrors will bring to the table. With that discussed, the gaming group feels no specific limitations are required.

Neil adds the Reanimate Power to his Dossier. Since he can't do anything with the 2 Event Points left, he leaves that on the Dossier and prepares for the next gaming session.

THE GAMING GROUP

As described under The Gaming Group sidebar (see p. 60), changing and/or adding Powers to a character should also involve all players.

EVENT BRIEF CREATION

While the *Valiant Universe RPG* includes a number of Event Briefs (not to mention all the excellent Events found in the various free PDFs online), players may decide they'd like to try their own hand at drafting one. While the Cue System is a shared gaming experience so that no single player is overburdened with running the game for the entire evening, players may soon discover that one of them is excellent at crafting new Event Briefs more suited to their style of play and enjoyment than preexisting Briefs. Or a group may simply want to enjoy the insight every player brings to the game, so for each session they play an Event Brief created by a different player.

Regardless of how Events are created, players can use the following guidelines when crafting their stories.

To create an Event), download the blank Event sheets from www.catalystgamelabs.com/valiant (they are also also found at the back of this book) and use the following guidelines.

REVIEW

Right out of the gate, review published Briefs. They generally follow a set format that works best for unfolding adventures at the gaming table using the Cue System. While players can make the game their own and mix and match or experiment as they will, following the format of preexisting material will likely make the creation easier, at least the first few times.

Comics

While this volume is designed as a standalone work for the enjoyment of roleplaying in the Valiant Universe, it can't possible encapsulate all the hundreds of issues and literally thousands of fantastic storytelling moments that have occurred in the comics.

Read a few Valiant comics. We certainly did, and the lion's share of the Event Briefs in this book are drawn directly from or inspired by those stories. A player might quickly find the perfect story not already covered in a preexisting Event, and they'd like to turn it into an evening's gaming session, or that story might spark an idea for a completely original story. Let the creative juices flow!

A THEME

Just as with creating a character, a theme is going to be the best guideline for the style of Event Brief to be played. The theme isn't which characters will be involved, or which settings.

Once you have a good handle on the theme, that'll usually lend itself directly to the setting and characters. For example, are you looking for in-your-face guns and explosions? Then bring H.A.R.D. Corps to the party. Looking for the difficult moral choices, where right is too often wrong? Then the characters and situations from *Harbinger* may be your best bet. And of course any type of horror or mystery is perfect for Shadowman.

That doesn't mean you can't mix and match. Armstrong likes to blow stuff up just as much as the next guy, while a H.A.R.D. Corps mission might find the characters stuck in a haunted mansion that's partly in the Deadside. If a group has specific characters or settings they prefer, by all means, keep them. But if they're looking for a style of play without caring about specifics, then peruse the appropriate Tags for the *Title Exposés* and *Organizations* sections (beginning on pages 10 and 28, respectively) to find the flavor of characters and setting best suited for the theme.

OBJECTIVES

Another important aspect of any Event Brief are the objectives. After all, gaming sessions will end either in victory for achieving those objectives, or in defeat for not fulfilling the requirements.

Once more, review a few Event Briefs. Notice most of them list just three objectives; doesn't seem that hard. But not only do those lines determine how and when players will end a game, they also set the bar for how challenging the gaming will be. Just one sentence can make a Scene a cakewalk or leave most of a group Staggered or Knocked Out. Be sure the objectives are tailored to the group's desire for difficulty and game length.

CUES AND TAGS

Whether these are generated is completely up to the author. However, the entire Cue System is built around their use, and they can make maintaining the game's flow easier. Those quick words and phrases can remind the LN if he's lost his way, or they can spark ideas for a new direction to push if the game seems to have stalled.

ENEMIES/OBSTACLES

This is where all the previous foundation work pays off. The bulk of an Event Brief is found in this section. And let's face it, without enemies and obstacles, we're just sitting around rolling dice.

But the theme, objectives, Cues, and Tags are all the shorthand notes and ideas from which players can build an entire gaming session. Can't decide who should show up in a given Scene? Glance back over your theme and Tags, then flip through the Dossiers in this volume to find similar Tags, and you've instantly got a plug-and-play option for additional NPCs. These could even be primary enemies that sets the stage for the *where* and potentially the *when* for the Event.

CONTEXT

Just as the Enemies/Obstacles is built from the previous work, the fiction of the Context builds on all of the previous steps. What's more, this is where the creator can truly let her imagination soar by giving life to the fantastic images rolling around in her head after reading parts of this volume or a comic or even a movie.

Since the Context is the first thing read to the group, make sure it's short but evocative, as it should set the stage for the entire evening's game and whet everyone's appetite for the fun to come. Don't hesitate to read it out loud to one or more players beforehand. A test audience is always a good idea to ensure that when the gaming group experiences this masterpiece, it's as enjoyable for the author to run as it was to create.

RANDOM EVENT GENERATOR

If you're having a hard time coming up with ideas to flesh out a blank Event Brief, use the Random Event Generator (see p. 203). Just roll on each of the tables as specified. Then look at the examples and they'll cue you where to look for inspiration from pre-existing Valiant Universe materials.

Of course the examples are just that—examples.

First, if you rolled Future and then City, you could use San Francisco, but you might consider switching it to where there's some great content to brainstorm from, such as in the forty-first century Japan as depicted in the *Rai* comics.

Second, you can springboard from these and let your imagination soar. If *you* want your Event to forge all new territory by having a civilization even before the City of Ur, populated by aliens using psionics to enslave time traveling humans…by all means, enjoy creating and running those Events!

VITAL FACTORS

Name: Alexander Dorian
Title: CEO, Orb Industries
Affiliation: Vine
Character Level: Hero
Event Points: _____

Tags: ● Vine ● planting ● CEO ● hedonist ● opportunist

HISTORY

Alexander Dorian grew up knowing what he was: a descendant of a Vine planting of Pict ancestry in northern Scotland. His connections to other plantings across the globe quickly put him into a position of power and prestige. With this power, Dorian adopted a playboy lifestyle and indulged in all manner of Earthly vices. Despite his proclivities, he rose to the head of military contractor Orb Industries. Dorian then used this position to further the Vine's goals of controlling the planet's population.

When Aric of Dacia brought the sacred X-O Manowar armor to Earth, Dorian's Vine masters sent a fleet to Earth. The fleet was to bring the Vine plantings back to the Vine homeworld and purge the planet's human population for having witnessed the sacred armor. Over the years, Dorian had come to embrace humanity as a race that enjoyed life rather than merely surviving, so he joined forces with Aric to stop the annihilation of all life on Earth.

PERSONALITY

Though indulgent in all manner of vices, Dorian is pragmatist when it comes to his own personal goals. His smooth confidence lets him manipulate others into getting what he wants.

MIGHT	INTELLECT	CHARISMA	ACTION	LUCK	
D8	D8	D10	D6	8	VALIANT

POWERS

Business Acumen *Replace*	D12	Access Vine Gatherings *Keep Both*	D8	Friends in High Places *Add+3*	D6

CUES

That's not necessary.	Such a waste.
What's done is done.	I hope this is worth it.
Wait! Take me with you!	We're on our own.
London is calling.	Are you not paying attention?

ACTION CUES

Only my mind is Vine. The rest is all man.	It's much worse than you imagine.
I'll talk him down.	We are all that stands in their way.
I can hold my own, I assure you.	This is the spy business. We're all liars and con men.
I speak the Vine's language because I'm one of them.	Forgive my misdirection.
I have business to attend to.	Let's start pruning.

DISPOSITION

Hides his identity as a Vine planting.	Chases after opportunity.
Usually puts himself before others.	Difficult to rattle.

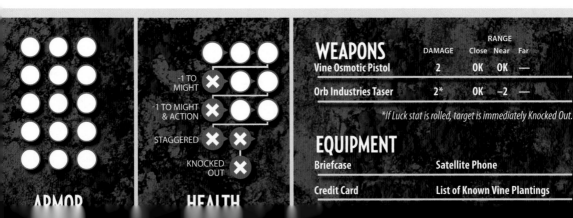

	-1 TO MIGHT
	-1 TO MIGHT & ACTION
	STAGGERED
	KNOCKED OUT

WEAPONS

	DAMAGE	RANGE Close	Near	Far
Vine Osmotic Pistol	2	OK	OK	—
Orb Industries Taser	2*	OK	−2	—

*If Luck stat is rolled, target is immediately Knocked Out.

EQUIPMENT

Briefcase	Satellite Phone
Credit Card	List of Known Vine Plantings

ARMOR   **HEALTH**

ALYSSA

VITAL FACTORS

Name: Alyssa Myles
Title: Apprentice
Affiliation: Abettors
Character Level: Sidekick
Event Points: _____

Tags: ● necromancer
● magic ● dedicated
● avid learner ● dependable

HISTORY

A young Abettor, Alyssa Myles studied under the tutelage of Dox and honed her magical powers in preparation for the day when the Host would reappear and return Shadowman to the world once again. When that day finally came, she saved the new Shadowman, Jack Boniface, from Deadside monsters. She also introduced him to the concept of necromantic energy—magic—and helped him understand his newfound powers. At Shadowman's side, Alyssa has faced all manner of dark entities, including Deadside ghosts, Baron Samedi, and Master Darque himself.

Alyssa is a capable and resourceful necromancer dedicated to using her abilities to assist Shadowman and the other Abettors in any way she can. On one occasion, however, the Abettors believed Jack was growing too dangerous, and they convinced Alyssa to help them strip the Shadowman loa spirit from Jack, a process that would kill him. In the end, Alyssa came to Jack's aid and persuaded her fellow Abettors that this was the wrong course.

PERSONALITY

A fiercely loyal Abettor, Alyssa is not one to back down from a fight, especially to protect those she loves. She hopes to someday become a full Abettor and take on her own apprentice.

MIGHT	INTELLECT	CHARISMA	ACTION	LUCK
D6	D6	D8	D8	8

VALIANT

POWERS

Cold Flame (Weapon)
Replace — D12

Sight Trance
Keep Both — D6

CUES

That's an excellent question.

Strange night?

Welcome to my world.

I *told* you!

Overpriced piece of crap. What is wrong with you?

The real question is, who are you?

Why would you say that?

He's here.

ACTION CUES

Oh crap. Oh crap! OH CRAP!

I really hate Plan B.

I could use a hand here.

This is going to hurt.

The police will be here in about five seconds.

So very, very not good.

Raise a hand like that to me again…and I'll break it.

Don't worry … I've got this.

We can protect you.

And what if you don't come back?

DISPOSITION

Always happy to help.

Treats Dox like a father.

Eager to learn.

Knows the Shadowman is worth protecting.

WEAPONS	DAMAGE	RANGE Close	Near	Far
Cold Flame	3	OK	OK	−2
Martial Arts	2	OK	—	—

-1 TO MIGHT

-1 TO MIGHT & ACTION

STAGGERED

KNOCKED OUT

EQUIPMENT

Goggles

Cell Phone

Veve Tattoos

ARMOR

HEALTH

VITAL FACTORS

Name: Monica Jim
Affiliation: Generation Zero
Character Level: Super
Event Points: _____

Tags: ● psiot ● Generation Zero ● creative ● fun-loving ● young

HISTORY

Being raised in PRS custody, Monica Jim has had no real contact with the outside world. When her psionic abilities surfaced, she was able to form a solid, opaque field around herself, which took the shape of an animal. However, her exposure to children's television programming and picture books had caused her field to mimic the appearance of cartoon animals—lions, bulls, gorillas, and other animals, including extinct creatures like pterosaurs.

Monica Jim loves creating and drawing her own cartoon characters. Her favorites are Humble Bumble, the dashingly handsome bumblebee; Samurai Sue, the honorable cat samurai; and Boran the Puppy Pirate and his sidekick Skeleton Pelican.

PERSONALITY

A lover of books and cartoons, Monica Jim likes to crack jokes and make bad puns. She is also fiercely loyal to Generation Zero and is always ready to jump into action.

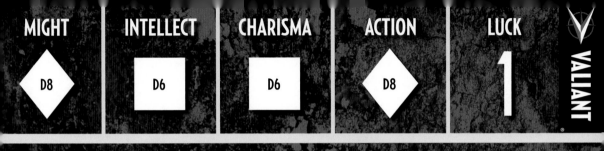

MIGHT	INTELLECT	CHARISMA	ACTION	LUCK	
D8	D6	D6	D8	1	VALIANT

POWERS

Lion Form (Weapon) — D10
Replace—Close only

Pterosaur Form (Weapon/Flight) — D6
Add+3—Any range

Bull Form (Weapon) — D8
Keep Both—Close/Near only

Cheetah Form — D10
Keep Both

CUES

Maybe I'll be a vet someday. Who knows?

Am I the only imaginative one here?

Fly, run, charge—I do it all.

Yeah, I like animals. So what?

What's a "cartoon"?

"Dinosaurs are extinct"? Yeah, *right*.

What would Samurai Sue do?

Not *every* animal form is useful. Like dodos.

ACTION CUES

What does a bull say?

Don't worry! I got this!

Outrun *this*!

He was certainly lion around on the job.

I'm queen of the jungle!

Animalia to the rescue!

I'm gonna pterodactyl your head off!

Still haven't gotten used to the taste of blood.

Cheetahs never prosper!

Bull in a china shop—that's me!

DISPOSITION

Loves to read but prefers picture books.

Only trusts close friends.

Unafraid to charge into dangerous situations.

Longs to have a "real" pet that looks like a cartoon.

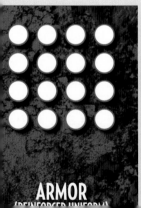

ARMOR
(REINFORCED UNIFORM)

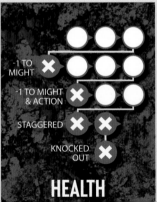

-1 TO MIGHT
-1 TO MIGHT & ACTION
STAGGERED
KNOCKED OUT

HEALTH

WEAPONS	DAMAGE	RANGE		
		Close	Near	Far
Animal Form	Power Die	*	*	*

*See Power description

EQUIPMENT

PRS A-team Uniform

Micro-shrapnel Brain Explosive

Animal Picture Book

ARCHER

VITAL FACTORS

Name: Obadiah Archer
Affiliation: Archer & Armstrong
Character Level: Hero
Event Points: _____

Tags: ● Dominion ● the Sect ● assassin ● religious ● driven

HISTORY

Obadiah Archer lives to do what is right. Raised by the Dominion—a quasi-fundamentalist church dedicated to defeating the evil one known as He Who is Not to be Named—Archer trained his whole life to be an assassin in the holy war. Blessed with the capability to "download" the known abilities of others, Archer did not doubt he was chosen by God…until he learned his mission of murder had nothing to do with God and his beloved Dominion was one faction of the Sect, a secret organization bent on controlling the world. Realizing what had to be done, Archer joined forces with Armstrong to stop the Sect.

Between knowing his life has been a lie and the only honorable man he's found being a drunken immortal who scoffs at God, Archer's faith has taken a beating. But he knows there is an ultimate good, even if he can't see or understand it, and he'll spend his life fighting for it.

PERSONALITY

Brilliant but unworldly, Archer believes in absolutes. There is little gray in his world and less fear. When he sees the right thing to do, he does it—no matter what it costs him.

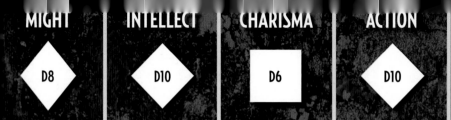

MIGHT	INTELLECT	CHARISMA	ACTION	LUCK
D8	D10	D6	D10	10

VALIANT

POWERS

Martial Arts Master (Weapon)
Discard Lowest — D10

Weapon Expert (Weapon)
Discard Lowest — D10

Access to Akashic Record
Discard Lowest — D8

CUES

I have been expertly homeschooled.

I am true kin to Mr. Armstrong.

I'm living for eternity.

H-E-double hockey sticks!

I cannot pollute my body with toxins.

There is no true faith without doubt.

I have sworn never to strike an innocent lady.

That's a load of flipping bullcorn!

ACTION CUES

I'm afraid I have to stop you right there.

You are not in control of the situation.

Leave Mary-Maria alone!

I am on a holy mission.

I can't allow that.

Let's flipping go for it!

I'm taking over the Sect for the good of mankind.

If only there was another way.

Do that and I'll hurt you.

I could detect you in my sleep.

DISPOSITION

Lives by a strict code of ethics.

Immune to humor.

Patient with those who try; no time for those who give up.

Will do what is right even if it kills him.

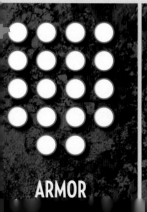

ARMOR

-1 TO MIGHT ✗
-1 TO MIGHT & ACTION ✗
STAGGERED ✗ ✗
KNOCKED OUT ✗

HEALTH

WEAPONS	DAMAGE	RANGE Close	Near	Far
Crossbow	3	OK	OK	−2
Martial Arts	2	OK	—	—

EQUIPMENT

Bible — Journal w/ Pen

Religious Medal

VITAL FACTORS

Name: Aram Anni-Padda
Title: He Who is Not to be Named
Affiliation: Archer & Armstrong
Character Level: Super
Event Points: _____

Tags: ● immortal ● Sumerian ● patient ● drinker ● resilient

HISTORY

Aram Anni-Padda of Ur enjoyed life; he believed man's highest purpose was to live in harmony. While his older brother Ivar hungered for knowledge and his younger brother Gilad lived for combat, Aram sought beauty and good conversation. Millennia ago the brothers looted the fabled Faraway and carried off the Boon—a monolith said to sustain life—but Gilad was killed during their escape. Despite Aram's warnings against invoking a magic they did not understand, Ivar was convinced the Boon could restore their brother. He activated it, but at a terrible cost. The Boon could not create life. It drained the life force of everything within its sphere and poured it into Aram. All of Ur, all the world they knew, died imbuing Aram with immortality and great physical strength. (Gilad was restored and made immortal, but by the Earth, not the Boon.)

Aram has since roamed the Earth for a hundred centuries, doing good when he can, taking love where he finds it, and struggling to still the cries of the thousands of lives lost within him.

PERSONALITY

Takes pleasure where he finds it; always stops to smell the roses. Tries to stay in the moment because he knows nothing lasts. He has no faith but believes in the basic goodness of people.

MIGHT	INTELLECT	CHARISMA	ACTION	LUCK	
D12	D8	D10	D8	10	VALIANT

POWERS

Physical Strength *Add+1*	D12	
Accelerated Healing *Add+1—Heals D4 – 1 pips of Health*	D4	

Persuasion *Discard Lowest*	D8
	○

Combat Sense *Discard Lowest*	D10
	○

CUES

I see the inevitable.	Someday I'll be all outta cats.
Whatchoo got there?	I have a million stolen lifetimes screaming inside of me.
I think I remember this.	Don't worry about me, I can amuse myself.
What matters is what you've got now before it's gone.	Keep your magic underwear on, kid.

ACTION CUES

Make 'em hurt!	'Sup.
Wrong answer.	Ooh, that can't be good.
When in doubt…*run*!	Crappity Crap!
Now it's personal.	If I don't come back, burn my porn!
Game over.	Smoke 'em if you got 'em!

DISPOSITION

Pretends not to care but seldom fools anyone.	A well of sadness beneath his celebration of life.
Lover of beauty—in art, nature, literature, women.	A teller of stories—true or otherwise.

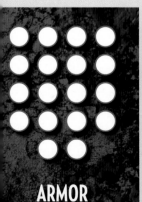

ARMOR

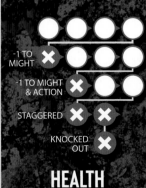

HEALTH

-1 TO MIGHT

-1 TO MIGHT & ACTION

STAGGERED

KNOCKED OUT

WEAPONS	DAMAGE	RANGE Close	Near	Far
Fists and Feet	4	OK	—	—
Hurled Found Objects*	4	OK	OK	-2

trees, vault doors, assailants, tables, trucks, boulders, etc.

EQUIPMENT

Bottomless Satchel of Useful Things	Spear
Goblet	Tesla Lightning Gun

BLOODSHOT

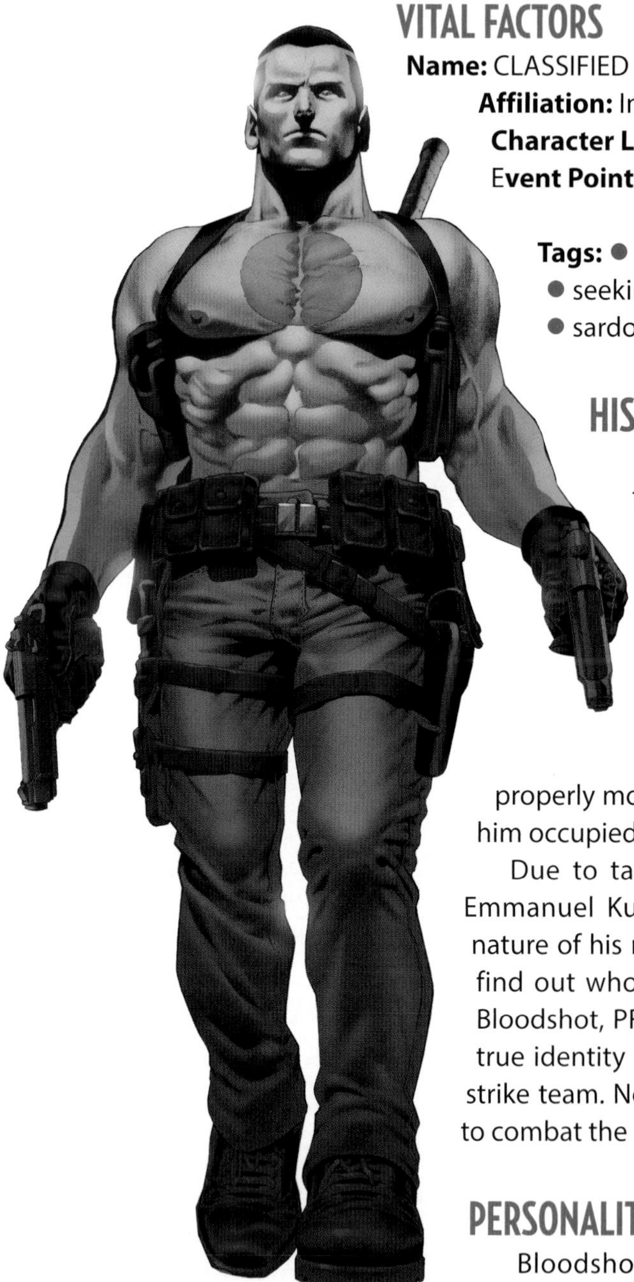

VITAL FACTORS

Name: CLASSIFIED
Affiliation: Independent
Character Level: Legend
Event Points: _____

Tags: ● killer ● determined ● seeking ● dedicated ● loyal ● sardonic ● Project Rising Spirit

HISTORY

The subject known as Bloodshot is the focal point of Project Bloodshot, part of Project Rising Spirit. This program infused Bloodshot with nanites that provide enhanced physical attributes, electronic communication, rapid healing, and a limited ability to alter the subject's appearance. Bloodshot was then fed a series of false memories to properly motivate him for his next mission and keep him occupied until he was needed.

Due to tampering by former PRS employee Dr. Emmanuel Kuretich, Bloodshot discovered the true nature of his memories, and he fought against PRS to find out who he really was. After Kuretich betrayed Bloodshot, PRS offered Bloodshot information on his true identity if he agreed to lead their H.A.R.D. Corps strike team. Now Bloodshot works with H.A.R.D. Corps to combat the psiot threat, Toyo Harada.

PERSONALITY

Bloodshot has two main motivations in life— finding out his true identity and trying to get out from under PRS control. Outside of that, he spends most of his time healing from his most recent battle or planning the next one.

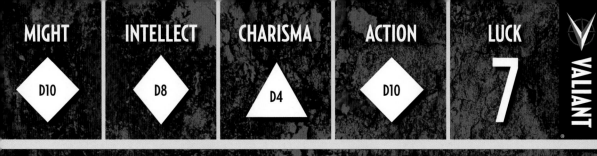

MIGHT	INTELLECT	CHARISMA	ACTION	LUCK	
D10	D8	D4	D10	**7**	**VALIANT**

POWERS

Control Computers *Keep Both*	D10	**Change Appearance** *Discard Lowest*	D8
Nanite Regeneration *Keep Both—Heals 2 Armor and 2 Health. May still use if Staggered or Knocked Out.*	D10	**Psionic Resistance** *Discard Lowest*	D12

Pain Resistance *Discard Lowest*—Ignore dice modifiers on the Health track. D10

CUES

I don't have a problem with that.	I need protein.
Kid, you there?	This isn't over!
God . . . I'm *hungry*!	I'm not what you think I am.
I was talking to the machines in my blood.	The rest of me heals, but this wound never goes away.

ACTION CUES

I'm going to watch you *die*.	I'm everybody's problem.
Blam, blam, blam, blam.	It's us or them. And I'd rather it be them.
Something horrible is headed this way.	Take cover. It's about to get messy.
My whole body is Kevlar.	You know what I am. I'm a damn walking weapon.
So. New plan. Go with what works.	Why can't you people just leave me alone?!

DISPOSITION

Looking for life and answers.	Often displays unrestrained rage.
Protects the weak.	Vengeful.

ARMOR (NANITES)

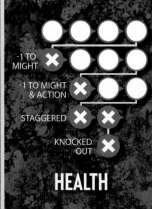

-1 TO MIGHT
-1 TO MIGHT & ACTION
STAGGERED
KNOCKED OUT

HEALTH

WEAPONS	DAMAGE	RANGE Close	Near	Far
NEMO Omen Rifle	3	−2	OK	OK
Marauder Combat Knife	2	OK	—	—

EQUIPMENT

C4 Detonator	Utility Belt
Dog tags	

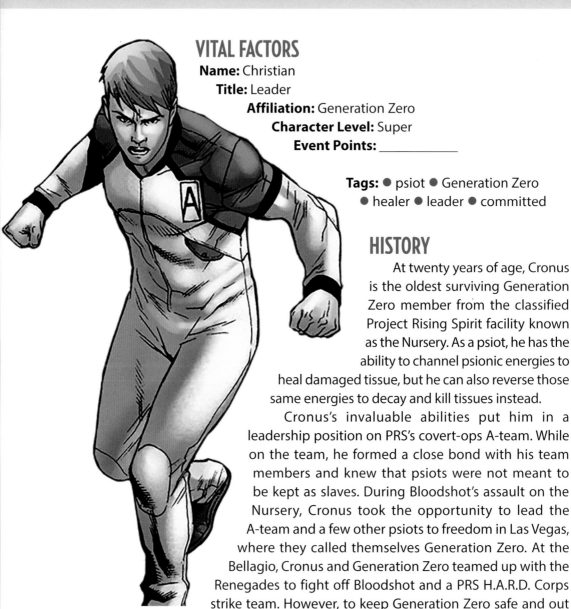

VITAL FACTORS

Name: Christian
Title: Leader
Affiliation: Generation Zero
Character Level: Super
Event Points: _____

Tags: ● psiot ● Generation Zero ● healer ● leader ● committed

HISTORY

At twenty years of age, Cronus is the oldest surviving Generation Zero member from the classified Project Rising Spirit facility known as the Nursery. As a psiot, he has the ability to channel psionic energies to heal damaged tissue, but he can also reverse those same energies to decay and kill tissues instead.

Cronus's invaluable abilities put him in a leadership position on PRS's covert-ops A-team. While on the team, he formed a close bond with his team members and knew that psiots were not meant to be kept as slaves. During Bloodshot's assault on the Nursery, Cronus took the opportunity to lead the A-team and a few other psiots to freedom in Las Vegas, where they called themselves Generation Zero. At the Bellagio, Cronus and Generation Zero teamed up with the Renegades to fight off Bloodshot and a PRS H.A.R.D. Corps strike team. However, to keep Generation Zero safe and out of PRS's hands, Cronus ultimately surrendered himself and his teammates to Toyo Harada's Harbinger Foundation.

PERSONALITY

Though young, Cronus is a leader to his friends, and he is determined to ensure the freedom of every Generation Zero member. He would put himself in harm's way to protect his friends.

MIGHT	INTELLECT	CHARISMA	ACTION	LUCK
 D8	 D8	 D10	 D8	 6

VALIANT

POWERS

Channel Energy (Weapon)
Replace — D10

Healing Energies
Add+3—Heal target for D6+1 Health — D10

Leadership
Keep Both — D8

Tactics
Discard Lowest — D8

CUES

We're alive, aren't we?	Everyone still breathing?
So, how do we do that?	You need to trust me.
Is something wrong?	Looks like a trap to me.
Our lives could be very, very short . . .	We're in no position to bargain.

ACTION CUES

Everybody, follow me!	We need some place to make our stand.
They don't deserve to live.	It's the only way out!
You think you're in charge, but you're not.	Not even I can heal everything.
PRS taught us predeterminism. I am fighting that idea.	This is going to sting.
Do what you have to.	If we keep fighting, what do we gain?

DISPOSITION

Strong and confident in the face of opposition.	Idealistic to a fault.
Values freedom above all else.	Never gives in.

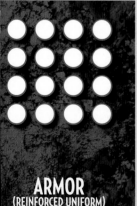

ARMOR
(REINFORCED UNIFORM)

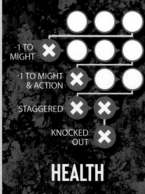

-1 TO MIGHT ✖

-1 TO MIGHT & ACTION ✖

STAGGERED ✖ ✖

KNOCKED OUT ✖

HEALTH

WEAPONS

	DAMAGE	RANGE Close	Near	Far
Damaging Energies	D6	OK	—	—
Martial Arts	2	OK	—	—

EQUIPMENT

PRS A-team Uniform — Micro-shrapnel Brain Explosive

Digital Copy of *Gray's Anatomy*

VITAL FACTORS

Name: Aaron Frye
Affiliation: H.A.R.D. Corps
Character Level: Super
Event Points: _____

Tags: ● borrowed time ● devout ● focused ● Southern ● honest

HISTORY

Aaron Frye spent his early adult years as an auto mechanic and a youth minister for his local congregation. When he applied for missionary work, his blood test results revealed his DNA was compatible with the H.A.R.D. Corps implant procedure. Director Kozol then approached Frye and offered him a chance to make a difference .

Disciple is one of the youngest of H.A.R.D Corps's new generation, yet in many ways he carries a wisdom and strength surpassing even Major Palmer's. His first kill in the field took a toll on him, but he prayed on it and decided his actions saved the lives of his team. Fellow H.A.R.D. Corps member Superstar worries that someday Disciple will run into something the Bible won't have an answer for.

PERSONALITY

Aaron draws strength from his faith. He approaches life with the joy of someone certain of his life and path. His ability to justify what he has experienced allows him to weather the strongest trials.

MIGHT	INTELLECT	CHARISMA	ACTION	LUCK	
D10	D6	D6	D8	7	VALIANT

POWERS

Shield (Armor)
Add+3—Reduce damage taken by 1 — D6

Detonation (Weapon)
Add+3 — D6

Lifeline Uploads
Add+3—May request any of the active Lifeline Bio-configs. Note: Powers are only available one at a time. — D4

Flight
Add+3 — D6

CUES

Trust in God, but keep the powder dry.	Because my heart is pure, I have no fear.
It's a gift from God. An opportunity to serve His will.	I fight for a cause greater than myself.
Praise God.	I may never be perfect, that does not mean I will not try.
Forgiveness is between them and God. I won't.	It's ginger ale.

ACTION CUES

Jesus, give me strength.	My faith is stronger than your gun.
I shall fear no evil!	Do unto others, et cetera.
Yes, they deserve to die, and I hope they burn in hell.	The path of the righteous man is beset on all sides.
You ready to die? God is waiting for me, so I'm ready.	God helps those who help themselves.
Justice will be done.	The devil take you!

DISPOSITION

Strong as long as his faith is.	God and his team are his only ties.
Always ready to talk to his flock.	Calm to the point of seeming comatose.

HEALTH
-1 TO MIGHT
-1 TO MIGHT & ACTION
STAGGERED
KNOCKED OUT

WEAPONS

WEAPONS	DAMAGE	Close	Near	Far
Explosive Concussion	3	OK	−2	—
Berretta 90two Pistol	2	OK	−2	—

EQUIPMENT

Lifeline Uplink	Multi-function Nanoskin Suit
Gideon Bible	Micro-shrapnel Brain Explosive

ARMOR

VALIANT

VITAL FACTORS

Name: Shan Fong
Title: Doctor Mirage
Affiliation: Independent
Character Level: Hero
Event Points: _____

Tags: ● parapsychologist ● medium ● TV personality
● lost love ● paranormal investigator

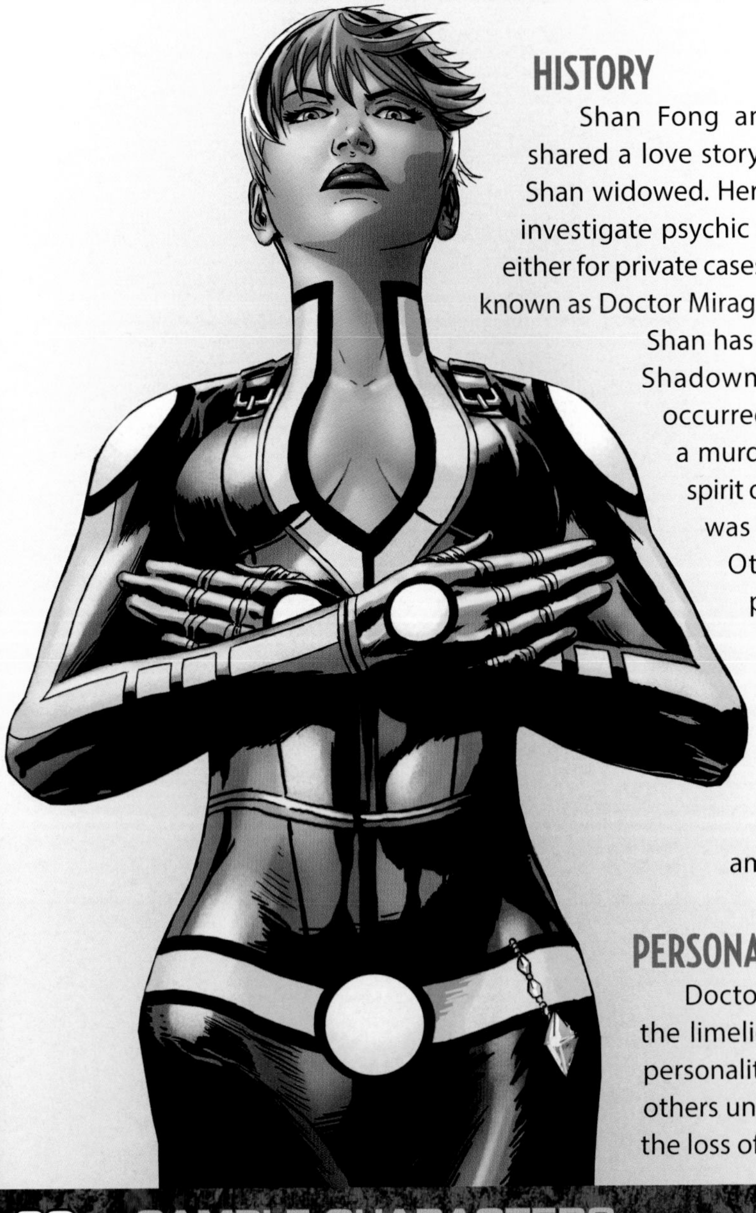

HISTORY

Shan Fong and her husband Hwen once shared a love story for the ages, but tragedy left Shan widowed. Her ability to see spirits led her to investigate psychic and supernatural phenomena, either for private cases or as the television personality known as Doctor Mirage.

Shan has crossed paths with the current Shadowman a few times. The first occurred while she was investigating a murder case in California, when the spirit of a young girl told Shan that she was running from Master Darque. Other ghosts flocked to Shan, prompting her to visit to New Orleans to deliver the ghosts' message to Shadowman and the Abettors: Darque had given Baron Samedi, a forgotten New Orleans deity, enough power to walk amongst the living once more.

PERSONALITY

Doctor Mirage is reluctant to be in the limelight, despite being a television personality, and she rarely interacts with others unless needed. She struggles with the loss of her husband.

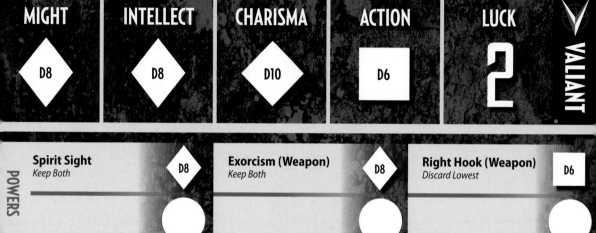

MIGHT	INTELLECT	CHARISMA	ACTION	LUCK	
D8	D8	D10	D6	2	VALIANT

POWERS

Spirit Sight	Exorcism (Weapon)	Right Hook (Weapon)
Keep Both — D8	*Keep Both* — D8	*Discard Lowest* — D6

CUES

It's all right. He can't hurt you.	This city's got enough problems as it is.
I came here to deliver a message.	You've probably seen me on television.
Relax ... it's just me.	I'd prefer not to talk about my husband.
I want to focus on my cases.	I'll send you my invoice.

ACTION CUES

Every once in a while, I deal with *human* monsters.	Get out!
Leave the host!	I'm saving lives, you moron!
... I get these impressions ...	I don't think I can hold it all back ...
I seem to have come down with a ghost infestation.	Shh! Ghost whispers can be hard to hear sometimes.
This impression is strong...	Something unsettles the spirits here.

DISPOSITION

Seeks to bring justice to the dead.	Calm and rational.
Hopes to one day find the spirit of her lost love.	Always acts in a professional manner.

-1 TO MIGHT
-1 TO MIGHT & ACTION
STAGGERED
KNOCKED OUT

WEAPONS	DAMAGE	RANGE Close	Near	Far
Exorcism*	6	OK	OK	OK
Fist	2	OK	—	—

*Only effective against spirits or undead

EQUIPMENT

Ghost Light   Cell Phone

Photo of Hwen Fong

ARMOR   **HEALTH**

DOX

VITAL FACTORS

Name: Alessandro Paradojo Del Verdad

Title: Fearless Leader

Affiliation: Abettors

Character Level: Hero

Event Points: _____

Tags: ● mentor
● protective
● diminutive
● necromancer
● inscriber

HISTORY

Dox has been fighting against the forces of the Deadside for a long time. As an Abettor, he served Shadowman Josiah Boniface when Master Darque first tried to break through into the realm of the living. Now, decades later, Josiah's son Jack has been revealed as the new Shadowman host, and Dox and his protégé Alyssa have pledged themselves to train and protect Jack at all costs.

Familiar with many aspects of channeling necromantic energies, Dox knows how to hit the forces of the dead where it hurts. He can craft weapons that utilize this macabre energy against the denizens of the Deadside. Grand veves—complex magical symbols—cover Dox's body, making him a reservoir for incredible amounts of necromantic power. Unfortunately, this also makes him an attractive target for the secretive Brethren.

PERSONALITY

Dox doesn't let his small stature hamper his ability to wage war against the dead. Fiercely loyal to Shadowman, he will do anything to further the cause of the living, even risking his own life.

MIGHT	INTELLECT	CHARISMA	ACTION	LUCK
D8	D8	D8	D8	4

VALIANT

POWERS

Veve Inscription Carving — D8
Discard Lowest

Necromantic Ammo — D10
Discard Lowest—Add +1 damage to the next successful pistol attack

Magical Lore — D12
Discard Lowest

CUES

Oh, terrific.	Everything's a trick.
Well, boring works.	Evil is not a toy.
Here's the problem.	There's plenty of blame to go around, starting with me.
Truth be told, I'm making this up as I go.	I didn't do enough.

ACTION CUES

Hold the perimeter!	Not likely. Not here. Not now.
I hope you choke on me.	I hope this hurts.
We're too late!	Go to hell.
You can't beat him alone.	Damnit, damnit, damnit.
They shouldn't have gotten this far!	Make this matter.

DISPOSITION

Treats Jack Boniface like a long-lost relative.	Always tries to do the *right* thing, not the easy thing.
Dedicated to furthering Alyssa's training.	Sees magic as a tool, not a crutch.

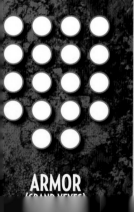

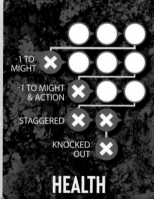

-1 TO MIGHT ❌
-1 TO MIGHT & ACTION ❌
STAGGERED ❌ ❌
KNOCKED OUT ❌

WEAPONS	DAMAGE	RANGE Close	Near	Far
Magnum Revolver Pistol	3	OK	OK	−2
Grand Veve Blast*	6	OK	OK	OK

*Costs 2 Health pips per use

EQUIPMENT

Magnification Goggles	Surgical Tools
Magical Tome	Inscription Toolkit

ARMOR
(GRAND VEVES)

HEALTH

FAITH

HARBINGER

VITAL FACTORS

Name: Faith Herbert
Affiliation: Renegades
Character Level: Super
Event Points: _____

Tags: ● psiot ● optimistic ● heroic ● idealistic ● loyal

HISTORY

Faith Herbert has lived in a world of superheroes since, like, forever. After losing her parents in a car crash at a young age, Faith was raised by her grandmother, who was sooo super-kind and encouraged her to read her parents' comic books and surround herself with everything they loved. She geeked out on *Star Trek*, *Doctor Who*, and *Firefly* (especially *Firefly* … mmm Captain Tightpants …), and all those comics and TV shows taught her what a hero is supposed to be.

Her life finally changed when Edward Sedgewick approached her on her favorite MMORPG. He wasn't really interested in her (jerk!), but he recruited her for the Harbinger Foundation. There, the cutie Peter Stanchek activated her powers, and she totally saved him from that creepy Harada dude later. Going on the run with Petey, she became the heart of his Renegades.

PERSONALITY

Faith is idealistic to a fault. She doesn't care what people think about her looks, and she is determined to be a true superhero. She has a crush on Peter but knows he is in love with Kris Hathaway.

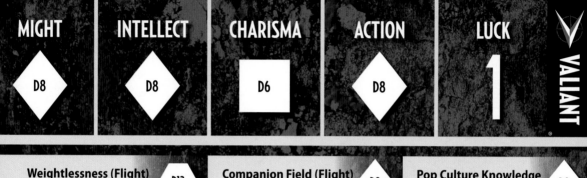

MIGHT	INTELLECT	CHARISMA	ACTION	LUCK	
D8	D8	D6	D8	1	VALIANT

POWERS

Weightlessness (Flight)	D12	Companion Field (Flight)	D8	Pop Culture Knowledge	D8
Keep Both		*Discard Lowest*		*Discard Lowest*	
Optimism	D10				
Discard Lowest					

CUES

Don't be a jerk!	Ghaa! You're so heavy!
White's not great camouflage . . .	We're totally superheroes!
The world needs me.	Do you like *Firefly*?
I AM this team.	We can be a pretty intense crew.

ACTION CUES

I totally save lives and stuff!	I'm sick of all this bull hockey!
This is what heroes do, right?	I'm trying to save you!
This is gonna be awesome!	This is really going to hurt . . .
Thank you for this life.	I have to go faster.
Everything I've ever dreamed about, it's all real!	Please fly! Please fly!

DISPOSITION

A true superhero.	Eternally cheerful.
Wants to do the right thing.	Comfortable in her own skin.

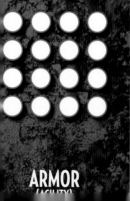

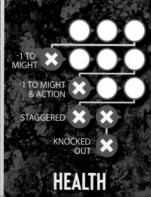

-1 TO MIGHT ✖
-1 TO MIGHT & ACTION ✖
STAGGERED ✖ ✖
KNOCKED OUT ✖

ARMOR (AGILITY)

HEALTH

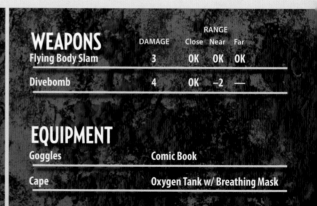

WEAPONS	DAMAGE	RANGE		
		Close	Near	Far
Flying Body Slam	3	OK	OK	OK
Divebomb	4	OK	–2	—

EQUIPMENT

Goggles	Comic Book
Cape	Oxygen Tank w/ Breathing Mask

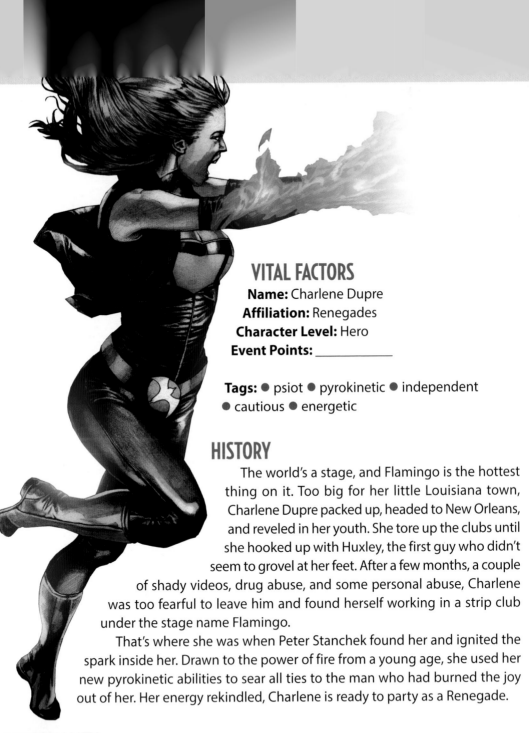

VITAL FACTORS

Name: Charlene Dupre
Affiliation: Renegades
Character Level: Hero
Event Points: _____

Tags: ● psiot ● pyrokinetic ● independent
● cautious ● energetic

HISTORY

The world's a stage, and Flamingo is the hottest thing on it. Too big for her little Louisiana town, Charlene Dupre packed up, headed to New Orleans, and reveled in her youth. She tore up the clubs until she hooked up with Huxley, the first guy who didn't seem to grovel at her feet. After a few months, a couple of shady videos, drug abuse, and some personal abuse, Charlene was too fearful to leave him and found herself working in a strip club under the stage name Flamingo.

That's where she was when Peter Stanchek found her and ignited the spark inside her. Drawn to the power of fire from a young age, she used her new pyrokinetic abilities to sear all ties to the man who had burned the joy out of her. Her energy rekindled, Charlene is ready to party as a Renegade.

PERSONALITY

Charlene's past somewhat prepared her for the rough parts of her new life, but living an underground existence does not agree with her. Used to being front and center, she yearns for the attention she once received.

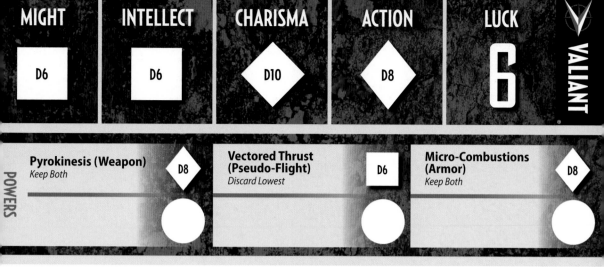

MIGHT	INTELLECT	CHARISMA	ACTION	LUCK	VALIANT
D6	D6	D10	D8	6	

POWERS

Pyrokinesis (Weapon)
Keep Both — D8

Vectored Thrust (Pseudo-Flight)
Discard Lowest — D6

Micro-Combustions (Armor)
Keep Both — D8

CUES

Did I hit anybody?

Don't look at me.

You'd better slow your roll, or this is gonna get real.

Nobody looks like me. I'm a snowflake.

I don't know what that means, but I'll take it.

Let's just keep our heads down and stick to our groove.

I'm pretty clued into these things.

Don't worry about that, darlin'.

ACTION CUES

Let's go be awesome, I guess.

Isaac Newton in the house!

Please don't let me die here!

That burning sensation you feel is probably me.

Well, hell! Let's do that!

I'm going after them!

Roast, you son of a bitch!

Get back . . . gonna be hot!

Can you take it?

Oh, God, please don't let me die here!

DISPOSITION

Living life to its fullest.

Pyromaniac.

Can't go home again.

Ready for action.

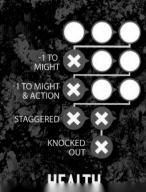

-1 TO MIGHT

-1 TO MIGHT & ACTION

STAGGERED

KNOCKED OUT

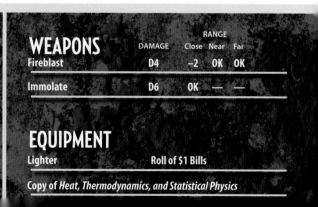

WEAPONS

WEAPONS	DAMAGE	Close	Near	Far
Fireblast	D4	−2	OK	OK
Immolate	D6	OK	—	—

RANGE

EQUIPMENT

Lighter

Roll of $1 Bills

Copy of *Heat, Thermodynamics, and Statistical Physics*

ARMOR

HEALTH

VITAL FACTORS

Name: Kay McHenry
Title: Geomancer
Affiliation: House of the Earth
Character Level: Super
Event Points: _____

Tags: ● determined ● untrained ● feisty ● impatient ● smart

HISTORY

Kay McHenry was a public relations spokesperson for Zorn Capital. While she was good at her job, her personal life was a mess, and she was slowly becoming numb. She began hearing voices, and those voices brought her back to Zorn Capital, only to stumble into a meeting between Zorn and the One Percent, part of the Sect. She was captured, thrown into an old subway car, which was then dumped into the water.

At first, Kay thought she was dying when she found herself having tea with a monkey dressed as Mother Nature. The monkey, actually the voice of the Earth, offered Kay the then-vacant position of Geomancer.

With the Geomancer's powers, she escaped from the trap, and she, Gilad Anni-Padda, Archer, and Armstrong stopped the Null from destroying existence.

PERSONALITY

Kay is attractive, smart, and unafraid to speak her mind. She finds this new job very different yet more rewarding than her old one.

MIGHT	INTELLECT	CHARISMA	ACTION	LUCK	
D6	D10	D8	D8	7	VALIANT

POWERS

Elemental Control (Weapon)
Discard Lowest — D10

Communicate with Mother Earth
Keep Both — D10

Lockpicking
Discard Lowest — D10

Earth Sense
Discard Lowest — D10

CUES

There's got to be some truth out there.

My business is words, not meanings.

It was nothing—I just asked nicely.

Could you turn down the testosterone a few hundred notches?

I'm not having a good day, all right?

I feel the proverbial disturbance in the Force.

I should be doing something for myself!

Darjeeling tea, my favorite.

ACTION CUES

I am the Speaker of the Earth.

I am the key, and I just changed the combination.

The Earth doesn't just speak to me; she sings.

It's not nice to fool Mother Nature.

Nothing is forever, but being is now.

Reality is written in code, and I have the master key.

Let me ask the source.

This is not like palm reading.

Hey! Get out of my way!

Eat this!

DISPOSITION

Still growing into her position.

Scared and reverential of her power.

Doesn't have a stable personal life.

Quick thinker.

WEAPONS

	DAMAGE	RANGE Close	Near	Far
Elemental Blast	4	OK	OK	−2
Fist	1	OK	—	—

HEALTH
-1 TO MIGHT
-1 TO MIGHT & ACTION
STAGGERED
KNOCKED OUT

EQUIPMENT
Book of the Geomancer   Geomancer's Seal

Journal

ARMOR
(EARTH'S EMBRACE)

GILAD ANNI-PADDA

ETERNAL WARRIOR

VITAL FACTORS

Name: Gilad Anni-Padda
Title: Fist and Steel of the Earth
Affiliation: The House of Earth
Character Level: Legend
Event Points: _____

Tags: ● immortal ● Sumerian ● patient ● fierce combatant ● Geomancers ● resilient

HISTORY

For over six thousand years, Gilad Anni-Padda has been a warrior for the Earth, serving the planet as its champion. The youngest of the three Anni-Padda brothers, Gilad served the Earth long and well, fighting and killing whomever and wherever the Earth's Geomancer directed him.

After millennia of killing, Gilad began to harbor doubts and grew tired of the everlasting war. Finally, he walked away from it. For years, he lived alone on the African savannah, killing only to eat.

But the Earth and the forces Gilad fought against for thousands of years would not just let him retire. His daughter Xaran interrupted Gilad's self-exile and sought the help of a father she hasn't seen in six thousand years.

The Eternal Warrior is back on the battlefield, but this time he's fighting his own war, on his own terms.

PERSONALITY

Gilad is a consummate warrior, with knowledge of all forms of ancient and modern warfare. While he's ruthless in combat, he adheres to a rigid code of honor.

MIGHT	INTELLECT	CHARISMA	ACTION	LUCK
D10	D8	D6	D10	**10**

VALIANT

POWERS

Weapon Mastery *Discard Lowest*	D12	**Tactical Genius** *Discard Lowest*	D8	**Combat Sense** *Discard Lowest*	D10
Accelerated Healing *Keep Both*—Heals D4 – 1 pips of Health	D10	**Sure Shot** *Keep Both*—On successful Test, adds +2 to next Action roll result	D10		

CUES

I hate being late.

I'm the oldest living thing in the hemisphere.

Go away. I won't ask you again.

There's always a war going on.

You're really never quite so alive as when you're killing something.

This won't end well.

The world is watching. There will be consequences.

An immortal can afford to be patient.

ACTION CUES

My war is eternal.

I was around when war got invented.

I'm the Fist and Steel of the Earth.

The only thing I know is war.

Get the innocents out of the line of fire.

I will protect the Geomancers—or avenge them.

You can't escape me.

I do what I was put on Earth to do.

It's not the weapon that's dangerous; it's the warrior using it.

I expect no quarter from you, nor should I give you any.

DISPOSITION

Not one to mince words.

Relentless in pursuit of his mission.

Aware of his surroundings at all times.

Has a strong warrior's code.

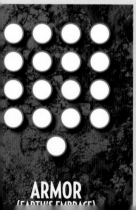

ARMOR (EARTH'S EMBRACE)

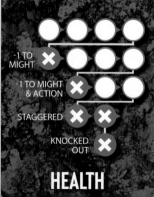

- -1 TO MIGHT
- -1 TO MIGHT & ACTION
- STAGGERED
- KNOCKED OUT

HEALTH

WEAPONS	DAMAGE	RANGE Close	Near	Far
Axe	3	OK	–2	—
Submachine Gun*	2	OK	OK	–2

*May target two enemies with the same attack action

EQUIPMENT

Token of the House of Earth	Spiked Gauntlet	
Combat Suit	Armored Sleeve	Cloak

GRANITE

VITAL FACTORS

Name: Erica Connelly
Affiliation: H.A.R.D. Corps
Character Level: Super
Event Points: _____

Tags: ● borrowed time ● sensitive ● athletic ● trusting ● direct

HISTORY

In a crashing economy, Erica Connelly tried raising her two children in a home she could no longer afford. Even when her parents moved in to help, the plummeting job market made keeping up on those payments even harder. With her credit tapped out, working three jobs, and her mother ill, Connelly was looking for a miracle to save her family.

Morris Kozol offered her that miracle. Connelly was willing to commit to H.A.R.D. Corps for her family's sake, even if she knew it meant endangering her own life down the line. However, even with her dedication, the firsthand reality of a mission's lethal danger sometimes lets her fear show through the cracks in her otherwise rock-hard resolve.

Granite has experienced much in her short time with H.A.R.D. Corps, but sometimes she needs to spend time with her family to remind herself the reason for her dedication.

PERSONALITY

Erica's entire being revolves around her family's safety and well-being. If she can see a link between family and the job in front of her, she is solid and focused. Otherwise, doubt swiftly creeps in.

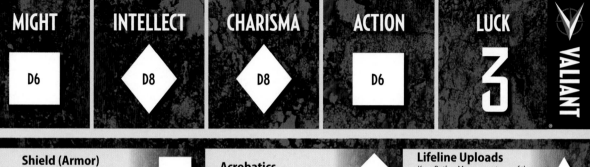

MIGHT	INTELLECT	CHARISMA	ACTION	LUCK	
D6	D8	D8	D6	3	VALIANT

POWERS

Shield (Armor)
Add+3—Reduce damage taken by 1 — D6

Flight
Keep Both — D8

Acrobatics
Keep Both — D10

Lifeline Uploads
Keep Both—May request any of the active Lifeline Bio-configs. Note: Powers are only available one at a time. — D4

CUES

None of us want to die. But we all know we could, and we accept that.

If we don't do it, then who will?

That could have been any of us.

All this power, it's nothing compared to what we have to face.

This is my "I don't care" face.

I'm gonna call my kids.

I'm human, not perfect.

I am a strong woman with or without these powers.

ACTION CUES

Sit down!

Lifeline, now!

Sister, I'm just getting started.

The difference is I make this look good.

Pig!

Be bold, be brave, be true to yourself.

That's presumptuous.

Quit your whining.

We've got a job to do.

Even my *kids* have better manners.

DISPOSITION

Brave, despite her fear.

Strong willed and stubborn.

Unafraid to cry.

All is done for her family.

ARMOR

HEALTH

-1 TO MIGHT

-1 TO MIGHT & ACTION

STAGGERED

KNOCKED OUT

WEAPONS	DAMAGE	RANGE Close	Near	Far
Berretta 90two Pistol	2	OK	−2	—
Berretta 90two Pistol	2	OK	−2	—

EQUIPMENT

Lifeline Uplink	Multi-function Nanoskin Suit
Picture of Her Family	Micro-shrapnel Brain Explosive

GUNSLINGER

VITAL FACTORS

Name: Charles Palmer
Rank: Major
Affiliation: H.A.R.D. Corps
Character Level: Super
Event Points: _____

Tags: ● borrowed time
● disciplined ● loyal
● professional ● teamwork
● sarcastic

HISTORY

A professional soldier to the core, Charles Palmer held to a strict "no man left behind" code, which served him well in the Harbinger Active Resistance Division. Ten years of serving and then leading H.A.R.D. Corps never took away his underlying sense of duty.

This explains why he agreed to return to active duty when Director Kozol personally sought him out. Palmer holds no illusions about the morality or rightness of Project Rising Spirit, but he knows he can do more good working for them than he can dead, which is his only other option.

Palmer has adjusted to being back in H.A.R.D. Corps far more easily and quickly than he did trying to adjust to civilian life after his initial retirement in the mid-'90s.

PERSONALITY

The weight of command, his past, and the agents who died under his watch have caused Palmer to withdraw more and more from the life around him. He wears his sarcasm and cynicism like a well-worn coat.

MIGHT	INTELLECT	CHARISMA	ACTION	LUCK	VALIANT
D8	D8	D8	D12	3	

POWERS

Shield (Armor)
Keep Both—Reduce damage taken by 1 — D8

Flight
Keep Both — D8

Arc Charge (Weapon)
Keep Both — D8

Lifeline Uploads
Add+2—May request any of the active Lifeline Bio-configs. Note: Powers are only available one at a time. — D6

CUES

Rule number one: guns for offense, shields for defense.

Let's earn our healthcare.

Take out the brain or the healer will just put them back in the fight.

What do you say we put an end to this Mickey Mouse crap?

All we can do now is keep breathing.

You don't know anything about me!

You unbelievable bastard.

I do it my way or not at all.

ACTION CUES

Okay, everybody, work out your hypotenuse. We're going in.

Lifeline, Sequence Four!

You want to dance with me?! Then let's dance!

This isn't about powers.

Give me Muscle, Lifeline! Now!

Shut up and finish it!

Give me Fire!

Gah! (shouted in pain)

Check in, H.A.R.D. Corps!

You with us, soldier?

DISPOSITION

Feels the weight of age and experience.

Places the team above all.

Barely restrains his rage.

Chronically distrustful of bureaucrats.

WEAPONS	DAMAGE	RANGE Close	Near	Far
Electrical Blast	3	OK	OK	—
NEMO Omen Rifle	3	−2	OK	OK

-1 TO MIGHT
-1 TO MIGHT & ACTION
STAGGERED
KNOCKED OUT

EQUIPMENT

Multi-function Nanoskin Suit   Lifeline Uplink

Unit Patches of Deceased Agents   Micro-shrapnel Brain Explosive

ARMOR   **HEALTH**

HARADA

VITAL FACTORS

Name: Toyo Harada
Title: Founder and CEO, Harada Global Conglomerates
Affiliation: Harbinger Foundation
Character Level: Legend
Event Points: _____

Tags: ● psiot ● Omega ● Harbinger ● visionary ● driven

HISTORY

Sand ripples like water through the garden, but it must flow around the rock. Through most of the last century, Toyo Harada has been that rock, quietly exerting his will to bend the world around him.

Born outside Hiroshima in the first half of the twentieth century, Harada was just a boy when the atomic bomb activated his powers and annihilated his old life. He wandered without purpose until the Bleeding Monk, a mysterious precognitive, guided him with visions of the future and Harada's grand role in shaping it. Having witnessed mankind's potential for self-destruction firsthand, Harada realized that only those with great power could unite humanity against the coming darkness.

A psiot with unmatched mental abilities, Harada can bend people to his will, raise force shields, disperse a target's atoms, and accomplish many other psionic feats. With a combination of nearly limitless power and natural business sense, Harada has crafted a mighty organization capable of redirecting the path of the world as he sees fit.

PERSONALITY

Possibly the most powerful psiot to ever walk the Earth, Harada takes the long view in all situations. He seeks loyalty from his followers but refrains from tyrannical behavior unless absolutely necessary.

MIGHT	INTELLECT	CHARISMA	ACTION	LUCK	
D6	D12	D10	D8	3	VALIANT

POWERS

Levitation (Flight) *Discard Lowest*	D8	**Atomize (Weapon)** *Add+2*	D10	**Psionic Shield (Armor)** *Keep Both*—Reduce damage taken by 2	D10
Mind Wipe *Add+2*—Target forfeits its next action	D8	**Telepathy** *Discard Lowest*	D10		

CUES

What you need is me.	Calm yourself. Listen closely.
I know you better than you know yourself.	Loyalty must be a choice.
We have very little time.	Victory has its own trappings.
I'm the first man of the Atomic Age.	Just do what I tell you to do.

ACTION CUES

The world is mine.	There's no need for pretense.
Protect me from yourselves.	You were born to lose.
This is the end of the line.	You are incapable of comprehending my limits.
I am the Omega…the Paragon…the True Harbinger.	Everything is under control.
Tonight we are the gods of war!	The time is thrust upon us all.

DISPOSITION

Has a vision for the future.	Will not waste resources.
Does not accept failure.	More exhausted than he lets on.

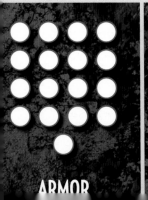

ARMOR

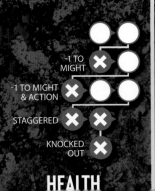

HEALTH

-1 TO MIGHT
-1 TO MIGHT & ACTION
STAGGERED
KNOCKED OUT

WEAPONS

		RANGE		
	DAMAGE	Close	Near	Far
Disintegration Field	D10	OK	OK	−2
Psychic Scream	D6*	OK	OK	−2

*Can target D4 targets at once. Ineffective against non-living targets

EQUIPMENT

Expensive Suit	Datapad
Business Card Holder	

HIGH PRIEST

VITAL FACTORS

Name: Unknown
Title: High Priest of Shanhara
Affiliation: Vine, Aric of Dacia
Character Level: Hero
Event Points: _____

Tags: ● Vine ● elder ● religious ● hopeful ● reverent

HISTORY

When the current High Priest of Shanhara joined the priesthood, he abolished his birth name and boarded the Vine colony ship to preach the word of Shanhara throughout the galaxy. Like all other priests before him, he took a vow never to return to his homeworld of Loam. This vow he would be unable to keep.

The priest rose through the ranks of the clergy, eventually reaching the vaunted high priesthood due to his ancestry. As High Priest, he personally oversaw the rituals by which brave Vine warriors attempted to bond with the Armor of Shanhara. When the human Aric of Dacia bonded with Shanhara, the High Priest's world was thrown on its ear: the armor had chosen a *human*. When he returned to Loam under orders, he witnessed Aric liberate the planet from the High Council's lack of faith.

PERSONALITY

The Vine High Priest takes a deferential role to the wearer of Shanhara, but he exercises his authority whenever necessary. He avoids violence but knows it is often a necessary evil.

MIGHT	INTELLECT	CHARISMA	ACTION	LUCK	VALIANT
D6	D8	D10	D4	4	

POWERS

Prophecy			Access Vine Gatherings		First Aid	
Add+3	D6		Discard Lowest	D10	Discard Lowest—Heals target for D4 Health	D8

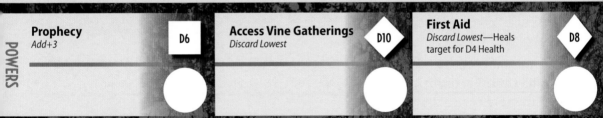

CUES

It is not possible!

You know I am right.

Chk-ree!

Earth is not the only world my kind has visited.

The armor will only bestow its gifts on the worthy one.

Pray there is still time.

What is the meaning of this?

There must be another way.

ACTION CUES

I am a practitioner of faith, not science.

Shanhara's will is paramount and unerring.

You will not bring violence here!

Sacrilege!

May Shanhara find you worthy.

The day will come when all is revealed.

The armor deserves your reverence.

Shanhara is our most sacred relic.

You blaspheme the name of God.

Shanhara, help me believe . . .

DISPOSITION

Seeks to serve Shanhara in any way.

Embraces the true, not the popular.

Desires to see others share his beliefs.

Fights only when necessary.

WEAPONS

WEAPONS	DAMAGE	RANGE		
		Close	Near	Far
Vine Plasma Knife	2*	OK	—	—
Vine Osmotic Pistol	2	OK	OK	—

*Deals 2x damage to Armor pips

EQUIPMENT

Priesthood Vestments

Bottle of Ovariole

Copy of *The Book of Hara*

Plasma Power Pack

ARMOR (VINE HIDE)

HEALTH

-1 TO MIGHT

-1 TO MIGHT & ACTION

STAGGERED

KNOCKED OUT

VITAL FACTORS

Name: Kara Anne Murphy
Affiliation: Bloodshot
Character Level: Sidekick
Event Points: _____

Tags: ● merciful ● loyal ● optimistic ● teamwork ● friendly

HISTORY

Kara Murphy was an army nurse who served three tours in Afghanistan. After her contract was up, she returned to Nebraska to look after her brother, also a military veteran. He had been wounded badly in Afghanistan and was in need of full-time care. She parlayed her medical skills into a job as an EMT, dealing primarily with agricultural accidents and domestic disputes. At this point she came into contact with the subject known as Bloodshot while responding to reports of an airplane crash.

After attempting to provide him with immediate aid, she has been helping him escape the pursuit of PRS. She has tried to avoid violence, especially fatalities, but she caused injuries during the escape from a PRS research facility.

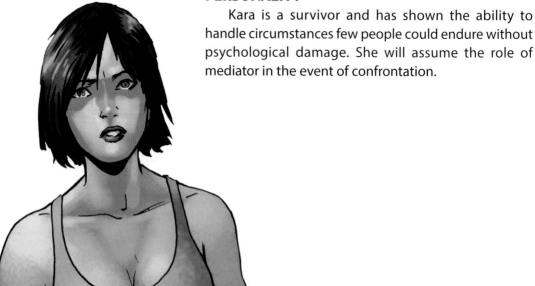

PERSONALITY

Kara is a survivor and has shown the ability to handle circumstances few people could endure without psychological damage. She will assume the role of mediator in the event of confrontation.

MIGHT	INTELLECT	CHARISMA	ACTION	LUCK	
D6	D8	D10	D8	1	VALIANT

POWERS

Army Medic Training
Keep Both—Heals target for D6 Health — D6

Take Aim
Discard Lowest—Add +2 to next Action roll result — D6

CUES

So tell me, who's the psycho here?

Will everybody please stop killing everybody!

Once you've stuck your hands inside someone's chest, you develop a bond.

Great, now I'm hearing voices.

Wait—who the hell's after us *now*?

Sometime it *sucks* being the only adult in the room.

Huh. That's odd.

Oh, gimme a break . . .

ACTION CUES

Get your hands off me!!!

I'm an EMT, not a killer, for God's sake.

Don't make me do this.

Hold still, will you?

Take cover!

This may sting a little . . .

Be glad you don't need stitches.

I'm out of practice, but I still know my way around a gun.

Hold this over the wound! Quick!

Haven't they ever heard of the Geneva Convention?!

DISPOSITION

Strives to help friends.

Fights to save the injured.

Just wants to make it through this.

Always wants to do the right thing.

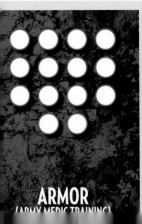

ARMOR
(ARMY MEDIC TRAINING)

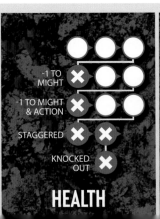

✖	-1 TO MIGHT
✖	-1 TO MIGHT & ACTION
✖ ✖	STAGGERED
✖	KNOCKED OUT

HEALTH

WEAPONS

	DAMAGE	Close	Near	Far
			RANGE	
Barrett M98 Rifle	3	–2	OK	OK
Martial Arts	2	OK	—	—

EQUIPMENT

Medkit	Radio
Latex Gloves	

KRIS HATHAWAY

HARBINGER

VITAL FACTORS

Name: Kris Hathaway
Affiliation: Renegades
Character Level: Hero
Event Points: _____

Tags: ● normal ● girl genius ● spotter ● strategist ● anti-authority

HISTORY

Raised by parents who put the news on television, a chessboard in the living room, and thought-provoking works on her bookshelf, Kris had already polished her bright mind to brilliance by her late teens. The young suburban revolutionary raged against the corporate oligarchy running the world and had little time for "sheeple" who refused to stand up. But when Peter Stanchek dropped back into her life, Kris learned that "the Man" she longed to fight against was an actual person.

Peter briefly used his powers to manipulate Kris's emotions and forced her to love him. But that was before his first encounter with Toyo Harada's Harbinger Foundation. After escaping the Foundation's Pittsburgh facility, he sought to atone for his sins by giving Kris the opportunity to kill him. Instead of agreeing to let Peter off the hook so easily, Kris chose to help him. Since she knew Toyo Harada was pulling the world's strings, her plans formed the Renegades to oppose him. Though Peter is the field general, Kris's strategies guide their war against Harada and his Foundation.

PERSONALITY

Despite her undeniable genius, Kris is haunted by the idea that her plans could possibly get others killed. She presents a bold face to the Renegades but is privately wracked with doubt.

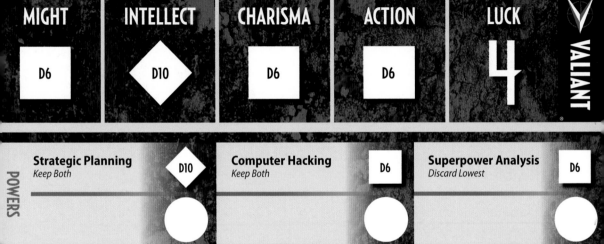

MIGHT	INTELLECT	CHARISMA	ACTION	LUCK	VALIANT
D6	D10	D6	D6	4	

POWERS

Strategic Planning *Keep Both* — D10 ○

Computer Hacking *Keep Both* — D6 ○

Superpower Analysis *Discard Lowest* — D6 ○

CUES

Leave me alone.	It means something, something bad.
I don't want to hear this.	This is a life you have to choose with full understanding.
This is somehow Peter's fault.	Something horrible has to happen.
Never again. You understand?	Your chess game must suck.

ACTION CUES

I'll gouge your eyes out, you bastard!	Do we understand each other?
Crazy just seems to be the natural order of things for me now.	We're spoiling for a fight.
Are we going to be all right?	We die plotting.
We have to move *now*.	I believe in it. I'm dedicated to it.
I guess I do think I'm smart.	You're never powerless!

DISPOSITION

Calm and collected in the heat of battle.	Distrustful of happiness.
Adaptive to new situations.	Concerned for her family.

HEALTH

- -1 TO MIGHT
- -1 TO MIGHT & ACTION
- STAGGERED
- KNOCKED OUT

WEAPONS

	DAMAGE	RANGE Close	Near	Far
9mm Pistol	2	OK	OK	−2
Fists	1	OK	—	—

EQUIPMENT

Tablet Computer — Harbinger Foundation Uniform

Binoculars

ARMOR

HEALTH

LITTLE CASTLE

VITAL FACTORS

Name: Isiah
Affiliation: Generation Zero
Character Level: Hero
Event Points: _____

Tags: ● psiot ● Generation Zero ● isolated ● silent ● young

HISTORY

When Isiah's psionic force shield activated, it effectively cut him off from direct contact with the outside world, and he appears unable to drop the shield for any reason. Since then, he has only communicated via nonverbal facial expressions. Observation indicates he is able to see and hear through his force bubble but is simply unable to reciprocate, and attempts to pierce the shield have met with dangerous feedback.

As part of Project Rising Spirit's A-team, Isiah accompanied the rest of Generation Zero to Las Vegas when they escaped PRS's Nursery facility. When a PRS H.A.R.D. Corps strike team attacked the Bellagio to try eliminating Generation Zero, Isiah fought fiercely to protect his fellow Generation Zero members and his new friends from the Renegades.

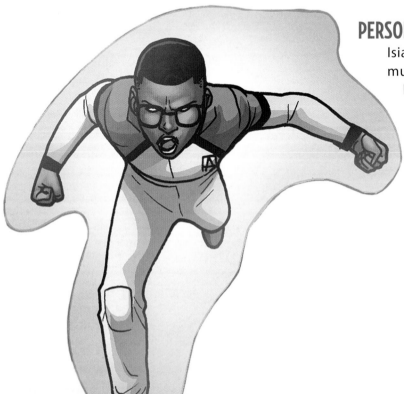

PERSONALITY

Isiah is unable to communicate verbally, but he still tries to connect with others. Though he is usually passive and reserved, he will not hesitate to jump in to protect a friend in danger.

MIGHT	INTELLECT	CHARISMA	ACTION	LUCK	
D6	D6	D6	D8	3	VALIANT

POWERS

Force Shield (Armor)
Keep Both—Reduce damage taken by 3 — D10 ◯

Feedback
Discard Lowest—Inflicts 3 damage when hit by a Close weapon — D8 ◯

Athletics
Discard Lowest — D6 ◯

CUES

...
...
...
...

...
...
<blink>
<stare>

ACTION CUES

...
<smile>
...
<laugh>
...

<frown>
...
<glare>
...
<rage>

DISPOSITION

Quiet and reserved.

Unable to communicate through his psionic bubble.

Easily amused.

Unafraid to protect those he considers friends.

ARMOR

HEALTH

-1 TO MIGHT ✖
-1 TO MIGHT & ACTION ✖
STAGGERED ✖ ✖
KNOCKED OUT ✖

WEAPONS

WEAPONS	DAMAGE	Close	Near	Far
Forcefield Slam	D6+1	OK	—	—
Forcefield Punch	2	OK	—	—

RANGE

EQUIPMENT

PRS A-team Uniform — Micro-shrapnel Brain Explosive

Eyeglasses — Paperback of *A Wrinkle in Time*

VITAL FACTORS

Name: Amanda McKee
Title: Kodenbushi (former)
Affiliation: Harbinger Foundation (former), Unity
Character Level: Super
Event Points: _____

Tags: ● psiot ● teletechnopath ● machine god ● apt pupil ● samurai

HISTORY

In a world full of technology, Amanda McKee lives by an old code, one that far predates smartphones, tablets, and the Internet: *bushido*, the way of the warrior. Toyo Harada rescued her from a group orphanage, but he did not wish to raise a daughter. He intended to train a samurai.

A capable teletechnopath able to communicate directly with machines and electronics, Livewire learned from Harada and pledged herself to his service. Over time, however, she began to realize her master was not limited by true challenges and so could not claim true honor. She betrayed Harada by releasing Peter Stanchek back into the world, indirectly triggering the birth of the Renegades and the Harbinger Wars. After serving a self-imposed exile, she joined Harada again but found him even more unworthy of her loyalty. Amanda finally committed to the path of the *ronin*, swearing to bring down her former master. To that end, she is a key member of Unity.

PERSONALITY

Livewire spent years serving Harada but never accepted the excesses his vision demanded. She will not violate her code of honor at anyone's command, and she opposes casual brutality.

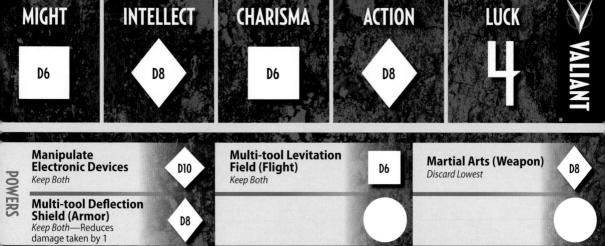

MIGHT	INTELLECT	CHARISMA	ACTION	LUCK
D6	D8	D6	D8	4

VALIANT

POWERS

Manipulate Electronic Devices
Keep Both — D10

Multi-tool Deflection Shield (Armor)
Keep Both—Reduces damage taken by 1 — D8

Multi-tool Levitation Field (Flight)
Keep Both — D6

Martial Arts (Weapon)
Discard Lowest — D8

CUES

Please shut up.	There is a code I live by.
Just try to be less of a punk, will you?	Do you mind turning that thing off?
There must be balance.	All this technology. You can't begin to understand it.
How goes the world?	A few more seconds is all we need.

ACTION CUES

I've a unique relationship with machines.	You reap what you sow.
We'll be better off with you gone.	I have yet to meet a technology I couldn't understand.
Forgive me, master.	You're in over your head.
You have to live!	Just keep doing whatever you're doing.
I need you to come with me!	Technology is my friend.

DISPOSITION

Willing to question orders.	Still discovering her powers.
Thinks for herself.	Lives by a code of honor.

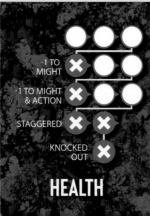

-1 TO MIGHT ✖ ⭕
-1 TO MIGHT & ACTION ✖ ⭕
STAGGERED ✖ ✖
KNOCKED OUT ✖

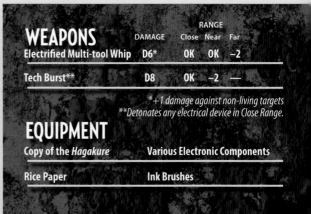

WEAPONS

	DAMAGE	Close	Near	Far
Electrified Multi-tool Whip	D6*	OK	OK	−2
Tech Burst**	D8	OK	−2	—

RANGE

*+1 damage against non-living targets
**Detonates any electrical device in Close Range.

EQUIPMENT

Copy of the *Hagakure*	Various Electronic Components
Rice Paper	Ink Brushes

ARMOR
(DEFLECTION SHIELD)

HEALTH

MARY-MARIA

VITAL FACTORS

Name: Mary-Maria Archer
Title: Sister Superior
Affiliation: The Sisters of
Perpetual Darkness
Character Level: Super
Event Points: _____

Tags: ● naïve ● determined
● possessed ● driven ● survivor

HISTORY

Mary-Maria's father sold her for seventy-five dollars. The Archers adopted her, brought her into their home, and raised her to love God and kill in his name without hesitation. When the Evil One ensorcelled her brother Obie, only love for him kept her from killing him.

Mary-Maria soon discovered her parents had used her to give them control of the Boon, so she turned on them and rescued Obie moments before the Boon extracted her life force.

Only, she didn't die. She awoke when the Boon was destroyed, but she wasn't alone. The life forces and minds of her parents resided in hers. They cannot control her—they couldn't make her kill Obie—but they can advise.

Able to draw on the knowledge and cunning of her parents, Mary-Maria began her conquest of the Sect, starting with the Sisters of Perpetual Darkness.

PERSONALITY

A lifetime of betrayal and abuse has pushed Mary-Maria beyond the naïveté of trust. Cynical suspicion protects her. If she sometimes hears the girl she once was asking to come out, she doesn't listen.

MIGHT	INTELLECT	CHARISMA	ACTION	LUCK
 D8	 D10	 D10	 D8	1

 VALIANT

POWERS

Strategist
Discard Lowest — D8

Combat sense
Keep Both — D8

Accelerated Healing
Discard Lowest—Heals D4 – 1 pips of Health — D8

Persuasion
Keep Both — D8

CUES

The world is a lot stranger than you think.

It's okay. I've been tested for cooties and everything.

We have bigger problems than worrying about the inevitable.

You don't know what it's like to be adopted.

Here comes the bleeding heart.

I'm going to carry on my adopted parents' work.

That's a good plan you had there. So I'm going to hijack it.

That works.

ACTION CUES

Shut up and fight!

You've had your chance.

No one does that to me.

My turn.

Don't be weak.

How many dudes do I have to shiv?

I see what the problem is here.

Fash darndit!

I didn't join the Sisterhood—they joined me.

Attack!

DISPOSITION

Determined to never again be hurt.

Sees her love for her brother as a weakness.

Always aware of her surroundings and the people around her.

Believes the world owes her for all it's taken.

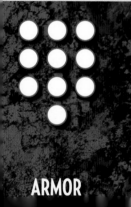

WEAPONS	DAMAGE	RANGE Close	Near	Far
Katana	4	OK	–2	—
Crossbow	2	OK	OK	–2

EQUIPMENT

Night Vision Contact Lenses   Habit Communications Suite

Religious Medal   Journal w/ Pen

ARMOR   **HEALTH**

-1 TO MIGHT

-1 TO MIGHT & ACTION

STAGGERED

KNOCKED OUT

VITAL FACTORS

Name: Nicodemo Darque
Affiliation: Independent
Character Level: Legend
Event Points: _____

Tags: ● necromancer ● trapped ● Deadside ● powermonger ● veves

HISTORY

Nicodemo Darque and his twin sister Sandria grew up learning magic on a plantation in New Orleans nearly two centuries ago. As their necromantic power grew, their father used them as a stepping stone toward gaining entry into the heavenly realm of Lyceum, so Darque killed his father before his father could kill Sandria.

When Sandria later fled from her brother's growing power, Darque attempted to kill Sandria's lover, Marius Boniface. Sandria summoned a powerful loa spirit, which bonded with Marius, creating the Shadowman.

As Darque's bitterness grew, he came to believe that the demiurgic force of creation itself was monstrous, so he sought the means to destroy it and "break the wheel." Darque tricked Josiah Boniface—father of the current Shadowman—and used him to travel to Lyceum by transiting through the Deadside. Once in Lyceum, Darque sought the Universitas Divinum and acquired the knowledge he needed to attempt to destroy the force of creation itself. When his teachers had taught him everything they could, he slew them all and attempted to return to Earth.

Since then, the Shadowman has thwarted Master Darque's many schemes to reach the realm of the living, and no one knows where or when the Darque will come again.

PERSONALITY

Darque is an immensely powerful necromancer, completely confident in his abilities. He believes all life suffers due to an endless wheel, and he dedicates his every breath toward destroying this cycle.

MIGHT	INTELLECT	CHARISMA	ACTION	LUCK	VALIANT
D6	D10	D8	D6	6	

POWERS

Steal Life Energy (Weapon) — *Replace*	D12
Shape Life Energy — *Keep Both*—Raise or lower a target's Stat Die by one level	D8
Restorative Energies — *Add+2*—Heal target for D6+1 Health	D10
Knowledge of Lyceum — *Keep Both*	D10
Necromantic Energy Construct (Armor) — *Discard Lowest*—Reduce damage taken by 2	D12

CUES

All things endure.	You disagree with my methods?
Regrettable.	Pathetic.
And how much did that cost you?	Why are we delayed?
You would do well to stop talking.	Are you really that foolish?

ACTION CUES

I am not amused.	You are on the wrong side.
You cannot. And you will not.	We are all monsters.
I will harvest the life of everything that lives and dreams.	I am going to places even you have never dreamed of.
I will break the wheel. I will end all suffering.	I read the signs, uncovered the mysteries, and found the impossible.
It'll all be over soon.	Are you frightened as well?

DISPOSITION

Feels like he is alone against the universe.	Seeks to attain perfect knowledge.
Fully devoted to his sister.	Sees an end to pain and suffering.

ARMOR
(NECROMANTIC ENERGY)

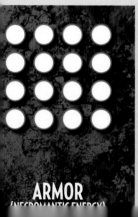

HEALTH

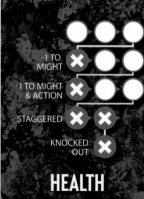

-1 TO MIGHT
-1 TO MIGHT & ACTION
STAGGERED
KNOCKED OUT

WEAPONS

	DAMAGE	RANGE Close	Near	Far
Steal Life Energy	D6*	OK	—	—
Veve Blast	4	OK	OK	OK

*Heal Darque's Health pips by this same amount

EQUIPMENT

Grand Veve Tattoos   Necromantic Charm

Memento from Lyceum

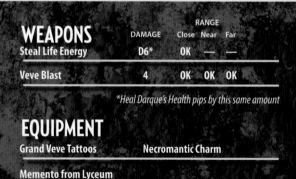

NINJAK

VITAL FACTORS

Name: Colin King
Title: CLASSIFIED
Affiliation: MI-6, Unity
Character Level: Legend
Event Points: _____

Tags: ● precise ● relentless ● skilled ● freelancer ● super-spy

HISTORY

Ninjak is the assassin you hire when you want a job done right, with no loose ends. Although on paper he is an MI-6 operative for the British government, he also performs freelance jobs for undisclosed reasons. His impressive array of training and gadgetry ensures he always has the right equipment for the job at hand.

His background is the speculation of most world intelligence agencies. This consummate professional has never left a job incomplete, though the means of completion and its ultimate form is not always what the employer envisioned. Whether Ninjak makes his own equipment or has it manufactured in secret is unknown, but it's of the highest quality and technology.

His allegiance to MI-6 shows his love for Crown and Country surpasses his mercenary sensibilities.

PERSONALITY

Ninjak has a mercenary's mindset, and he's extremely dedicated to his craft. His skills are peerless among normal humans, and his drive to complete any job is total.

MIGHT	INTELLECT	CHARISMA	ACTION	LUCK
D8	D10	D10	D12	9

VALIANT

POWERS

Smart Gloves/Boots (Climbing) *Add+3*	D10
Ninjutsu Reflexes *Add+2—Reduces damage taken by 2*	D8
Hologram Belt *Discard Lowest*	D8
Explosive Foam *Discard Lowest*	D8
Adaptive Camouflage *Discard Lowest*	D10
	○

CUES

I'd'a done this job for free.	Voilà.
When I fight someone, they don't realize it until it's over.	Only one chance . . .
Blunt-force trauma will suffice.	I guess you didn't get my "It's a trap" memo?
Alien tech or not, a locked door is a locked door.	One can never be too prepared.

ACTION CUES

Go wage your war in the open. I'll wage mine in the shadows.	I don't retreat. I maneuver.
You can take away my equipment. But you can't take away my training.	There's no one more lethal.
Not a problem.	Through the heart usually works best.
You may be tough. But everyone has to breathe.	Time to pay your tab.
It's time.	You have no idea what I'm about.

DISPOSITION

Prefers solitude to company.	Suspicious of others.
Confident in his abilities.	A consummate professional in all regards.

-1 TO MIGHT

-1 TO MIGHT & ACTION

STAGGERED

KNOCKED OUT

WEAPONS

	DAMAGE	RANGE Close	Near	Far
Katana	4	OK	−2	—
Customized Shuriken*	2	OK	OK	OK

Drugged: Target must pass a Might Test or fall unconscious for D4 turns
Poisoned: Target suffers 1 additional damage over the next D4 turns
Explosive: Target suffers D6 additional damage; nearby targets take D4 damage

EQUIPMENT

Stealth Drone Vehicle   **Wing Suit**   **Pocket Computer**

ARMOR   HEALTH

PETER STANCHEK *Harbinger*

VITAL FACTORS

Code Name: Sting
Title: Leader
Affiliation: Renegades
Character Level: Super
Event Points: _____

Tags: ● psiot ● Harbinger
● aloof ● challenger ● troubled

HISTORY

For some people, it's just a land of milk and honey and nice, happy lives, isn't it? Everything works out and everyone gets what they deserve, right? But Peter Stanchek never asked for any of this—being a psiot with vast telepathic and telekinetic powers, getting shipped off to a mental institution as a child, and spending his teenage years desperately trying to drown out the voices clawing into his brain.

Then came Harada and his damn Foundation, which tried to hold Peter up to another set of standards and offer him another place he'd never fit in. Peter barely escaped, but his salvation led him to a group of psiot misfits every bit as damaged as he. Now the Renegades look to him, not as a resource or a project but as their leader against Harada, the Harbinger Foundation, and the new world order the Foundation wishes to create. Peter's mistakes are in the past. He's here now, and there's no room for doubt.

PERSONALITY

Peter is a broken god, a profoundly powerful Omega-level psiot who barely survived a rough childhood and life on the streets. He is equally terrified of his responsibility and furious at those who would exploit him.

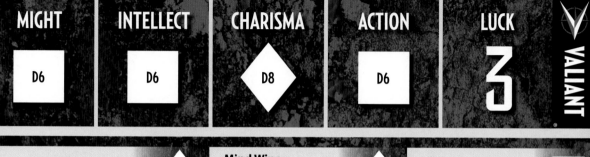

MIGHT	INTELLECT	CHARISMA	ACTION	LUCK	VALIANT
D6	D6	D8	D6	3	

POWERS

Telepathy — D8
Add+2

Psionic Shield — D10
Keep Both—Reduce damage taken by 2

Mind Wipe — D8
Keep Both—Target forfeits its next action

Levitation (Flight) — D6
Add+1

CUES

Stop. Talking.	I'm learning something new every day.
I was born to die.	You don't know anything about me.
I'm going to make it right. I swear.	I think I can help you here.
Great . . . more jackasses with guns.	Okay, hold on. Everybody just be cool.

ACTION CUES

Forget. Forget everything you've ever known. Everything you've ever loved.	Wave goodbye, asshat!
You want to dance with me?! Then let's dance!	I'll see you all in hell.
Let's see you put me down!	It's cavalry time, yo!
You've all made a terrible mistake.	This has to be the end. Here and now.
I'm way past talking.	Why won't you leave us alone?!

DISPOSITION

Runaway, grinder, addict.	Deeply distrustful of authority.
Uncomfortable with leadership.	Still pushing his limits.

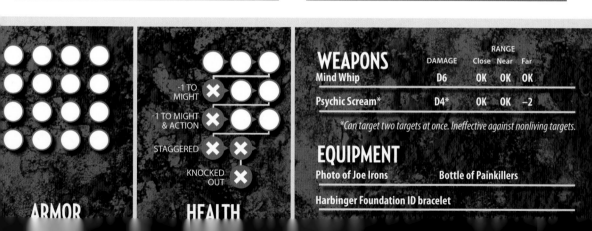

WEAPONS

	DAMAGE	RANGE Close	Near	Far
Mind Whip	D6	OK	OK	OK
Psychic Scream*	D4*	OK	OK	−2

Can target two targets at once. Ineffective against nonliving targets.

EQUIPMENT

Photo of Joe Irons   Bottle of Painkillers

Harbinger Foundation ID bracelet

−1 TO MIGHT
−1 TO MIGHT & ACTION
STAGGERED
KNOCKED OUT

ARMOR   HEALTH

VITAL FACTORS

Name: Melissa Sophia Krajnak
Affiliation: Bloodshot
Character Level: Sidekick
Event Points: _____

Tags: ● psiot ● EMP ● scared ● angry ● lost ● lonely

HISTORY

Melissa Kranjak is a young psiot with the ability to emit a powerful EMP burst. She has been raised by PRS since being discovered as a young girl, and twice she has been involved in the capture of the subject known as Bloodshot. Due to her ability, she has been given the code name Pulse. During her most recent operation, she escaped and joined forces with Bloodshot. PRS's evaluation noted her EMP ability and a Taser-like discharge of electrical energy, but she displayed the ability to shut down the neurological impulses in her handler's brain, killing him.

PRS recaptured her and subjected her to disciplinary action which has since shown to be counterproductive. Bloodshot's attempt to liberate her resulted in an altercation between Melissa and the former operative called Gamma.

PERSONALITY

Melissa is a teenager filled with anger and fear from being isolated from her parents and raised in PRS's Nursery facility. She wants to escape and live a normal life, but she will also exact revenge on PRS if the opportunity shows itself.

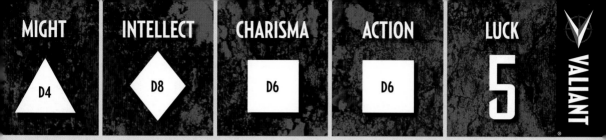

MIGHT	INTELLECT	CHARISMA	ACTION	LUCK	VALIANT
D4	D8	D6	D6	5	

POWERS

EMP (Weapon)		Shock (Weapon)			
Discard Lowest	D10	*Replace*	D10		

CUES

What, you want me to stop him?	I'm not a kid anymore.
You lied to me and kept me in the Nursery for three years!	Cut the crap.
They're going to need you now.	No! No more drugs.
You saved me, you can save them.	I just want to go home.

ACTION CUES

Going to kill you.	Fat chance.
I said, stop it!	You'll regret that.
You sick, evil witch . . . I'll give you your fill!	I'll do what I want.
There's just something I have to do.	You can't hurt me anymore.
I'm not afraid of you!	Do your worst.

DISPOSITION

Young and scared.	Finds it hard to trust others.
Hates government.	Looking for home.

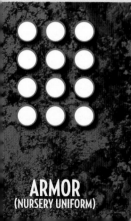

ARMOR
(NURSERY UNIFORM)

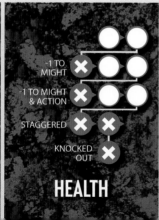

HEALTH

-1 TO MIGHT
-1 TO MIGHT & ACTION
STAGGERED
KNOCKED OUT

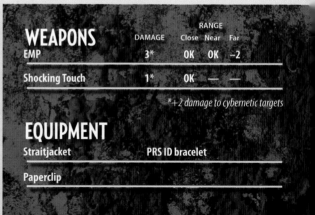

WEAPONS

	DAMAGE	RANGE Close	Near	Far
EMP	3*	OK	OK	−2
Shocking Touch	1*	OK	—	—

*+2 damage to cybernetic targets

EQUIPMENT

Straitjacket	PRS ID bracelet
Paperclip	

QUANTUM

VITAL FACTORS

Name: Eric Henderson
Affiliation: Quantum and Woody
Character Level: Super
Event Points: _____

Tags: ● earnest
● straitlaced ● ex-military
● "superhero" ● *KLANG!*

HISTORY

Eric Henderson always wanted to be a hero, to do the right thing. In pursuit of this dream, he earned top grades in school and enlisted in the US Army after graduation. A proven marksman, Eric hoped to take up Army Ranger training, but his plan to take revenge on a fellow soldier for getting their commander dishonorably discharged ended up getting him thrown out of the service.

He was working with the private security firm Magnum Security when he learned that his father died—and was possibly murdered. He and Woody—his estranged and irresponsible adopted brother—infiltrated their dad's lab at Quantum Energy Solutions to find clues, but a disagreement between them triggered an explosion that infused the pair with incredible energy. To keep their bodies from destabilizing, Eric and Woody need to *klang* their control bracelets together once every twenty-four hours.

As the superhero Quantum, Eric uses his energy force fields to stop various threats. He's not always successful, but it's the thought that counts.

PERSONALITY

Unlike his brother Woody, Quantum takes this superhero thing seriously—maybe a bit too seriously at times. He is a firm believer in doing an honest day's work and taking responsibility for one's actions.

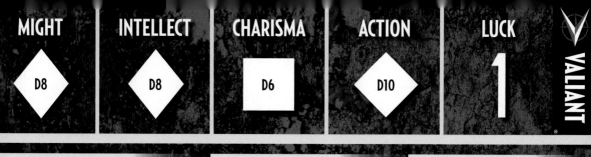

MIGHT	INTELLECT	CHARISMA	ACTION	LUCK	
D8	D8	D6	D10	1	VALIANT

POWERS

Quantum Shield (Armor) — D10
Keep Both—Reduce damage taken by 3. Can target others.

Power Field (Weapon) — D8
Discard Lowest

Force Field Catch — D8
Add+2—Can prevent falling damage

Martial Arts (Weapon) — D8
Discard Lowest

CUES

Well, I'd definitely call that suspicious.	I just rescued you from like, *three* kinds of certain death!
If I get killed, I am absolutely taking you with me.	Oh, jeez, um . . . sorry about that.
I feel like you guys are just mocking me.	I mean, that's what *I'd* do.
Would it kill you to say "thanks"?	Woody started it!

ACTION CUES

¡Suelta el arma! (Drop the gun!)	Get the hell out of the way, people!
That is EVERY kind of wrong.	I'm a @#$&@#*% superhero, bitch.
I'd save my ammo if I were you.	Everyone stay calm! I've got this!
Ah! Ah! CRAMP! CrampCRAMPCramp!	Are *all* scientists working on psychotic #$@% like this?!
This place is getting weird as &%*@.	You can't run from justice!

DISPOSITION

Strives to do the right thing.	Means well but isn't always successful.
Has zero tolerance for foolishness.	Blames Woody for most things.

WEAPONS	DAMAGE	RANGE Close	Near	Far
Force Field Shove	D6	OK	OK	−2
Martial Arts	2	OK	—	—

EQUIPMENT

Spandex Uniform and Mask	Binoculars
Handheld Radio	Tracking Device

HEALTH
-1 TO MIGHT
-1 TO MIGHT & ACTION
STAGGERED
KNOCKED OUT

ARMOR

SHADOWMAN

VITAL FACTORS

Name: Jack Boniface
Title: Shadowman
Affiliation: Abettors
Character Level: Super
Event Points: _____

Tags: ● driven ● reckless ● Deadside ● Abettors ● Master Darque

HISTORY

Destined by blood for a life of sacrifice, Jack Boniface knew nothing of his fate growing up, yet an unknown father and the loss of his mother at a young age sending him into foster care hardened him to life's vagaries.

After foster care Jack began investigating his parents. Disgusted at revelations of their apparent crime-ridden histories, he cast a strange medallion, his only memento of his mother, into a lake. However, the artifact kept a voodoo loa from finding Jack. No longer hidden, the creature bonded with him as it has done with generations of Bonifaces, and this brutal legacy from his father's blood turned him into … the Shadowman.

Now Jack finds himself alongside an ancient order, the Abettors, in the midst of a struggle against demons and necromantic powers from the Deadside who want nothing but the destruction of the human race! A mantle he finds unfit for his shoulders, yet there appears to be no one else ….

PERSONALITY

Jack is a loner, a product of his lost father and his nature as Shadowman. Though he struggles to accept help from others, he feels destined for eternal solitude.

MIGHT	INTELLECT	CHARISMA	ACTION	LUCK	
D8	D6	D4	D10	2	VALIANT

POWERS

Strength Against Deadside Creatures *Keep Both*	D10	**Transit to/from Deadside** *Replace*	D12	**Deadside Sight** *Keep Both*	D6
Superlative Healing *Keep Both—Restore D6 Health*	D10				

CUES

Nauseating . . .

Show me.

I'm listening.

I've always been alone.

You have got to pull it together, Jack.

Get off of me.

On it.

Faith, trust, and pixie dust.

ACTION CUES

I didn't ask for this.

Do you know what I'm going to do to you?

Terrific. Awesome. Zombies.

Not good.

Back off! She's with me!

Sure. Put down your guns.

What's in it for you?

Tell me what you are when you are alone in the dark?

If we destroy them, we won't need a legacy.

That's because I'm the one dressed like a superhero.

DISPOSITION

Always feels as though he's alone.

Utterly ruthless when the need arises.

Brooding.

On the edge of holding it together.

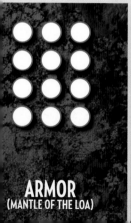

ARMOR
(MANTLE OF THE LOA)

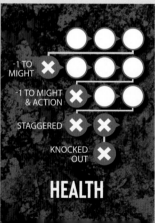

-1 TO MIGHT ✖

-1 TO MIGHT & ACTION ✖

STAGGERED ✖ ✖

KNOCKED OUT ✖

HEALTH

WEAPONS	DAMAGE	**RANGE**		
		Close	Near	Far
Shadow Scythe	4*	OK	−2	—

* +3 damage against Master Darque

EQUIPMENT

Utility Belt	Gris-gris Amulet
Mendacem Stone	

SUPERSTAR

VITAL FACTORS

Name: Victor Salas
Rank: Lieutenant
Affiliation: H.A.R.D. Corps
Character Level: Super
Event Points: _____

Tags: ● borrowed time ● soldier ● orders ● quick ● repressed ● proud

HISTORY

Victor Salas never forgot he was raised in a trailer park, and he spent his entire life trying to rise to the standard of life his mother wanted for him. He graduated top of his class at West Point, served two tours in Afghanistan, and he continued pushing for greater heights. As long as he focused, he could excel at anything he tried—everything except eradicating the lung cancer slowly killing his mother.

Director Kozol approached Salas with an offer to be one the most elite soldiers in the world. If he accepted, his mother would get the best treatment science could provide, so he needed only seconds to give up his skyrocketing military career. For Salas, taking care of his mother meant more than anything he could ever obtain for himself.

PERSONALITY

Only two things matter to Superstar: his mother and his duty, in that order. Having overcome every challenge set before him, he tends towards overconfidence, which he constantly fights to overcome.

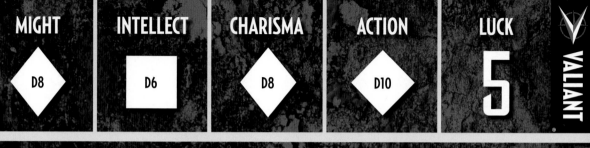

MIGHT	INTELLECT	CHARISMA	ACTION	LUCK	VALIANT
D8	D6	D8	D10	5	

POWERS

Shield (Armor)
Add+3—Reduce damage taken by 1 — D6

Flight
Keep Both — D8

Fire (Weapon)
Add+3 — D6

Lifeline Uploads
Keep Both—May request any of the active Lifeline Bio-configs. Note: Powers are only available one at a time. — D6

CUES

We know the risks.

I've been living with risks like this every day since I was eighteen.

If I were going to be careful, I'd have joined the Air Force.

How'd you do that?

We make it possible for the common man to despise what we do.

We all die, I just want to live before I do.

No, I'm good.

Stay in school, kids.

ACTION CUES

Outstanding, out-freaking-standing.

Sir, yes, sir!

Stay frosty. Let them make the first mistake.

Remember! Short, controlled bursts.

We should be *training*, not talking.

I've got this!

I may be good at what I do, but I'm not *crazy*.

Don't you *dare* bring my mother into this.

What do *you* fight for?

Prepare to face your mortality.

DISPOSITION

Confident but knows he has limits.

Conflicted because duty and right are not always the same.

Pride is his Achilles heel.

Uncomfortable around non-H.A.R.D. Corps women.

WEAPONS	DAMAGE	RANGE Close	Near	Far
Fire Blast	2	OK	OK	—
NEMO Omen Rifle	3	–2	OK	OK

-1 TO MIGHT
-1 TO MIGHT & ACTION
STAGGERED
KNOCKED OUT

EQUIPMENT

Lifeline Uplink   Psionic Dampener   Multi-function Nanoskin Suit

Willie Mays Autographed Baseball   Micro-shrapnel Brain Explosive

ARMOR   HEALTH

TIMEWALKER

VITAL FACTORS

Name: Ivar Anni-Padda
Title: Timewalker
Affiliation: Archer and Armstrong, Eternal Warrior
Character Level: Super
Event Points: _____

Tags: ● resourceful ● Sumerian ● inventor ● scientist ● curious

HISTORY

The oldest Anni-Padda brother, Ivar was an inventor, builder, and scientist in his home city of Ur. Always looking for new intellectual challenges, Ivar was just as eager as his brothers to travel to the Faraway and retrieve the Boon. But when Gilad died during the Boon's retrieval, a grief-stricken Ivar activated the Boon. In the aftermath of the activation, Ivar wandered throughout Earth's time and history.

Ivar was later sealed inside the Aleph, a prison that trapped him in the timestream. Freed from the device by Obadiah Archer, Ivar helped his brother Aram (better known as Armstrong) to stop General Redacted in the Faraway. Now free again, he travels through time, staying ahead of pursuers known only as the Prometheans.

PERSONALITY

As the eldest, Ivar was responsible for his younger brothers and would do anything for them. He is cheerful, friendly, and willing to help anyone who's in trouble.

MIGHT	INTELLECT	CHARISMA	ACTION	LUCK
D8	D12	D10	D8	12

VALIANT

POWERS

Time Perception
Discard Lowest — D8

Technology
Discard Lowest — D12

Accelerated Healing
Keep Both—Heals D4 – 1 pips of Health — D6

Gadget-building
Add+3 — D8

CUES

It'll be an adventure.

The past doesn't allow itself to be changed—that is why it's called the past.

There are some outcomes I refuse to repeat.

I've been gone too long, changed too much.

There is someone very special to me I must protect.

I'm sorry—that hasn't happened yet, has it?

I can no longer be my brothers' keepers.

Would you like some gum?

ACTION CUES

Any moment now . . .

Give me a moment to rewire this.

I know I can solve this!

Now, what would have Roy Rogers done?

Just so you know, I was taught by the best swordsmen in history.

It can't be any worse than the Charge of the Light Brigade.

Genghis Khan was tough—these guys, not so much.

Let's see if I have anything left in my bag of tricks.

As an immortal, you always survive your stupid mistakes.

I have to do something.

DISPOSITION

Friendly and outgoing.

Enjoys traveling through time.

Quick to blend in with the time and place he's in.

Hates injustice in any form.

-1 TO MIGHT

-1 TO MIGHT & ACTION

STAGGERED

KNOCKED OUT

WEAPONS	DAMAGE	RANGE		
		Close	Near	Far
Fist	2	OK	−2	—
Kick	3	OK	−2	—

EQUIPMENT

Tachyon Compass

Multi-tool

Pack of Gum

Language Translation Chip

ARMOR
(BOON'S BLESSING)

HEALTH

TORQUE

VITAL FACTORS

Name: John Torkelson
Affiliation: Renegades
Character Level: Hero
Event Points: _____

Tags: ● psiot ● psionic projectionist ● "brobarian" ● tenacious ● self-denial

HISTORY

John "Torque" Torkelson wasn't always like this. He was frail and sickly and jacked-up for so long, so when Peter Stanchek asked him to join the Renegades instead of staying in Georgia and feeling sorry for himself, Torque didn't need to be asked twice.

Torque doesn't care if his mega-strong body he got from his activated powers isn't "real." Pssh, now he can walk, throw down, pound brews, and (maybe?) get down with the ladies. Why should he worry about his muscles being a psionic projection? His brother died saving Torque's life. His home is gone. This is what he has left.

Well, this and Torquehalla, his own personal heavy-metal, reality-TV fantasy paradise! If his new, slammin' bod is "real," why can't Torquehalla be real, too? There's so much going on in real life, so sometimes he likes to get away for awhile and spend some time in his imaginary world…

PERSONALITY

The mighty shell of Torque shields the frail form of John Torkelson, who lives his heavy-metal dreams through his ripped avatar. Torque is eager to deal out the pain but is terrified of letting anyone else in.

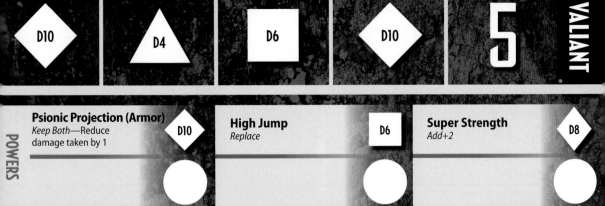

MIGHT	INTELLECT	CHARISMA	ACTION	LUCK	VALIANT
D10	D4	D6	D10	5	

POWERS

Psionic Projection (Armor) — D10
Keep Both—Reduce damage taken by 1

High Jump — D6
Replace

Super Strength — D8
Add +2

CUES

You're harshing my buzz, man!

How can it hurt so much?

Life in Torquehalla ain't nothing but fightin' bastards and bangin' hotties.

This doesn't happen in Torquehalla, man!

This is stupid crazy!

Why you disrespect me all'a time?

I—I never know what's real anymore.

You better believe it, hottie!

ACTION CUES

Here comes the Condition!

Ha ha! I took out a helicopter with my bare hands!

I'll be the only one still standing.

Just leave me alone!

C'mon little man. I'll take care of you.

I'm gonna go completely ape balls back here!

You ain't never gonna be juiced like me.

Boom! Gun show!

Freight train! Coming through!

BAM! Right in the *face*!

DISPOSITION

King of his realm.

Living the dream.

Terrified to open up.

Working through some issues.

	-1 TO MIGHT
	-1 TO MIGHT & ACTION
	STAGGERED
	KNOCKED OUT

WEAPONS	DAMAGE	RANGE		
		Close	Near	Far
Fist	4	OK	OK	−2
Fist	4	OK	OK	−2

EQUIPMENT

Baseball Cap   *Heavy Metal* Magazine

First Aid Kit

ARMOR   HEALTH

VAGABOND

VITAL FACTORS

Name: Classified
Affiliation: H.A.R.D. Corps
Character Level: Super
Event Points: _____

Tags: ● borrowed time ● carefree ● sloppy ● uninhibited ● unflappable

HISTORY

Even from a young age, Vagabond coasted through life at his own speed. In high school he partied rather than studied, and his history of substance abuse distanced him from his wife and young daughter. When his wife and daughter died in a car crash that he survived, he found no reason to even get out of bed. He began a long, slow slide into the gutter, a constant state of chemical intoxication that allowed him to dull the pain.

Director Kozol's promise of a chance to right the scales gave Vagabond a reason to stop trying to die. His implants prevented him from being impaired, and his life has already started to change.

PERSONALITY

Vagabond revels in every cliché for slackers, losers, and bums. Under the stereotypes and poor hygiene, he hides a keen eye and active mind that carefully takes in the world around him.

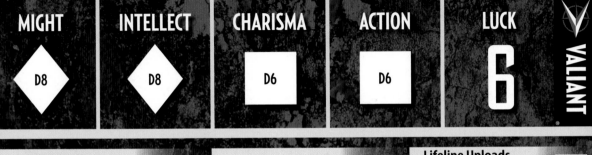

MIGHT	INTELLECT	CHARISMA	ACTION	LUCK	VALIANT
D8	D8	D6	D6	6	

POWERS

Shield (Armor)
Add+3—Reduce damage taken by 1 — D4

Flight
Add+3 — D6

Muscle
Add+3 — D6

Lifeline Uploads
Add+3—May request any of the active Lifeline Bio-configs. Note: Powers are only available one at a time. — D6

CUES

Yeah, well, you know, that's just, like, your opinion, man.

One for the road.

I have a prescription for it.

What?

Dude . . .

I'm just gonna sit here for a minute.

Ease off, man.

I'll take care of that tomorrow.

ACTION CUES

Wicked!

Gnarly!

No dice!

You are so ruining my high.

Hey man, truce.

I've always been lucky.

This one's for the history books.

Talk about Mr. *Buzzkill* here . . .

You do things your speed; I'll do things my speed.

Wouldn't want to waste that kind of opportunity.

DISPOSITION

Never met a drink he didn't like.

Thinks it's never too early to relax.

Believes life is meant to be lived, not understood.

Why worry?

WEAPONS	DAMAGE	RANGE Close	Near	Far
Berretta 90two Pistol	2	OK	−2	—
Berretta 90two Pistol	2	OK	−2	—

HEALTH: -1 TO MIGHT / -1 TO MIGHT & ACTION / STAGGERED / KNOCKED OUT

EQUIPMENT

Lifeline Uplink — Multi-function Nanoskin Suit

Stash Pouch — Micro-shrapnel Brain Explosive

ARMOR | **HEALTH**

WOODY

VITAL FACTORS

Name: Woodrow Henderson
Affiliation: Quantum and Woody
Character Level: Super
Event Points: _____

Tags: ● unapologetic ● screw-up
● irreverent ● clueless ● *KLANG!*

HISTORY

As a kid, Woody went from one bad foster home to the next until Derek Henderson adopted him. Woody and his brother Eric became inseparable, and Woody always stuck up for Eric at school. When Eric blew up a chemistry lab, Woody took the rap for it and skipped town, believing Eric and his father would be better off without a screw-up like him.

He spent the next several years living it up with stolen credit cards until he learned his father was dead—possibly murdered—and he and Eric were potential suspects. To hunt for clues, the two brothers infiltrated their dad's lab at Quantum Energy Solutions, but a disagreement between them triggered an explosion that infused the pair with incredible energy. To keep their bodies from destabilizing, Eric and Woody need to *klang* their control bracelets together once every twenty-four hours.

Woody uses his explosive energy blasts to charm the ladies, blow up things that are trying to kill him, and look as cool as humanly possible.

PERSONALITY

Unlike Quantum, Woody thinks being a superhero is all fun and games. He believes a flashy grin or a snarky rejoinder can get him out of anything, and he fails to see the consequences of his actions.

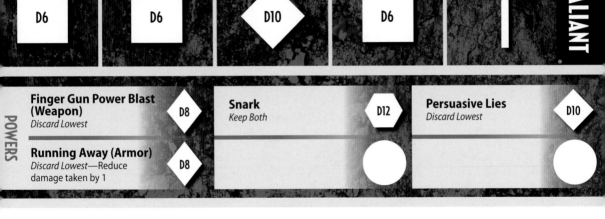

MIGHT	INTELLECT	CHARISMA	ACTION	LUCK	VALIANT
D6	D6	D10	D6	1	

POWERS

Finger Gun Power Blast (Weapon) *Discard Lowest*	D8	**Snark** *Keep Both*	D12	**Persuasive Lies** *Discard Lowest*	D10
Running Away (Armor) *Discard Lowest—Reduce damage taken by 1*	D8				

CUES

You're just a hater because it's *my* plan.

Less boring—more hiding!

Okay, I'm willing to admit . . . that got a *little* out of hand.

I know this wasn't what you were expecting.

I'm gonna pretend that never happened.

Screw this noise.

That would be a weird thing to make up.

Er . . . I *really* gotta figure out how to do that right.

ACTION CUES

I'm Woody, and I'll be your ass-kicker for this evening!

You can all relax now! We're superheroes!

I ruin lots of stuff.

You're lucky I have no idea how to control these powers!

Suck on some super powers!

We're about to be famous!

Ah, crap. It's the fuzz.

I've been hit harder by *drag queens*.

Why does everyone who knows science use it to try and kill me?!

If you're going to hit me—just avoid the face.

DISPOSITION

Thinks the world is his oyster.

Doesn't understand why people blame him for things.

Believes his stupid ideas are genius.

Doesn't see what the fuss is about.

| | | -1 TO MIGHT |
| -1 TO MIGHT & ACTION |
| STAGGERED |
| KNOCKED OUT |

WEAPONS

	DAMAGE	RANGE Close	Near	Far
Pew! Pew! Pew!	D10	OK	OK	−2
Bang! Bang!	2	OK	OK	OK

EQUIPMENT

Stylish Suit & Blue Shades	Four Driver's Licenses
Smartphone	Stolen Credit Cards

ARMOR (RUNNING AWAY)

HEALTH

X-O MANOWAR

VALIANT

VITAL FACTORS

Name: Aric of Dacia
Title: King of the Visigoths
Affiliation: Independent
Character Level: Legend
Event Points: _____

Tags: ● Visigoth ● warrior
● resolute ● bellicose ● displaced

HISTORY

Born at the tail end of the fourth century, Aric of Dacia was destined for greatness. His uncle Alaric, king of the Visigoths, ensured Aric was trained in martial combat, and when Aric reached adulthood he used those skills during the Visigoth invasion of the Roman Empire. After a major defeat at the hand of the Romans in 402 AD, Aric was captured by Vine agents and forced to work as a slave on their colony ship. He engineered a prison break and stole the Armor of Shanhara, the Vine's most sacred relic.

Upon returning to Earth, Aric found 1,600 years had passed. His homeland of Dacia was gone, and he would forever be a man out of his time. Together he and the Armor of Shanhara strive to protect what remains of his people's descendants and challenge any who would stand in their way.

PERSONALITY

A natural leader and dyed-in-the-wool warrior, Aric is brash and always ready to throw down at a moment's notice. He is slowly learning that restraint is often prudent in modern society.

MIGHT	INTELLECT	CHARISMA	ACTION	LUCK	
D12	D8	D10	D12	**3**	VALIANT

POWERS

Armor Regeneration (Armor) — D8
Keep Both—Restores 2 Armor and 2 Health, even if Staggered or Knocked Out

Anti-gravity (Flight) — D10
Keep Both

Energy Weapons (Weapon) — D6
Keep Both

Wrist Rockets — D8
Keep Both—Deals 2 damage to targets in Close or Near ranges

Sensor Array — D8
Keep Both

CUES

Let them face me.

This is not my own time.

I have no fight with you.

My home is no more.

Show yourself, coward!

There is ALWAYS someone to fight.

I do not know what makes a hero now.

Everything I have ever known is gone.

ACTION CUES

ARE THERE NO MORE?

Your blood will stain my boots!

Name the battlefield and I will meet you on it.

A true warrior stares his foe in the eye!

I did not come this far to surrender.

The armor is a weapon. And weapons grant power.

I am finished arguing.

You will not escape so easily.

Leave none alive!

If it's war they want, they will have it.

DISPOSITION

Mourns the loss of his wife.

Slow to adapt to the modern world.

Often acts without thinking.

Unafraid to pick a fight.

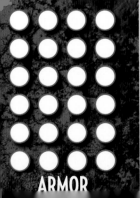

ARMOR

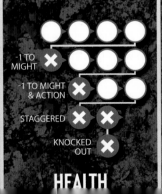

HEALTH

-1 TO MIGHT

-1 TO MIGHT & ACTION

STAGGERED

KNOCKED OUT

WEAPONS	DAMAGE	RANGE		
		Close	Near	Far
Energy Blast	3	OK	OK	OK
Energy Sword	3	OK	−2	—

EQUIPMENT
The Sacred Armor of Shanhara

Visigoth Knife   Visigoth Sigil

XARAN

VITAL FACTORS

Name: Xaran Anni-Padda
Title: Wild Child
Affiliation: House of the Earth
Character Level: Super
Event Points: _____

Tags: ● immortal ● warrior ●
Sword of the Earth ● wild child ●
impatient

HISTORY

Xaran is like her father, the Eternal Warrior. Six thousand years ago, she disobeyed her father and slaughtered the women and children of a death cult. When Gilad and her brother Mitu tried to stop her, Xaran killed Mitu and left Gilad wounded on the battlefield. The rest of the tribe Gilad had led was slaughtered by a second death cult army. Xaran then lost her mind, killed the cultists, and escaped into the wilds. She spent a few millennia living like an animal.

For two thousand years she served the God of the Wild as one of his Swords, but during that time she was secretly serving the Earth. On orders from the Geomancer, she massacred the God of the Wild's inner circle and fled. Now hunted by former comrades, she turned to the only person who could help—her estranged father.

PERSONALITY

Xaran is very much like her father, only she's far more ruthless. She cannot understand why Gilad walked away from the war, and she is determined to bring him back.

MIGHT	INTELLECT	CHARISMA	ACTION	LUCK	
 D8	 D6	 D8	 D10	 **10**	**VALIANT**

POWERS

Weapon Mastery — D8
Keep Both

Accelerated Healing — D8
Add+1—Heals D4 – 1 pips of Health

Wild Sense — D8
Add+2

Markswoman — D8
Keep Both—On successful Test, adds +1 to next Action roll result

CUES

I'm my father's daughter.

I'm good enough to be Earth's Sword!

I'm trying to bring balance back to the Houses.

I'm with the old man.

When the Earth called, I answered.

A few thousands years alone does things to one's mind.

Don't know why kids were scared of me. I never ate any of them.

When I was a child, all I wanted to do was kill.

ACTION CUES

I always prefer hunting a moving target.

I don't let enemies live.

Kill them all!

I came here to kill you.

This is where I belong!

I always knew my life would end with screaming and blood.

Mow 'em down!

To hell with that!

Come on then!

That's it, you stupid monster!

DISPOSITION

Trying to prove herself to her father.

Quick to anger.

Solitary hunter, uncomfortable in crowds.

Savage in battle, relentless in pursuit.

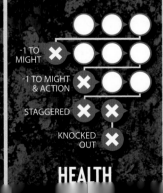

-1 TO MIGHT ✗
-1 TO MIGHT & ACTION ✗
STAGGERED ✗ ✗
KNOCKED OUT ✗

ARMOR

HEALTH

WEAPONS

	DAMAGE	RANGE		
		Close	Near	Far
Spear	3	OK	OK	—
Submachine Gun*	2	OK	OK	–2

May target two enemies with the same attack action

EQUIPMENT

Token of the House of Earth   Predator Tooth Necklace

Sharpening Stone

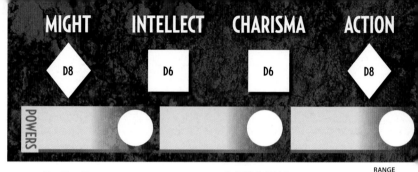

SECT SECURITY GUARD

MIGHT	INTELLECT	CHARISMA	ACTION
D8	D6	D6	D8

POWERS

ARMOR
(BODY ARMOR)

HEALTH

-1 TO MIGHT
-1 TO MIGHT & ACTION
STAGGERED
KNOCKED OUT

WEAPONS

	DAMAGE	RANGE Close	Near	Far
H&K MP5K PDW	2	OK	OK	−2
Sleep Gas	*	OK	−2	—

*Target must pass a Might Test or pass out for D4 rounds.

EQUIPMENT

Tactical Helmet

Gas Mask

BLACK BLOC WARRIOR

MIGHT	INTELLECT	CHARISMA	ACTION
D8	D8	D6	D8

POWERS

ARMOR
(BODY ARMOR)

HEALTH

-1 TO MIGHT
-1 TO MIGHT & ACTION
STAGGERED
KNOCKED OUT

WEAPONS

	DAMAGE	RANGE Close	Near	Far
H&K USP9	2	OK	OK	−2
H&K USP9	2	OK	OK	−2

EQUIPMENT

Block-shaped Helmet

Utility Vest

THE ONE PERCENT

MIGHT	INTELLECT	CHARISMA	ACTION
D6	D8	D8	D6

POWERS

ARMOR
(TAX EVASION)

HEALTH

-1 TO MIGHT
-1 TO MIGHT & ACTION
STAGGERED
KNOCKED OUT

WEAPONS

	DAMAGE	RANGE Close	Near	Far
Ritual Dagger	3	OK	—	—

EQUIPMENT

Tailored Suit	Golden Bull/Bear Mask
Copy of *The Wall Street Journal*	Checkbook

HASHISH EATER

	MIGHT	INTELLECT	CHARISMA	ACTION
	D8	D6	D6	D8

POWERS

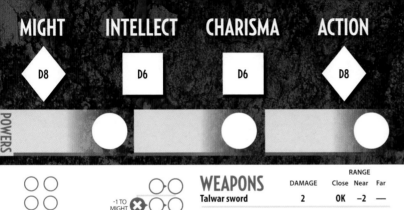

ARMOR (CHOLA ROBE)

HEALTH

-1 TO MIGHT
-1 TO MIGHT & ACTION
STAGGERED
KNOCKED OUT

WEAPONS	DAMAGE	RANGE Close	Near	Far
Talwar sword	2	OK	−2	—
Garrote	3	−2	—	—

EQUIPMENT
THC Rebreather

Dime Bag

SISTER OF PERPETUAL DARKNESS

	MIGHT	INTELLECT	CHARISMA	ACTION
	D8	D8	D4	D10

POWERS

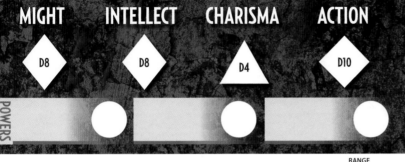

ARMOR NANOCARBON HABIT

HEALTH

-1 TO MIGHT
-1 TO MIGHT & ACTION
STAGGERED
KNOCKED OUT

WEAPONS	DAMAGE	RANGE Close	Near	Far
Crossbow	2	OK	OK	OK
Sai	1	OK	—	—

EQUIPMENT
Night Vision   Contact Lenses

Communications Suite

GREEN DRAGON LAMA

	MIGHT	INTELLECT	CHARISMA	ACTION
	D4	D10	D6	D8

POWERS

Telepathy *Keep Both*	D10	Martial Arts (Weapon) *Discard Lowest*	D8	Access Akashic Record *Discard Lowest— Download new skill/Power*	D8

ARMOR LAMA REFLEXES

HEALTH

-1 TO MIGHT
-1 TO MIGHT & ACTION
STAGGERED
KNOCKED OUT

WEAPONS	DAMAGE	RANGE Close	Near	Far
Downloaded Martial Art Style	D4	OK	−2	—

EQUIPMENT
Green Robe

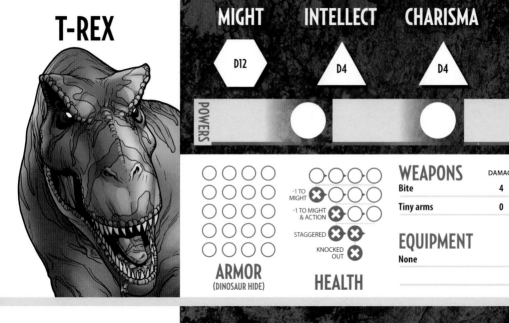

T-REX

	MIGHT	INTELLECT	CHARISMA	ACTION
	D12	D4	D4	D6

POWERS

ARMOR (DINOSAUR HIDE)

HEALTH
- -1 TO MIGHT
- -1 TO MIGHT & ACTION
- STAGGERED
- KNOCKED OUT

WEAPONS	DAMAGE	Close	Near	Far
Bite	4	OK	OK	—
Tiny arms	0	OK	—	—

EQUIPMENT
None

QUETZALCOATLUS

	MIGHT	INTELLECT	CHARISMA	ACTION
	D6	D4	D4	D6

POWERS
Flight
Replace — D12

ARMOR (DINOSAUR HIDE)

HEALTH
- -1 TO MIGHT
- -1 TO MIGHT & ACTION
- STAGGERED
- KNOCKED OUT

WEAPONS	DAMAGE	Close	Near	Far
Beak	2	OK	—	—
Wingtip	1	OK	−2	—

EQUIPMENT
None

ROANOKE TRIBESMAN

	MIGHT	INTELLECT	CHARISMA	ACTION
	D8	D6	D6	D8

POWERS

ARMOR (LEATHER ARMOR)

HEALTH
- -1 TO MIGHT
- -1 TO MIGHT & ACTION
- STAGGERED
- KNOCKED OUT

WEAPONS	DAMAGE	Close	Near	Far
Spear	2	OK	OK	−2
Stunner	*	OK	−2	—

Target is treated as Knocked Out for D4 −1 rounds

EQUIPMENT
Claw Necklace

Feathers

GENERAL REDACTED

MIGHT	INTELLECT	CHARISMA	ACTION
D6	D8	D8	D8

POWERS

Leadership			Rampant
Leadership *Discard Lowest*	D10	*Keep Both* ▬▬ ▬▬ D10	Rampant Paranoia *Add +3* D8

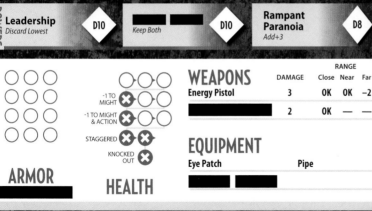

WEAPONS

	DAMAGE	RANGE Close	Near	Far
Energy Pistol	3	OK	OK	−2
▬▬▬▬▬	2	OK	—	—

EQUIPMENT

Eye Patch   Pipe

▬▬▬ ▬▬▬

ARMOR ▬▬▬▬

HEALTH
-1 TO MIGHT
-1 TO MIGHT & ACTION
STAGGERED
KNOCKED OUT

GREY

MIGHT	INTELLECT	CHARISMA	ACTION
D4	D6	D6	D6

POWERS

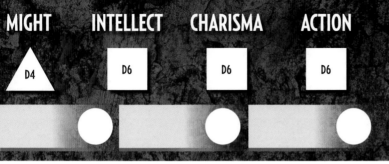

WEAPONS

	DAMAGE	RANGE Close	Near	Far
Energy Pistol	3	OK	OK	−2

EQUIPMENT

Helmet and Goggles   Scarf

Gloves

ARMOR (EVOLVED HIDE)

HEALTH
-1 TO MIGHT
-1 TO MIGHT & ACTION
STAGGERED
KNOCKED OUT

ARCHIE

MIGHT	INTELLECT	CHARISMA	ACTION
D6	D8	D6	D4

POWERS

Non-Intervention *Keep Both*	D10	Knowledge of the Future *Add +3*	D10	Martial Arts *Replace*	D12

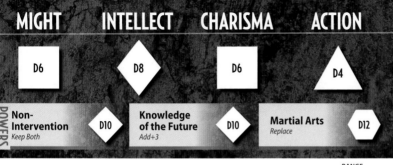

WEAPONS

	DAMAGE	RANGE Close	Near	Far
Martial Arts*	3	OK	—	—

*Can only be used in defense of The Timeless Word

EQUIPMENT

Blue T-Shirt   White Cloak

Copy of *The Timeless Word*

ARMOR (SEVEN SAGE CLOAK)

HEALTH
-1 TO MIGHT
-1 TO MIGHT & ACTION
STAGGERED
KNOCKED OUT

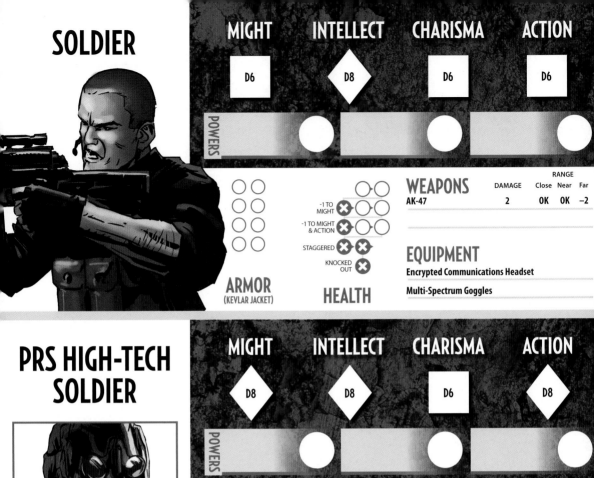

SOLDIER

	MIGHT	INTELLECT	CHARISMA	ACTION
	D6	D8	D6	D6

POWERS

ARMOR (KEVLAR JACKET)

HEALTH
- −1 TO MIGHT
- −1 TO MIGHT & ACTION
- STAGGERED
- KNOCKED OUT

WEAPONS	DAMAGE	RANGE Close	Near	Far
AK-47	2	OK	OK	−2

EQUIPMENT

Encrypted Communications Headset

Multi-Spectrum Goggles

PRS HIGH-TECH SOLDIER

	MIGHT	INTELLECT	CHARISMA	ACTION
	D8	D8	D6	D8

POWERS

ARMOR (BODY ARMOR)

HEALTH
- −1 TO MIGHT
- −1 TO MIGHT & ACTION
- STAGGERED
- KNOCKED OUT

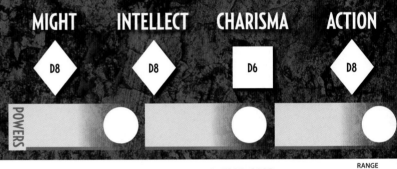

WEAPONS	DAMAGE	RANGE Close	Near	Far
M203 Carbine	2	OK	OK	−2
Synaptic Bomb	D4*	OK	−2	—

*Damage ignores Armor and applies directly to Health

EQUIPMENT

Psiot Jamming Helmet   Multi-Spectrum

Goggles   Encrypted Communications Headset

PRS COMMANDER

	MIGHT	INTELLECT	CHARISMA	ACTION
	D8	D8	D8	D8

POWERS

Leadership *Keep Both*   D10   Small-unit Tactics *Keep Both*   D8

ARMOR (KEVLAR VEST)

HEALTH
- −1 TO MIGHT
- −1 TO MIGHT & ACTION
- STAGGERED
- KNOCKED OUT

WEAPONS	DAMAGE	RANGE Close	Near	Far
Desert Eagle	3	OK	OK	—
Combat Knife	2	OK	−2	—

EQUIPMENT

Tactical Headset   PRS ID Badge

Cell Phone

CHAINSAW OPERATIVE

MIGHT	INTELLECT	CHARISMA	ACTION
D10	D6	D4	D8

POWERS

Leadership
Discard Lowest—
"Command" operative only — D12

ARMOR (CYBERNETIC GRAFTS)

HEALTH
-1 TO MIGHT
-1 TO MIGHT & ACTION
STAGGERED
KNOCKED OUT

WEAPONS	DAMAGE	RANGE Close	Near	Far
Sniper Rifle*	5	—	−2	OK
Cybernetic Claws**	4	OK	−2	—
Plasma Cannon***	3	OK	OK	OK
Rocket Launcher****	4	—	OK	OK

* "Cleaner" operative only ** "Recon" operative only
*** "Gunner" operative only **** "Point" operative only

EQUIPMENT
Private Communications Network

ROGUE PSIOT

MIGHT	INTELLECT	CHARISMA	ACTION
D6	D8	D6	D6

POWERS

Psionic Blast (Weapon) — D6
Keep Both

Non-Combat Psionic Power — D6
Discard Lowest—Choose a random non-combat power

ARMOR (PSIONIC SHIELD)

HEALTH
-1 TO MIGHT
-1 TO MIGHT & ACTION
STAGGERED
KNOCKED OUT

WEAPONS	DAMAGE	RANGE Close	Near	Far
Psionic Attack	2	OK	OK	−2
Pistol	2	OK	−2	—

EQUIPMENT
Fake ID

LYSANDER A.I. MEDBOT

MIGHT	INTELLECT	CHARISMA	ACTION
D8	D10	D6	D6

POWERS

Control Computers — D8
Discard Lowest

ARMOR (METAL PLATING)

HEALTH
-1 TO MIGHT
-1 TO MIGHT & ACTION
STAGGERED
KNOCKED OUT

WEAPONS	DAMAGE	RANGE Close	Near	Far
Arm Blades	D6	OK	−2	—

EQUIPMENT
None

RANGER OF THE WILD

	MIGHT	INTELLECT	CHARISMA	ACTION
	D8	D8	D6	D10

POWERS

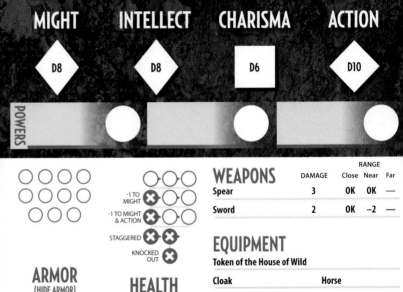

ARMOR (HIDE ARMOR)

HEALTH

-1 TO MIGHT ⊗
-1 TO MIGHT & ACTION ⊗
STAGGERED ⊗ ⊗
KNOCKED OUT ⊗

WEAPONS	DAMAGE	Close	Near	Far
Spear	3	OK	OK	—
Sword	2	OK	–2	—

EQUIPMENT
Token of the House of Wild

Cloak   Horse

SWORD OF THE WILD

	MIGHT	INTELLECT	CHARISMA	ACTION
	D8	D8	D8	D10

POWERS

Animal Mastery *Keep Both* D10

ARMOR (HIDE ARMOR)

HEALTH

-1 TO MIGHT ⊗
-1 TO MIGHT & ACTION ⊗
STAGGERED ⊗ ⊗
KNOCKED OUT ⊗

WEAPONS	DAMAGE	Close	Near	Far
Spear	3	OK	OK	—
Sword	2	OK	–2	—

EQUIPMENT
Token of the House of Wild

Cloak   Horse

RANGER OF THE EARTH

	MIGHT	INTELLECT	CHARISMA	ACTION
	D8	D6	D8	D10

POWERS

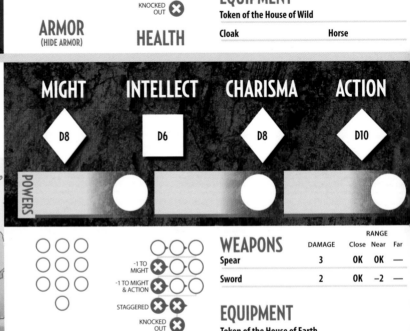

ARMOR (EARTH'S EMBRACE)

HEALTH

-1 TO MIGHT ⊗
-1 TO MIGHT & ACTION ⊗
STAGGERED ⊗ ⊗
KNOCKED OUT ⊗

WEAPONS	DAMAGE	Close	Near	Far
Spear	3	OK	OK	—
Sword	2	OK	–2	—

EQUIPMENT
Token of the House of Earth

BERSERKER OF THE DEAD

MIGHT	INTELLECT	CHARISMA	ACTION
D8	D4	D4	D8

POWERS

Berserker Potion
Keep Both—Increases Might to D12 and Action to D10 for D6 rounds — D10

HEALTH

- -1 TO MIGHT ✗
- -1 TO MIGHT & ACTION ✗
- STAGGERED ✗ ✗
- KNOCKED OUT ✗

ARMOR
(BERSERKER POTION)

WEAPONS

WEAPONS	DAMAGE	Close	Near	Far
Mace	3	OK	−2	—
Fist	3	OK	−2	—

EQUIPMENT

Token of the House of Dead

PRIEST OF THE DEAD

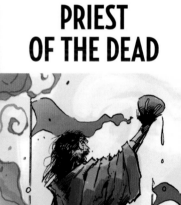

MIGHT	INTELLECT	CHARISMA	ACTION
D6	D8	D10	D6

POWERS

Death Magic
Discard Lowest — D10

HEALTH

- -1 TO MIGHT ✗
- -1 TO MIGHT & ACTION ✗
- STAGGERED ✗ ✗
- KNOCKED OUT ✗

ARMOR
(BLOOD SPELL)

WEAPONS

WEAPONS	DAMAGE	Close	Near	Far
Dagger	1	OK	—	—

EQUIPMENT

Token of the House of Dead

Berserker Potion	Robes

TECH OF THE WHEEL

MIGHT	INTELLECT	CHARISMA	ACTION
D6	D10	D6	D6

POWERS

HEALTH

- -1 TO MIGHT ✗
- -1 TO MIGHT & ACTION ✗
- STAGGERED ✗ ✗
- KNOCKED OUT ✗

ARMOR
(FLEXIBLE ARMOR)

WEAPONS

WEAPONS	DAMAGE	Close	Near	Far
Submachine Gun*	2	OK	OK	−2

*May target two enemies with the same attack action

EQUIPMENT

Token of the House of Wheel

Toolkit	Tablet

EGGBREAKER

	MIGHT	INTELLECT	CHARISMA	ACTION
	D6	D8	D6	D8

POWERS

Psionic Blast (Weapon) *Keep Both*	D6	Non-Combat Psionic Power *Discard Lowest—Choose a random non-combat power*	D6	

ARMOR (FOUNDATION UNIFORM)

HEALTH
- -1 TO MIGHT
- -1 TO MIGHT & ACTION
- STAGGERED
- KNOCKED OUT

WEAPONS

	DAMAGE	RANGE Close	Near	Far
Psionic Attack	D6	OK	OK	−2

EQUIPMENT

Harbinger Foundation ID   List of Latent Psiots

Harbinger Foundation Uniform

SECURITY GUARD

	MIGHT	INTELLECT	CHARISMA	ACTION
	D8	D6	D6	D8

POWERS

ARMOR (ARMORED VEST)

HEALTH
- -1 TO MIGHT
- -1 TO MIGHT & ACTION
- STAGGERED
- KNOCKED OUT

WEAPONS

	DAMAGE	RANGE Close	Near	Far
Pistol	2	OK	OK	—
Stun Baton	1*	OK	—	—

*Target suffers a −3 on next action

EQUIPMENT

Building Badge/Passkey   Radio

Cup of Coffee

PSIOT TRAINEE

	MIGHT	INTELLECT	CHARISMA	ACTION
	D6	D8	D6	D8

POWERS

Flight *Keep Both*	D8			

ARMOR (FOUNDATION UNIFORM)

HEALTH
- -1 TO MIGHT
- -1 TO MIGHT & ACTION
- STAGGERED
- KNOCKED OUT

WEAPONS

	DAMAGE	RANGE Close	Near	Far
Psionic Attack	D4	OK	OK	—

EQUIPMENT

Harbinger Uniform

Tablet Computer

HARBINGER FOUNDATION TECHNICIAN

MIGHT	INTELLECT	CHARISMA	ACTION
D6	D10	D4	D6

POWERS

ARMOR (FOUNDATION UNIFORM)

HEALTH

-1 TO MIGHT ❌ ◯
-1 TO MIGHT & ACTION ❌ ◯
STAGGERED ❌ ❌
KNOCKED OUT ❌

WEAPONS

	DAMAGE	Close	Near	Far
			RANGE	
Stun Baton	1*	OK	—	—

*Target suffers a −3 on next action

EQUIPMENT

Radio   Toolkit

Systems Manual

TORQUEHALLA TROLL

MIGHT	INTELLECT	CHARISMA	ACTION
D10	D6	D4	D8

POWERS

ARMOR (CHAINMAIL)

HEALTH

-1 TO MIGHT ❌ ◯ ◯
-1 TO MIGHT & ACTION ❌ ◯
STAGGERED ❌ ❌
KNOCKED OUT ❌

WEAPONS

	DAMAGE	Close	Near	Far
			RANGE	
Battle Axe	3	OK	−2	—
Knife	1	OK	—	—

EQUIPMENT

Leather Clothes

Wooden Shield

HELL BAT

MIGHT	INTELLECT	CHARISMA	ACTION
D8	D6	D4	D8

POWERS

Flight
Keep Both

D10

ARMOR (TOUGH HIDE)

HEALTH

-1 TO MIGHT ❌ ◯ ◯
-1 TO MIGHT & ACTION ❌ ◯
STAGGERED ❌ ❌
KNOCKED OUT ❌

WEAPONS

	DAMAGE	Close	Near	Far
			RANGE	
Bite	3	OK	—	—

EQUIPMENT

None

THE CRONE

MIGHT	INTELLECT	CHARISMA	ACTION
D4	D12	D10	D6

POWERS

Monologuing *Keep Both*	D10	Genetic Engineering *Keep Both*	D10	

HEALTH
- -1 TO MIGHT
- -1 TO MIGHT & ACTION
- STAGGERED
- KNOCKED OUT

ARMOR (FORCE FIELD)

WEAPONS

	DAMAGE	Close	Near	Far
Fingernail Needles	4	OK	—	—
Wheelchair Rockets	D4	—	–2	OK

EQUIPMENT

Face Staples	Intravenous Tubes
Thomas Edison Biography	Tablet Computer

NIGHTMARE BRIGADE

MIGHT	INTELLECT	CHARISMA	ACTION
D8	D4	D6	D8

POWERS

Clown Cackling *Replace—Target must pass a Charisma Test or suffer –4 on its next roll*	D10		

HEALTH
- -1 TO MIGHT
- -1 TO MIGHT & ACTION
- STAGGERED
- KNOCKED OUT

ARMOR (NIGHTMARE FUEL)

WEAPONS

	DAMAGE	Close	Near	Far
Needle Teeth	3	OK	OK	—
Spider Claws	D4	OK	–2	—

EQUIPMENT

None

CRONE-CLONE SOLDIER

MIGHT	INTELLECT	CHARISMA	ACTION
D6	D6	D8	D8

POWERS

HEALTH
- -1 TO MIGHT
- -1 TO MIGHT & ACTION
- STAGGERED
- KNOCKED OUT

ARMOR (EXPERIMENTAL FABRIC)

WEAPONS

	DAMAGE	Close	Near	Far
Incandescent Laser Rifle	2	OK	OK	OK

EQUIPMENT

Spare Battery Pack

Preserved Frame of Motion Picture Film

VINCENT VAN GOAT

MIGHT	INTELLECT	CHARISMA	ACTION
D8	D10	D6	D10

POWERS

Flight — D6
Discard Lowest

ARMOR
(GOAT HIDE)

HEALTH

-1 TO MIGHT
-1 TO MIGHT & ACTION
STAGGERED
KNOCKED OUT

WEAPONS

	DAMAGE	Close	RANGE Near	Far
Heat Vision	D6	OK	OK	OK
Hircine Appetite	1*	OK	—	—

*+3 damage to anything made of metal

EQUIPMENT
None

JOHNNY 2

MIGHT	INTELLECT	CHARISMA	ACTION
D4	D10	D4	D6

POWERS

ARMOR
(ARMORED HOVERCHAIR)

HEALTH

-1 TO MIGHT
-1 TO MIGHT & ACTION
STAGGERED
KNOCKED OUT

WEAPONS

	DAMAGE	Close	RANGE Near	Far
Tesla Pistol	3	OK	OK	OK
Hypodermic Cocktail	*	OK	—	—

*Reduces Might and Action Stat Dice by 2 levels for D4+1 rounds

EQUIPMENT
Nightmare Brigade Capsules (Just Add Water!)

Life-Sustaining Serums   Tablet Computer

MAD SCIENCE WARBOT

MIGHT	INTELLECT	CHARISMA	ACTION
D10	D6	D8	D6

POWERS

ARMOR
(TITANIUM ALLOY)

HEALTH

N/A

WEAPONS

	DAMAGE	Close	RANGE Near	Far
Death Ray	D4	OK	OK	OK
Robot Fist	2	OK	–2	—

EQUIPMENT
Mad Scientist Pilot

Nuclear Power Core

MR. TWIST

MIGHT	INTELLECT	CHARISMA	ACTION
D12	D6	D8	D8

POWERS

Parasite Fling *Replace*—Control target's actions while attached. Parasite has 5 Health.	D6	**Swap Places with Flesh Parasite** *Add+3* — D8	**Regeneration** *Keep Both*—Restores 2 Armor and 2 Health — D8

ARMOR (SACRIFICIAL FLESH)

HEALTH
- -1 TO MIGHT
- -1 TO MIGHT & ACTION
- STAGGERED
- KNOCKED OUT

WEAPONS	DAMAGE	RANGE		
		Close	Near	Far
Claw Swipe	4	OK	OK	—
Death Touch	*	OK	—	—

If this hits, roll a D20. The target is immediately Knocked Out if a 1 is rolled.

EQUIPMENT

Tailored Suit	Sacrificial Flesh
Parasite	

PARASITE MONSTER

MIGHT	INTELLECT	CHARISMA	ACTION
D6	D4	D6	D6

POWERS

Regeneration *Discard Lowest*—Restores 1 Armor and 1 Health	D8

ARMOR (SACRIFICIAL FLESH)

HEALTH
- -1 TO MIGHT
- -1 TO MIGHT & ACTION
- STAGGERED
- KNOCKED OUT

WEAPONS	DAMAGE	RANGE		
		Close	Near	Far
Parasite Claws	2	OK	—	—
9mm Pistol	1	OK	-2	—

EQUIPMENT

Embedded Sacrificial Flesh Parasite

Normal Clothing

DEADSIDE GHOST

MIGHT	INTELLECT	CHARISMA	ACTION
D4	D4	D4	D6

POWERS

Deathly Fear Target must pass a Charisma Test or lose its next action.	D4

ARMOR (INTANGIBILITY)

HEALTH N/A

WEAPONS	DAMAGE	RANGE		
		Close	Near	Far
Ghost Touch	1	OK	—	—

EQUIPMENT

None

JAUNTY

MIGHT	INTELLECT	CHARISMA	ACTION
D4	D8	D8	D6

POWERS

Deadside Knowledge — *Keep Both* — D10

WEAPONS	DAMAGE	Close	RANGE Near	Far
Monkey Bite	2	OK	–2	—

EQUIPMENT

Miniature Top Hat

ARMOR (AGILITY)

HEALTH

-1 TO MIGHT
-1 TO MIGHT & ACTION
STAGGERED
KNOCKED OUT

BRETHREN GOON

MIGHT	INTELLECT	CHARISMA	ACTION
D6	D6	D6	D8

POWERS

WEAPONS	DAMAGE	Close	RANGE Near	Far
Concealed Pistol	1	OK	–2	—
Silver Dagger	2	OK	—	—

EQUIPMENT

Tailored Suit

Arcane Talisman

ARMOR (DEMONIC PROTECTION)

HEALTH

-1 TO MIGHT
-1 TO MIGHT & ACTION
STAGGERED
KNOCKED OUT

LIONEL DEVEREAUX

MIGHT	INTELLECT	CHARISMA	ACTION
D6	D10	D8	D6

POWERS

Leadership — *Keep Both* — D10

Call Demon — *Discard Lowest* — D8

WEAPONS	DAMAGE	Close	RANGE Near	Far
Tommy Gun	2	OK	OK	OK
Runed Silver Kris	3	OK	—	—

EQUIPMENT

Tailored Suit — Arcane Talisman

Book of Rituals

ARMOR (DEMONIC PROTECTION)

HEALTH

-1 TO MIGHT
-1 TO MIGHT & ACTION
STAGGERED
KNOCKED OUT

VINE SLAVEMASTER

	MIGHT	INTELLECT	CHARISMA	ACTION
	D8	D6	D6	D8

POWERS

ARMOR
(VINE ARMOR)

-1 TO MIGHT

-1 TO MIGHT & ACTION

STAGGERED

KNOCKED OUT

HEALTH

WEAPONS

	DAMAGE	Close	Near	Far
Stun-stick	3*	OK	—	—

*Target suffers a −3 on next action

EQUIPMENT

Ring of Keys   Power Pack

Manacles

VINE COMMANDER

	MIGHT	INTELLECT	CHARISMA	ACTION
	D10	D6	D6	D8

POWERS

ARMOR
(VINE ARMOR)

-1 TO MIGHT

-1 TO MIGHT & ACTION

STAGGERED

KNOCKED OUT

HEALTH

WEAPONS

	DAMAGE	Close	Near	Far
Vine Ion Rifle	2	OK	OK	OK
Vine Plasma Knife	2*	OK	—	—

*Deals 2x damage to Armor pip

EQUIPMENT

Helmet

Battle Computer

VINE X-O COMMANDO

	MIGHT	INTELLECT	CHARISMA	ACTION
	D10	D6	D4	D10

POWERS

Anti-gravity (Flight) Keep Both	D8	Armor Regeneration (Armor) Discard Lowest—Restores 1 Armor and 1 Health	D6	Sensor Array Discard Lowest	D8

ARMOR
(X-O COMMANDO ARMOR)

-1 TO MIGHT

-1 TO MIGHT & ACTION

STAGGERED

KNOCKED OUT

HEALTH

WEAPONS

	DAMAGE	Close	Near	Far
Energy Blast	3	OK	OK	OK

EQUIPMENT

None

VINE WOLF-CLASS ARMOR

	MIGHT	INTELLECT	CHARISMA	ACTION
	D8	D6	D6	D8

POWERS

Strength — D10
Discard Lowest

ARMOR

HEALTH

-1 TO MIGHT
-1 TO MIGHT & ACTION
STAGGERED
KNOCKED OUT

WEAPONS	DAMAGE	RANGE Close	Near	Far
Energy Cannons	3	−2	OK	OK
Rending Claws	2	OK	−2	—

EQUIPMENT

Vine Soldier Pilot   Repair Kit

Spare Parts

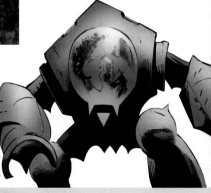

VINE PLANTING (OVERLORD)

	MIGHT	INTELLECT	CHARISMA	ACTION
	D8	D8	D8	D6

POWERS

ARMOR
(VINE PHYSIOLOGY)

HEALTH

-1 TO MIGHT
-1 TO MIGHT & ACTION
STAGGERED
KNOCKED OUT

WEAPONS	DAMAGE	RANGE Close	Near	Far
Vine Hold-out Pistol	2	OK	—	—
Stun Baton	2*	OK	−2	—

Target suffers a −3 on next action

EQUIPMENT

Satellite Phone   ID Card

Spy Drone

VINE PLANTING (MINION)

	MIGHT	INTELLECT	CHARISMA	ACTION
	D6	D8	D6	D8

POWERS

ARMOR
(VINE PHYSIOLOGY)

HEALTH

-1 TO MIGHT
-1 TO MIGHT & ACTION
STAGGERED
KNOCKED OUT

WEAPONS	DAMAGE	RANGE Close	Near	Far
Silenced Vine Pistol	2	OK	OK	—

EQUIPMENT

Radio Communicator   Pocket Computer

Surveillance Tools

EVENT BRIEFS

OBADIAH ARCHER'S JOURNAL

Dear Mary-Maria,

See? I'm already putting your journal to good use!

If I fail in my quest, and you—or any of our other brothers and sisters—must replace me, you'll have the benefit of my experience, and you'll already know the strange sights and sounds and smells of the outside world.

Particularly the smells. They are nasty.

The sacred artifact Mom and Dad gave me glowed even brighter when I explored what the locals call the Meatpacking District. In front of one slaughterhouse of morals, the artifact began to burn in my hand like the Eternal Fire.

Transcript of Coded Radio Traffic Intercepted by Black Bloc Agent J33t DO3

Gabriel One: Gabriel One to all Angels, the Chosen One is entering a bar called Sows and Cows.

Gabriel Three: Gabriel Three to Gabriel One. Do you think He Who is Not to be Named is there?

Gabriel One: He must be. The Chosen One has the sacred artifact in his hand. All Angels, surround the building and stand by.

Gabriel Three: Stand by for what?

Gabriel One: It is a pit of evil, and the Chosen One is walking into it. Now, we'll wait for all hell to break loose.

Suggested Characters: Archer, Armstrong

OBJECTIVES

- Find He Who is Not to be Named
- Discover the Sect's plans
- Get out alive

CUES

- sacred artifact ● drunks ● brawls ● knockout gas ● the One Percent ● captured

TAGS

- New York City ● Meatpacking District ● Federal Hall
- tunnels ● the Sect ● betrayal ● escape ● the Boon

THE SETTING

The Sows and Cows Bar in the Meatpacking District is a rough bar. The patrons are bikers and other hard-edged types. The most noticeable feature is the hundreds of bras stapled on the wall behind the bar. The place is noisy, crowded, and the beer is flowing.

ENEMIES/OBSTACLES

Scene 1: *Suggested NPCs: Armstrong (if not a player), Sect Security Guard*

Sows and Cows is primed for a fight. A biker gang in the bar, the Sons of Perdition, recently arrived in New York, and the rest of the clientele are rough drunks one insult or shove away from a bar fight.

A sacred artifact the players have will point toward He Who is Not to be Named, and in the crowded bar it will be difficult to reach the target: Aram Anni-Padda, now calling himself Armstrong, the bar's bouncer.

When the players enter the bar, they attract attention. Almost any actions they take—brushing against someone, interrupting conversation, looking at someone too long, etc.—forces a Charisma Test (plus any related Power) to placate the offended customer. If a player strikes anyone—customer, employee, or other characters—the bar will erupt into a massive brawl. The patrons will fight anyone, as drink makes it difficult to tell friend from foe. The weapons involved are a mix of beer bottles, chairs, a few knives, but no firearms. Customers have the following stats: Might D6, Intellect D6, Charisma D6, Action D6; Weapons are Close only, 2 Damage.

On the second round of Narrations, Armstrong (if not a player character) will enter the brawl and begin laying out anyone in his way. If anyone is holding the sacred artifact, the beam of light emitting from it will strike Armstrong.

At some point during the scene (LN's discretion), Sect Security Guards throw canisters of Sleep Gas through the front windows (see Dossier for rules). If all of the players pass out, they will be taken prisoner (along with Armstrong, if he is an NPC).

Scene 2: *Suggested NPCs: Armstrong (if not a player), Sect Security Guard, The One Percent*

The players wake up in a brick vault. Any obviously strong-looking characters are chained to the wall. The door is a locked vault door, and the characters have been stripped of all visible equipment. Outside the vault, Sect Security Guards are positioned at intersections and are making regular rounds. The halls are dark with plenty of shadows for the players to hide in if they escape from the vault.

In the central hall, members of the One Percent, a Wall Street-based demon-worshipping cult that wears golden bull and bear masks, are talking to Archer's parents—Reverend and Mrs. Archer—via teleconferencing. The Archers are part of the Dominion, a faction of a larger group called the Sect, which is trying to gain access to something called the Boon. The One Percent has two of the six pieces need to assemble the Boon. One of the pieces is the sacred artifact that the players used to locate Armstrong. The One Percent decides they will sacrifice the captured players to their demon god.

The players can either try to escape or take on the One Percent and their security to secure the two parts of the Boon in their possession: the Fulcrum (the sacred artifact) and the Inclined Plane. If the players beat the One Percent, they gain access to the cult's private jet.

If Armstrong is with the group—either as a player or an NPC—he will produce a sheet of paper from his satchel, claiming the location of another part of the Boon is on the sheet. If Armstrong is not with the group, the players can find the sheet in the One Percent leader's pocket.

The sheet says, "Mikey keeps the Torque in Chains," a reference to both Michelangelo and Rome.

OBADIAH ARCHER'S JOURNAL

Mary-Maria,

Mister Armstrong says we're going to go to Rome to get a piece of the Boon he hid there. He seems like a nice man—except for his drinking, his lustful eye for women, his singing, and his complete lack of belief in God.

And his stories...

He told me he helped Wilbur and Orville Wright perfect their airplane and was going to be their first test pilot, but he was too heavy for the aircraft! He then told me a story about him and three stewardesses at thirty thousand feet back in the early sixties, but I won't repeat it here because it's too sordid and I don't think the human body can move in the manner he described.

We'll be landing in Italy in seven hours, long enough to get some sleep, but I'm not sure that's a good idea. Mister Armstrong says he's a good pilot, but I think it's best I stay awake, just in case...

ALERT! ALERT! ALERT!

To: Sect Security Commanders, European Division
From: Sect Security Command, Eastern Seaboard, North American Division
Subject: He Who is Not to be Named

He Who is Not to be Named, along with the Dominion turncoat Obadiah Archer, have escaped Sect control in New York and stolen a plane from the One Percent. Air radar indicates the plane's last known location was over the Atlantic Ocean, heading east toward Europe. Most likely targets are France, Italy, Austria, or Greece, but other possible destinations cannot be ruled out.

Current pictures and description of both fugitives are attached to this email. Both men are high-priority targets and are considered extremely dangerous. Both are well-versed in unarmed combat and are to be shot on sight.

SSCO #4563

Suggested Characters: Archer, Armstrong

OBJECTIVES

- Find the Boon piece in Rome
- Get to Tibet
- Stop the Boon from being activated

CUES

- hunted ● puzzle ● the Sect ● Michelangelo ● Green Dragon Lamas
- the Fulcrum, the Inclined Plane, the Wedge, the Torque, the Axle, and the Sphere

TAGS

- Rome ● San Pietro in Vincoli ● catacombs
- library ● Tibet ● Himalayas ● the Boon ● Geomancer

THE SETTING

The search for the Boon has led to Rome, to the church San Pietro in Vincoli (Saint Peter in Chains). The church holds the tomb of Pope Julius II, which has a statue of Moses in front of it.

ENEMIES/OBSTACLES

Scene 1: *Suggested NPCs: Sister of Perpetual Darkness, Mary-Maria (if not a player)*

Sister Thomas Aquinas takes the group to a statue of Moses, part of Pope Julius II's tomb. Any player who passes an Intellect Challenge will notice something strange about the statue. After a successful Might Challenge, the statue will slide back to reveal a dial with images on it.

To solve the dial's puzzle, a player must succeed in an Intellect Challenge; the floor then slides open, revealing a staircase leading down into the catacombs. If no one succeeds, the church begins to collapse; each round that the puzzle goes unsolved, every character still inside the church takes 2 damage from falling debris.

Once in the catacombs, the players are confronted by the Sisters of Perpetual Darkness. The Sisters will not retreat under any circumstances.

In the catacombs library, a player who succeeds in an Intellect Challenge will find information about a piece of the Boon, the Torque: it is embedded in the Sistine Chapel ceiling between the fingers of Adam and God in the painting *The Creation of Adam*.

Inside the chapel, one of the Archers' children (use Mary-Maria's Dossier unless she is one of the players) is atop scaffolding and already removing the Torque. Should the thief escape, the players will learn that the last piece, the Axle, is in the La-Chen Monastery in Ladakh.

Scene 2: *Suggested NPCs: Green Dragon Lama, Sect Security Guard, Mary-Maria (if not a player)*

The monastery sits on an isolated mountain peak. A player who passes an Intellect Challenge will locate a secret entrance. Another Intellect Challenge will undo the lock. Other methods of gaining access to the monastery involve forcing the door, climbing the sheer ice-coated walls, and so on.

The monastery's main hall is filled with Green Dragon Lamas, Sect Security Guards, and the Archers and their children. A large box—the unfinished Boon—sits between two Nazi eagle statues. Another prisoner is also present: Geomancer Buck McHenry was tortured to reveal the Fulcrum's location. The Sect Security Guards and the Green Dragon Lamas will stop the players from preventing the Archers from rebuilding the Boon with all six pieces.

When the Boon is activated, the device drains life from everyone in the room. Each round, players must pass a Might Challenge or suffer 2 Health damage (ignoring Armor); treat Knocked Out characters and NPCs as dead. Players with an Accelerated Healing Power are immune to the Boon's effects.

Identifying the Boon's weak point requires a successful Intellect Challenge; a successful Action Challenge will then shatter the Boon. If that happens, the energy released will restore the closet D8 dead people (characters and NPCs) back to life, and at full Health.

AFTERMATH

If the Boon is destroyed

Armstrong: Ah, the Boon's finally gone, and it didn't kill everyone this time—thank goodness for that.

On the other hand…if there's one thing I've learned in all my millennia of walking this Earth, nothing is ever *truly* gone. I've split up the six pieces of the Boon, and we're all going to hide them in the far corners of the globe so this won't happen again—at least not for a good long while. So that means *more* walking…

"The woods are lovely, dark, and deep, / But I have promises to keep, / And miles to go before I sleep, / And miles to go before I sleep."

If the Boon isn't shut down

The Timewalker: I have seen this happen *again*. How many times is that now? How many times have I witnessed that accursed device explode and destroy this little monastery and take most of the mountaintop with it? I have lost track.

Perhaps next time…perhaps this next time will be different…

BREAKING STORY

Jeena Xavier: Good afternoon, we interrupt *Celebrity Court Battles* to bring you a KNMX exclusive. A strange car chase is happening in the metro area. We take you live to Paul Emerson in LiveCopter 6.

Paul Emerson: Thanks, Jeena. As you can see, we are following an ambulance heading away from the center of town, away from the major hospitals in the region. As we zoom out, it is being followed by a…well, I'm not sure what that is. Looks like some sort of cross between a construction vehicle and a steam locomotive. You'll notice there are no police cars around. I have no idea why law enforcement hasn't responded—

Oh my! Did you *see* that?

The ambulance just clipped a parked car and kept right on going. He's even running a red light—Mother of *God*! The pursuing vehicle just went *through* a semi-trailer! It hardly even slowed down, sending wreckage and—can we get a little closer?—yes, I believe those are chickens everywhere. Some still alive, running around the intersection.

The ambulance is turning onto Farmstead road, going against traffic. Luckily, it's not rush hour right now. The pursuer seems to be gaining on the ambulance, despite all the reckless moves the driver is making. Jeena, this is like something out of a Hollywood movie. Are we sure nobody's filming today?

We are now above this chase, as the two vehicles get closer. They are a bit out of town now, no other vehicles in the picture. Wait, the chasing vehicle is slowing down…and the ambulance just flipped—Holy— What's going on? We're—

Xavier: Emerson? Emerson? I'm sorry folks, we've lost the LiveCopter 6 feed. We'll keep you updated once we know more about this situation.

PRS Mission Briefing
  Okay, team: someone screwed up, and we have to go retrieve Bloodshot again. You ask me, it's time for a new model that doesn't go rogue like this one does. Let's try to keep the collateral damage down, but taking him down is job number one.
  This time, we go in on the ground. We've got satellite coverage, but the chopper mishap last time has made me aware that our psiot—code name Pulse—isn't terribly bright and is almost as loose a cannon as Bloodshot. Luckily I have a leash for her, complete with a simple, electronic-free termination device to keep her motivated. If all goes well, I'll just need you guys to keep him occupied and pinned down. If it goes all pear-shaped, then you might have to show off your heroic side. I'm sure Uncle Sam will award you some sort of secret Medal of Honor that will be declassified for your grandkids to see. The Freedom of Information Act is even more unstoppable than Bloodshot...
  Beers are on me if we bag him with no scratches!

Suggested Characters: Fugitives: Bloodshot and Kara Murphy. Captives: Pulse

FUGITIVE OBJECTIVES

- Evade Project Rising Spirit agents
- Avoid collateral damage and civilian casualties

CAPTIVE OBJECTIVES

- Escape captors
- Survive

CUES

● They're watching me ● shocking revelation! ● get out of Dodge ● making frenemies

TAGS

● hide ● escape ● firefight ● teamwork ● New Mexico ● daytime ● ambulance
● Project Rising Spirit ● Mr. Dodge● electromagnetic pulse

THE SETTING

For the fugitives: Albuquerque, New Mexico, was founded in 1706. With over half a million people in 190 square miles, one can get lost in the city pretty easily, even in the suburbs. Unfortunately, the Project Rising Spirit pursuers have some tricks up their sleeves and are hot on the trail. Time to skip town before it's too late.

For the captives: The interior of this Project Rising Spirit armored car is dark and filled with all kinds of instruments and readout monitors.

PRS obviously doesn't trust its captives, even when those captives are being coerced into helping. Straitjackets, mental dampeners, sedative cocktails, and kill switches keep all of the "special assets" in line.

ENEMIES/OBSTACLES

This Event begins with the players split into two groups: the fugitives and the captives. The fugitives are trying to escape Project Rising Spirit; they begin in an Albuquerque suburb, and have an ambulance for a getaway vehicle. The captives are aboard a PRS armored car, which is trying to chase down the fugitives. The two groups will act simultaneously, but they will remain apart until they find each other and choose to either work together or fight against each other.

Scene 1: *Suggested NPCs: Soldier, PRS Commander*

The fugitives need to get out of the city before PRS can find them: if they are caught, the resulting battle could cause lots of damage and injure too many innocents. To make it out of the city, the fugitives will need to find a path that their ambulance will not attract much attention.

PRS has a bead on the fugitives, but the PRS commander, Mr. Dodge, must rely primarily on electronic surveillance: satellites, local communications, traffic cams, etc. The more stealth the fugitives use trying to leave the city, the harder it will be for PRS to find them inside city limits.

Scene 2: *Suggested NPCs: Soldier, PRS Commander*

Finding the fugitives is one thing; catching them is another. Once the fugitives escape the city, there is nowhere to hide on arid country roads, so it will only be a matter of time before PRS finds them.

The ambulance has 15 Armor, and the driver must pass Action Tests to avoid being rammed, forced off the road, and so on. While actively driving the ambulance, the driver cannot use Powers or weapons that require hands or a high degree of concentration (LN's discretion).

The PRS pursuers will try to close with the ambulance to put the soldiers' and the captives' weapons and Powers in range. The PRS driver will attempt to run the fugitives off the road or wreck the ambulance. The PRS armored car has 20 Armor.

Scene 3: *Suggested NPCs: Soldier, PRS Commander*

If the ambulance stops for any reason, the fight continues on the side of the road. If the captives have not yet tried to turn on their captors, this is their best opportunity, as the PRS agents undo their restraints.

The fugitives can stay and fight, try to get away on foot, steal the armored car, or come up with any other viable escape plan. Otherwise, the soldiers will capture them and cart them off to some dark dungeon in a hidden PRS base.

AREA 51 S-4 IMPLOSION INCIDENT REPORT

When the unknown intruders were sucked through the Faraway portal, onsite Rising Spirit security continued to fire. Having followed the two male intruders across the compound, these security personnel were unfamiliar with the established safety protocols in the S-4 complex. The resulting gunfire destroyed the Einstein-Rosen Bridge, which created a reverse harmonic effect, essentially sucking a small portion of the Faraway through the bridge into the S-4 complex.

The anomaly immediately killed the security guards and displaced a considerable portion of the S-4 complex. The instability of the event threatened to expand and impact the S-7 power complex. We are uncertain what effects the anomaly would've had on the Project Magellan system. If Magellan had lost containment, the resulting catastrophe could have destroyed the better part of Nevada.

With conventional response unable to penetrate the anomaly and Generation Zero no longer available, the only available option was to deploy the new H.A.R.D. Corps agents, who were still training for their primary mission of neutralizing Project Bloodshot. It was a calculated risk, but since we have the backup Faraway arc in San Francisco, Director Kozol personally authorized this deployment.

H.A.R.D. Corps Mission Briefing
Listen up. It's time to take the lessons out of the Training Village. If you're going to succeed in your mission, we need to kick up the training to maximum.
We're heading to another operation site for your final training mission. This site has been equipped with an advanced holographic system that is hyper-real, genuine Star Trek holo fun. It's going to seem real, it's going to feel real, and if you screw up it's going to hurt like it's real.
The objective of the training mission is simple. Enter the training complex, find the holo generator, place this EMP device on the generator, and trigger it. Do that and the simulation is over and your mission is complete.
Any questions?

Suggested Characters: Granite, Disciple, Superstar

OBJECTIVES

- Secure S-4 Skunk Works complex
- Eliminate non-PRS personnel
- Avoid structural damage

CUES

- Is that a T-Rex? ● That looks like a ray gun from a pulp sci-fi movie
- We're not in Kansas anymore ● It's bigger on the inside…

TAGS

- dinosaurs ● strange beings ● reality askew
- first mission ● Einstein-Rosen bridge ● the Faraway

THE SETTING

Area 51 is a top-secret Project Rising Spirit base in southern Nevada. There's far more to the base that just the hangars and building visible from the desert outside. Who knows what kind of experiments are being performed in the classified sections that only the top brass have access to?

The klaxons are currently going off, which seems normal for a training run like this, but the shimmering anomaly looks pretty real. The holographic projection capabilities of this facility are nothing short of outstanding.

ENEMIES/OBSTACLES

Scene 1: *Suggested NPCs: None*

Unbeknownst to the team, this mission is not a simulation. In reality, the anomaly was created when the Einstein-Rosen bridge leading to the Faraway collapsed in on itself. The collapse created a mirror of the Faraway inside the S-4 complex, and this unstable pocket is slowly expanding, slowly replicating the contents of Faraway.

To stop the pocket's expansion, the team must find a safe way inside the anomaly. The edges of the anomaly—the "holographic construct," as the players are concerned—form a shimmering field of physical energy. A pair of Rising Spirit Security agents already tried to walk through the field before the players arrived; this resulted in the

smoking remains nearby, their equipment fused to their charred bodies.

The team needs to figure out how to penetrate the field and get inside the so-called simulation.

Scene 2: *Suggested NPCs: T-Rex, Quetzalcoatlus, Roanoke Tribesman, Grey*

Once the team is inside the anomaly, they will have entered a completely different world. When they first enter, the pocket reality is two miles across. The team has a locator to find the remains of the Einstein-Rosen bridge—or what they believe to be the "holo generator"—which sits at the very center of the Faraway pocket.

Between the team and the bridge lie a host of potentially hostile encounters. Rampaging dinosaurs, little grey men from outer space, flying saucers, and primitive humans are all in frenzying of conflict with one another and have little compunction in bring the team into the conflict with them. The environment itself is also potentially deadly: liquid metal water, crystalline trees, and flowers that explode on contact are just some of the strange hazards the team can expect to face.

Scene 3: *Suggested NPCs: T-Rex, Quetzalcoatlus, Roanoke Tribesman, Grey*

To collapse the Faraway pocket, the team needs to plant an EMP device near the remains of the Einstein-Rosen bridge and set it off. However, some of the Faraway's denizens see this site as a kind of holy place and will defend it with their lives.

KAY MCHENRY'S GEOMANCER'S JOURNAL

Gilad says that every Geomancer keeps a journal so future Geomancers can learn from their predecessors. I'm not used to writing things in longhand, but Gilad insists that writing imparts something of the Geomancer's soul that a printout can't do. I guess when you've been around as long as he has, you can make anything sound profound.

But he's several millennia old! Imagine all the history he's experienced, places he's visited, and the people he's seen. Pity he's so tight-lipped most of the time. Not like his brother, Armstrong—that's one guy I wouldn't mind going drinking with.

Anyway, Mother Earth says we have to go to New York City. Gilad's been tense since we left Greenland. I get the impression from Mother that Gilad did something bad, but neither will tell me what. I think it has to do with the Methuselah Tree, but when I brought it up, he gave me a menacing glare and told me to never mention the Tree. Guess it's still a sore point with him.

For some reason, Mother wants us to go by train. I can see Gilad isn't happy with the idea, but he's staying quiet.

We'll be there in twenty minutes. I hope I can do this job like Mother wants me to.

Intercepted Radio Traffic, Grand Central Terminal

Nex Leader: Nex Leader to all agents. The train is coming in. Our target will be aboard. As soon as you see the target, fan out. I want this done by the numbers.

Nex Three: Copy, Leader. Nex Three, standing by.

Nex Two: Nex Two, standing by.

Nex Four: Nex Four here. I can't see anything. Moving to new position.

Nex Leader: Stay alert, Nex Four. If we miss our target, we'll be lucky if the Priests flay us alive.

Nex Four: I know, Leader, I—Ah, Nergal's wrath!

Nex Leader: What? What's happening?

Nex Four: It's him! The Fist and Steel!

Nex Leader: Impossible! You must be mistaken!

Nex Four: It's him. He has the facial scars!

Nex Leader: Is he alone?

Nex Four: No, there's a blonde woman with him. I think he's protecting her.

Nex Leader: Nex Leader to all Nexes: change of plans. The woman with the Fist is probably the new Geomancer. Nexes Five and Six, use your potions and kill the Geomancer. Nexes Two, Three, and Four, locate the target and get her out of here. No witnesses.

Suggested Characters: Gilad Anni-Padda, Xaran, Geomancer

OBJECTIVES

- Stop the Berserkers
- Protect the Geomancer
- Rescue Doctor Barkley

CUES

- crowded ● no time to prepare ● public place ● element of surprise
- panic and chaos ● Manhattan street traffic

TAGS

- New York City ● Grand Central Terminal ● benches ● House of the Dead
- Berserkers ● innocents in the crossfire ● balcony ● kidnapping ● car chase

THE SETTING

Grand Central Terminal is crowded with people coming and going, along with vendors, station employees, and some security guards. The area is large and open, sunlight streaming down from large windows high in the walls. Stairs run up to a balcony overlooking the main floor, which is lined with long wooden benches. A kiosk sits in the center of the room.

ENEMIES/OBSTACLES

Scene 1: *Suggested NPCs: Berserker of the Dead, Security Guard*

As soon as the players enter the terminal's main area, Berserkers from a death cult kidnapping team spot them; this team has been sent to grab Doctor Regina Barkley, a noted virologist who is slated to arrive by train at any moment. These Berserkers are armed with Machine Guns (Damage 2, Close OK, Near OK, Far —). Two members of the cultist team use their Berserker Potion Power and try to kill the Geomancer (or whichever player character the LN designates as the Berserkers' target), and the rest of the cultist team tries to kidnap Doctor Barkley. When the Berserkers attack, some of the Security Guards will move immediately toward the Berserkers, guns blazing, and tell everyone to get out.

Scene 2: *Suggested NPCs: Berserker of the Dead, Security Guard*

The players witness the kidnapping of Dr. Barkley on the other end of the main area, and one of the players should realize this kidnapping attempt is why they were sent to this location. Two of the Berserkers are dragging a struggling Dr. Barkley toward the nearest exit, while the rest threaten anyone who gets in the way. If the Berserkers make it outside, a van is outside waiting for them; the van has 15 Armor. The Berserkers will try to throw Doctor Barkley into the van, then open fire on the station doors, then on anyone they see, causing as much chaos and carnage as they can before jumping into the van and driving off.

If the players defeat the Berserkers before they can drive off, then Scene 3 can be skipped.

Scene 3: *Suggested NPCs: Berserker of the Dead*

To chase after the kidnappers, the players will need to find some form of transportation—such as commandeering a car, grabbing a taxi, and so on—and go after the van in a car chase through the streets of Manhattan. Feel free to include police cars in the chase as well (either to hinder or aid the players).

The LN assigns an appropriate number of Armor to the pursuing vehicle, depending on the vehicle type (10–20 Armor). Maneuvering through the crowded streets requires the driving character to pass Action Tests; failed Tests inflict D4 damage caused by clipping nearby vehicles, fire hydrants, buildings, etc. Any dice rolls that passengers must take while inside the pursuing vehicle suffer a –1 modifier.

If the van is reduced to 0 Armor, it crashes. Regardless of how the players stop the van, the Berserkers inside will try to escape with their prisoner on foot, and they will fight to the death.

VALIANT

KAY MCHENRY'S GEOMANCER'S JOURNAL

Gilad is one scary dude. I guess being an immortal and having ten thousand years of war under your belt will do that for you. I didn't see him fight much back on Greenland, but at the train station…. Now I know why Armstrong was running away from him. Gilad's safe house isn't much to look at, but it's fully stocked with weapons and food.

So, the woman those lowlifes were trying to drag away was Dr. Regina Barkley, a noted virologist who's supposed to speak at the United Nations about a newly discovered Ebola strain that's more virulent than any previous strain. When Gilad heard that, he wasn't happy. Seem these clowns belong to a death cult—Mother Earth's biggest nemesis. This cult's kind of like the Null, except these guys just want to destroy all life, not the whole universe.

While Gilad and Xaran loudly debated our next actions, I listened to the Earth, who gave me direction to the House of the Dead's nearest base of operations. We spent a few hours driving around to find the place—an old meat-packing plant near the river.

Suggested Characters: Gilad Anni-Padda, Xaran, Geomancer

OBJECTIVES

- Infiltrate the House of the Dead's base
- Discover the Dead's plans
- Destroy the base
- Rescue the scientists and prisoners.

CUES

- deserted building complex ● smell of death ● shadows ● hostages ● Ebola virus

TAGS

- hidden lab ● infiltration ● rescue ● fanatical guards ● innocent victims
- containment ● death cult ● Berserkers ● bioweapons

THE SETTING

This shut-down meat processing plant near the river is surrounded by a chain-link fence that looks old but is actually solid. Only a few lights are on, and the rest of the plant is in darkness. The House of the Dead has guards patrolling the grounds, staying in the shadows as much as possible.

ENEMIES/OBSTACLES

Scene 1: *Suggested NPCs: Berserker of the Dead*

Given the amount of security in the area, the players should approach the facility with caution. The fence is wired with silent alarms, the padlocked gates are under observation from hidden guard posts, and the Berserker guards have night vision goggles. If the players make it into the plant without raising any alarms, they can make it all the way to where the cult's viral lab is located.

Scene 2: *Suggested NPCs: Berserker of the Dead, Priest of the Dead*

Inside the cult's lair, the players can explore the lab and the cultists' temple.

In the lab, the players will encounter captive scientists; if Dr. Barkley wasn't rescued in the previous Event, she will also appear here. The scientists explain that the cult wants to weaponize a new Ebola strain and cause countless thousands of deaths. Prison cells in the next room hold several prisoners that have been infected with test strains of Ebola.

If the players are captured, they will be taken to the death cult's temple, located near the labs. There, Priest of the Dead Karl Pestis decides to find out whether immortals can be infected by the virus. The players are then taken to the lab, to be injected with the newest strain.

Breaking out is a lot harder than breaking in, especially because all the prisoners and scientists are tired and in no shape to run for their lives.

Scene 3: *Suggested NPCs: Berserker of the Dead, Priest of the Dead*

Once the players are outside the plant's main building, the players will see a helicopter coming in to land on the roof to wait for Pestis, who's carrying a canister. One of the scientists realizes that the canister contains the Ebola strain, and the Priest is attempting to escape with it. The cultists will fight to the death to cover Pestis's escape. If Pestis can't escape, he will crack open the canister and spray the virus into the air to infect everyone nearby. None of the cult will be captured alive.

AFTERMATH

If the Priest is stopped

Gilad Anni-Padda: It was a narrow victory, for certain. The news will likely report this as an "attempted terrorist attack," and the story will fade from the headlines after a few days. The prisoners infected by the virus will be sent to the hospital, where Dr. Barkley and the other virologists we freed will synthesize a treatment for the virus.

If the Priest escapes

Kay McHenry: I can't believe this is happening. A lot of people are going to die horribly. I know Dr. Barkley and her colleagues will no doubt find a treatment for the virus, but that can't prevent this disease from spreading worldwide.

In the meantime, the House of the Dead could be hatching any number of horrendous schemes. Mother Earth, please show me how to right this wrong and restore balance!

HARADA GLOBAL CONGLOMERATES BREAKS GROUND ON NEW OFFICES

Local officials, community members, and spokespeople of Harada Global Conglomerates gathered Tuesday to officially break ground on a new office tower which will serve as the corporation's local home here in San Francisco.

The mixed-use development will include street-level retail space and some high-end residential suites. But the tower will primarily host office space and other research and development labs, according to documents filed with the city zoning department.

"We're thrilled to count San Francisco among the many communities who understand HGC's mission to improve the human experience," said Isabella Dupre, general manager of facility. "We've benefited every community that has provided us a home, and we're eager to count the City by the Bay among them."

The exact plans for the 30-story tower, and key hearings in the zoning process, were not available to the public due to "proprietary concerns," according to a spokesman for Mayor Jonathan Ford. However, if other HGC facilities are any indication, the San Francisco tower will boast bleeding-edge technology, including biometric security, an integral underground garage, a green roof and other LEED-certified environmental features, and next-generation architecture and construction.

"This is a great day for San Francisco," Ford said at the groundbreaking ceremony. "We know that Mr. Harada's new offices here will provide endless opportunities."

Recovered Security Audio, HGC SF Offices

Kris Hathaway: Tell me again why we're not taking her when she gets in a car.

Peter Stanchek: Because she only gets in a car in their underground parking garage, Kris. When they roll out, they roll deep. And I'm not sure we could hold off the Foundation's lackeys long enough for me to focus and grab what I need.

Kris: So we wait for a weak moment. Dupre is going to go for a sandwich or a DVD sometime.

Peter: Wait? How long? A month? Two? No way. We can't wait out Harada. Not now, not when he knows I'm collecting a list of latents. We might have been able to pull that off before, but after what we did to Rachel...no way. Even if we hit a convoy, he's more likely to order someone to put a bullet in her head than let me scan her.

Kris: Fine. I got a few details on this place from City Hall, but bottom line, there's only two ways to do this.

Peter: The easy way and the hard way?

Kris: What? No, genius. The quiet way and the loud way.

Suggested Characters: Peter Stanchek, Kris Hathaway, Faith

OBJECTIVES

- Gain entry to the Harbinger Foundation building
- Obtain information about latent psiots
- Escape premises

CUES

- Things are going to get ugly fast ● hovercams ● Myyy mind…scrambled
- most secure building in the world ● the lion's den ● reality lockdown
- invasive extraction ● Show me what you know

TAGS

- infiltrate ● assault ● Harada Global Conglomerates ● real estate
- recruiter ● latents ● mind scan ● Eggbreakers ● turret drones

THE SETTING

Harada Global Conglomerates maintains offices in nearly every major American city. Blended into the urban landscape, these mini-fortresses provide flexibility to Harada's Harbinger Foundation, allowing it to hide in plain sight while granting Harada and his followers a safe haven wherever they go. Though these offices seem like fortresses at first glance, the only thing Harada values more than security is anonymity.

This thirty-story San Francisco office includes access points for everyday citizens, and the building's standard commercial appearance offers some of the same security weak points as any other city building.

ENEMIES/OBSTACLES

Scene 1: *Suggested NPCs: Security Guard, Foundation Trainee*

The team must choose whether they want to covertly infiltrate the building or fight their way in. The main entrance to the building and surrounding retail areas are nondescript, and the lobby is manned by Security Guards. If the group chooses to fight, eventually a mixed contingent of Foundation trainees and/or Eggbreakers will respond to the intrusion.

The first twenty floors of the tower are typical commercial offices and residences, which offer little except a place to get lost or pinned down. Lobby elevators only go as high as the twentieth floor; from there, a private elevator accesses the next ten floors, where the Foundation makes its home.

On the top ten floors, security is tight: there will be sensors, security cameras, and keycard locks. If alarms are activated, Eggbreakers will confront the team with the intent to capture rather than kill, per Harada's standing orders.

Scene 2: *Suggested NPCs: Eggbreaker*

Isabella Dupre, a trained psiot and one of the Foundation's key recruiters, is going about her duties on the thirtieth floor. While security is relatively light at that level, as Harada does not believe in undue surveillance on his own employees, Dupre is an Eggbreaker with the Powers Mind Wipe (D6, Discard Lowest) and Mental Freeze (D8, Add+2); she is accompanied by one or more Eggbreaker attendants.

If the characters were overwhelmed and captured, they will find themselves interrogated by Dupre. A list of latent psiots is stored both in the Foundation's mainframe, accessed by a terminal in the open penthouse level, and in Dupre's mind.

Should Dupre be Knocked Out at any point, turret drones will swoop down from the roof (5 Armor, Action D6; Machine Gun, Damage 2, Close OK, Near −2, Far —).

Scene 3: *Suggested NPCs: Foundation Security Guards, Eggbreakers*

Once the players have obtained the information they want, they must flee the premises by whatever means necessary.

Several options are available: they can go back the way they came, discover a secret private elevator to the ground floor (tied to Dupre's palm print), or use the window. Groups which have diligently maintained a stealth approach could be rewarded with an easier escape.

If the alarm system is triggered at this stage, turret drones will begin hunting the group. However, once the characters are on the ground, the drones will not pursue them beyond the immediate city block, as strict programming prevents them from making a public spectacle at street level.

VALIANT

TORQUE NIGHT TONIGHT!

"Ladies and gentlemen, coming to you *live* from the impenetrable fortress crib of Anthrax Keep, this—is—*Torque Night Tonight*! We've got one heck of a program for you tonight, thanks to the return of our very own Dark Lord Torque, Monster Hunter. He's back, he's brought some friends, and our beholder cams caught all the action.

When our main man is on the scene, there's no doubt it's on like Donkey Kong. But his friends— including a pair of hotties we can't WAIT to see in the Miller Genuine Draft fountain—have kicked things up to the next level. Last night, we saw Lord Torque jump into a troll gladiator fight for the first time in months and take on a Hell Bat without even his personal guard for backup. What a show!

Before we get to the highlights of that battle, let's check in on some viewer mail. Grognak from the Wolf King's Forest asks: 'How long can Lord Torque keep this up? Sure, we've never really seen him get injured and he doesn't seem bored yet, but isn't he going to get tired of laying the smackdown eventually?'

Well, Grognak, I gotta tell you, asking questions like that is not the way to get an invite to the New Orleans Saints Hall of Feasts. Lord Torque's Trophy Room of Vanquished Terrors isn't getting any smaller, and this reporter is willing to bet Torque's new friends are just going to drive him to new heights of awesome.

Let's move on and take a look at that sweet footage from last night…"

+++*Personal Notes of Ingrid Hillcraft, Harbinger Foundation Psychologist. Psychic Encryption ACTIVE*+++

This isn't working.

How long can one human mind—or even two—suppress another? How long should we try?

No one doubts the Kalfus brothers' power. But I've begun to doubt anyone's ability to override an individual's own will and grasp of reality. I pushed for this experiment because I believed that we could change the way we imprison others, but this prison we've created seems barely capable of holding four average psiots and one normal human being.

Normally, this is the kind of problem Master would have seen coming miles away. But he's not fully here, not the way he used to be, and I know Stanchek is the reason. I've seen this kind of behavior in Harada-sama before. He is obsessed, totally focused on understanding—and worse, controlling—Stanchek. I tried to talk to him about it, but he brushed me off.

A short time ago, we felt a rumbling that could only be the pre-tremors of a mind squall. I have to try to reach Master one more time before he loses control. I owe him that much, and I still believe in the Foundation's mission. But I won't allow one man's fixation, even his, to jeopardize the human lives all around us.

Suggested Characters: Peter Stanchek, Faith, Flamingo, Torque, Kris Hathaway

OBJECTIVES

- Determine the nature of reality
- Escape from Torquehalla
- Survive Harada's mind squall

CUES

- legendary vacation ● Something is seriously wrong ● a man-child's id-driven fantasy world
- Listen to the sea ● I'm exhausted ● This place is made of *win* ● My mind! It's on fire!

TAGS

- Torquehalla ● shared construct ● hyper-psychics
- Harada sleep cycle ● tremors ● Animalia ● mind squall

THE SETTING

Torquehalla is a fantasy world that exists in the mind of John "Torque" Torkelson, created as a refuge where Avenged Sevenfold is always playing, the beer is always flowing, and the women are always willing. Here, Torque is king, and his subjects tune in each week to watch him battle mighty creatures and rock as hard as possible.

ENEMIES/OBSTACLES

Note: If Torque is not a member of the group, the LN can choose to include him as a friendly NPC. Additionally, if Peter Stanchek is being played, his player should ideally be the LN during Scene 2, to represent "fake Peter" in the group's shared construct.

Scene 1: *Suggested NPCs: Torquehalla Troll, Hell Bat*

Together, each player experiences the closest approximation of their best, most relaxing day. The sun is shining, everything they could want is at hand, and things are perfect—suspiciously so. Eventually, one or more characters should realize that all is a little too right with the world; any character who succeeds in an Intellect Challenge will cause the setting to jarringly shift to Torquehalla (or a similarly unrealistic, confusing reality of the players' design if Torque is not present).

Once in Torquehalla, the group should make their way to the bottom of the Sea of Woe; various denizens of the world should repeatedly point them in this direction. Along the way, the group may have to contend with various elements of Torque's perfect world, including Torquehalla Troll brawlers, the Hell Bat, and the Miller Genuine Draft fountain.

Scene 2: *Suggested NPCs: Peter Stanchek ("Fake Peter"), Harbinger Foundation Technician, Animalia*

Either en route to or at the bottom of the Sea of Woe (with Kardashian Mermaids helpfully providing D6 turns of oxygen), the players will face Fake Peter, a psychic construct with the Mind Whip and Levitation Powers of the real Peter, but no others.

If the players are struggling to find a way to exit the shared reality construct or overcome the Fake Peter, the LN may introduce Animalia, a young NPC psiot projectionist who has overcome her mental restraints and can help lead them out of their captivity.

Scene 3: *Suggested NPCs: Foundation Technician, Foundation Trainee, Eggbreaker*

When the group frees itself from the shared construct, Harada's mind squall begins in earnest as he temporarily loses control of his powers. The mind squall inflicts D10 damage to every unshielded mind in the area (LN's discretion).

If Peter is present, he can successfully shield the group with his Psionic Shield Power. Otherwise, the players can locate Ingrid Hillcraft, the Foundation's psiot psychologist, and convince or coerce her to shield them; use an Eggbreaker Dossier to represent her. Finally, the building is equipped with a psionic-suppression vault Harada usually uses to contain his mind squalls; however, the vault is empty and can protect those within from the mind squall raging outside. Unprotected building staff will be horribly slain by the squall, making the group's escape relatively easy if they manage to survive.

HALF STREET FAIRGROUNDS FLIER

Come one, come all, to the **70th Annual Edison's Carnival of Wonders**! For the next two weeks, get your fill of thrills and chills before this big top extravaganza disappears until next year!

The **Carnival of Wonders** features **fun** and **attractions** for the whole family!

Experience the dizzying **Wheel of Death**! Master the **Maze of Mirrors**! Get shocked at the mysterious **Freak Show**! Take a tour through the **Tunnel of Love** with that special someone! Or test your luck with numerous games of skill, chance, and strength! Grab some balloon animals for the kids or get your face painted by a real circus clown!

There's something for everyone of all ages!

The **70th Annual Edison's Carnival of Wonders** is brought to you in part by these generous sponsors:

Carny's Corn Dogs ✪ Colonel Popcorn ✪ The Washington Capitals
The Washington Post ✪ WUSA Channel 9

A portion of your ticket proceeds goes to the **Children's Science Foundation**: helping kids around the country grow to love **Science** and **Techn**—

[*The rest of the flier appears to have been eaten, and the bite marks are covered in animal slobber.*]

Woody's Ramblings

What's your problem, Eric? I know you didn't invite me on this gig, but...who doesn't like carnivals?

Hey, hey, don't blame me for inviting myself: this was all Cejudo's idea. She saw that flier and thought it might be worth us checking out—Lord only knows why. And I figured we could grab some carnival chow while we're here, since Vincent van Goat here keeps burning our breakfast...

Speakin' of food, you got a tenner I could borrow for a funnel cake and some popcorn? I'm a little broke right now. Hey, do you think they have any cotton candy here?

Anyways...I figured we'd all come and have a good time. Besides, Cejudo reminded me that I owe Sixty-nine a date. Like, a real date, not one of those crappy excuses for dates I've been giving her lately. I mean, she is my girlfriend, after all. And somehow our dates always end up with me giving away your car keys to homeless guys and walking in on mad scientists building giant warbots or something. She deserves a piece of the real Wood-meister charm, not lame-o "dates" like that...

...and she told me that if we went on a real date, she'd recite the Gettysburg Address for me later, if y'know what I mean...

And...

Oh god. Oh GOD! What's that clown doing here?! I HATE CLOWNS!!! GET IT AWAY FROM ME! GET IT AWAY FROM ME!!! OHMYGOD?! WHAT'S HAPPENING TO ITS FACE?!

Oh. OH. It's just makeup. Sheesh. Man, what is wrong with me these days, eh? Sorry about knocking over your popcorn, Sixty-nine. I'll get you another one.

...Say, Eric, you got another tenner I can borrow?

Suggested Characters: Quantum, Woody

OBJECTIVES

- Win some carnival-game prizes
- Protect the carnival-goers

CUES

- At least you'll blend in with all the other carnies ● You don't know where that's been
- I am *not* going in the Tunnel of Love with you, man ● I double-dog dare you to try the Wheel of Death
- That mirror makes you look like you put on a few pounds ● I think I'm going to be sick

TAGS

- carnival ● carnie games ● rides ● clowns ● fair food
- the Nightmare Brigade ● Edison's Radical Acquisitions

THE SETTING

The 70th Annual Edison's Carnival of Wonders is exactly what it sounds like—fair food, families, and fun. Old-timey incandescent bulbs light all of the classic carnival rides and stall signs, children scream from nearby rides (a sound that comes across as simultaneously thrilled and terrified), and the scent of fried dough and meat—corn dogs, one hopes—wafts on the air.

ENEMIES/OBSTACLES

Throughout this Event, the players are accompanied by the friendly NPCs Vincent Van Goat and "Sixty-nine" (Crone-clone Soldier).

Scene 1: *Suggested NPCs: Nightmare Brigade*

The players can wander around the carnival for as long as the LN deems appropriate (see below). While at the carnival, the players can do any number of things.

Games: If the players wish to try their hand at carnival games, use an appropriate Stat Die (Might, Intellect, or Action) for the game's Challenge/ Test—use multiple rolls if necessary—but Powers should be used at the player's own risk, as the stall attendants might not enjoy having their stall accidentally blown up…Prizes for the games are generally ridiculously large stuffed animals that are too big for the friendly NPCs to carry, so the player that won the prize will have to lug it along, which may incur an Action or Power penalty, depending on the situation.

Fair Food: If a player indulges in fair food, a successful Charisma Test will decide if he or she has enough money to buy it. A failed Might Challenge after eating said food will result in indigestion, which will temporarily lower the character's Might Die by one level for as long as the LN deems appropriate.

Rides: Any carnival rides also call for a Might Challenge. A failed roll means the character is dizzy and/or nauseous, and his or her Action Die is lowered by one level for as long as the LN deems appropriate.

Attractions: Things like the Tunnel of Love and the Maze of Mirrors don't have any adverse affect on the players, but the LN is free to invent some.

Once the LN deems the players have had enough "fun" at the carnival, one (or more) of the fair's clowns turns into a Nightmare Brigade monster: a fusion of clowns, spiders, and needle-like teeth. These clowns are triggered to turn into a Nightmare Brigade whenever they detect the quantum energy that Quantum and Woody emit.

Scene 2: *Suggested NPCs: Johnny 2, Nightmare Brigade*

Further investigation will reveal that Johnny 2, the inventor of the Nightmare Brigade, is at the carnival testing how scary his creations are. When the players encounter him, he will say, "Ah, not you two idiots *again*!" and try to speed away in his hoverchair, and possibly try to lose them in the Maze of Mirrors.

Feel free to create a major public spectacle of over-the-top destruction and chaos here; the more ludicrous, the better.

Scene 3: *Suggested NPCs: Johnny 2, the Crone, Crone-clone Soldier*

Johnny 2 will run to a seemingly innocuous, wheelchair-bound carnival goer. It turns out this is the Crone, who was observing Johnny 2's experiment. She has a few Crone-clone soldiers in disguise with her; they throw off their disguises and reveal their weapons. "Great," she says. "These imbeciles *again*?"

The Crone and Johnny 2 will try to flee as best they can, and they will pull out all of the stops, including sacrificing Crone-clones and innocent bystanders to escape.

WASHINGTON D.C. 911 DISPATCH TRANSCRIPT

Dispatch: This is 9-1-1 Dispatch. Please state the nature of your emergency.

Male Caller: [smoke alarm going off in background] Hello? Hello? Can you hear me over all this racket?

Dispatch: Yes, I can hear you just fine. Go ahead. What's your emergency?

Caller: Well, uh…

Dispatch: Do you actually *have* an emergency, sir? You do know that calling emergency services in D.C. without having an actual emergency can be a felony?

Caller: I *know* that, ma'am. I'm just—[muffled] oh goshdarnit, will *one* of you grab the goat for a blasted second?—Sorry. Things are a little hectic at the moment—[muffled] Seriously, you guys?

Dispatch: Sir. *Sir!* What is your emergency? And did you say something about a *goat*?

Caller: [smoke alarm stops] Yes, ma'am. Sorry. We've had a bit of an incident. The goat set a fire in our apartment—

Dispatch: Wait. You have a *goat*…in your *apartment*?

Caller: [crackling fire sounds getting louder] Yeah. Grease fire, I think. Little guy burnt the pancakes and bacon. Which is weird because he makes breakfast all the time and *never* burns it bad enough to cause an actual fire.

Dispatch:…Can I get your last name, sir?

Caller: Sure. It's Henderson. H-E-N-D-E-R-S-O-N. Eric Henderson. E-R-I-C.

Unknown Male Voice: [in background] Hey, Eric—hang up, man. I think I got the fire under control. I *knew* all those ugly clothes in your closet would come in handy someday. Used 'em to smother the fire.

Caller: Agh! *WOODY!* So *help* me—! [to dispatcher] Sorry, ma'am. Looks like everything's under control here.

[End of call]

Woody's Ramblings

Of all the luck—can you believe it? Forget the clones and rednecks and science weirdos always trying to kill us—We can't even eat a proper breakfast at home these days. So, today's off to a wonderful start already, and it's not even noon yet.

Where's the waitress? I am starving…

Eric, will you stop shaking your leg under the table? It's starting to drive me up the wall. Geez. You need to chill with the coffee, partner.

Anyway, as I was saying, I could really go for some not-burned pancakes right about now, but it wouldn't surprise me if some more of those crazy, weird-science types showed up and threw a wrench in the ol' breakfast gears.

Waitress? Geez. Where is she?

Okay. Seriously. Quit it with the nervous leg shaking. I mean it. You're about to make me start feeling all jittery…Gah!

Whaddaya mean it's not you? If not you, then who?

Oh.

Cripes.

I hate being right…

Suggested Characters: Quantum, Woody

OBJECTIVES

- Get some real breakfast
- Follow the warbots
- Avoid getting arrested

CUES

- I'll never get the smoke out of these clothes ● Why you gotta interrupt my breakfast?
- Those things are not street legal ● Stop shooting! We're on your side!

TAGS

- fire alarm ● the goat ● mad scientists ● warbots ● stolen car ● police station ● disaster relief

THE SETTING

The goat's gone and burned the pancakes (again), so now breakfast is in the far more capable hands of the local pancake house. The smell of grease-fire smoke from the apartment still lingers in the air and in everyone's clothes, and it's probably not going away anytime soon. The waitress is a little absentminded, but at least she's nice. And the pancakes smell really good.

ENEMIES/OBSTACLES

Throughout this Event, the players are accompanied by the friendly NPCs Vincent Van Goat and "Sixty-Nine" (Crone-clone Soldier).

Scene 1: *Suggested NPCs: Mad Science Warbot*
Sometime during breakfast at the pancake house, the players will feel slight tremors nearby. Some Mad Science Warbots are running down the street outside the restaurant; if the players investigate before they see the Warbots, then they'll almost get trampled as the robots charge past them. These Warbots aren't slow and ponderous like those Quantum and Woody have fought in the past; these towering robots are fast, and they're running like their pilots stole something. Since the Warbots are fast, the players will need to figure out the best method of chasing them down before they can do some real damage: driving a car, using Powers to slow them down, etc. These Warbots are concentrating on evading the players, so they'll be more focused on speed than on accuracy or stopping to fight, and they're not making a conscious effort to keep from accidentally harming pedestrians.

If a Warbot needs to make a maneuver to keep from crashing into a building, other cars, etc., they must pass an Action Challenge/Test or lose 1 Armor pip from the collision.

If all but one of the Warbots is destroyed before they reach the police station (see Scene 2), at least one other Warbot will appear from a side street and join the other one.

Scene 2: *Suggested NPCs: Mad Science Warbot, Security Guard*
The Warbots run right past a police station; use the Security Guard NPC for police officers. Any police outside will shoot at the Warbots, but they might also try to arrest the players due to guilt by association.

The Warbots realize they've taken a wrong turn and head in the opposite direction to flee from the cops.

Scene 3: *Suggested NPCs: Mad Science Warbot, Johnny 2, Crone-clone Soldier, Nightmare Brigade*
The Warbots lead the players to an abandoned warehouse, where Johnny 2 is conducting some really freaky experiments. "How could you lead *them* here?!" he shouts at the Warbot scientists, who stole an item he needs for his experiments.

Johnny 2 will do everything in his power—including releasing a Nightmare Brigade and or calling for some nearby Crone-clone Soldiers, if necessary—to flee the scene. Johnny 2's experiments are extremely combustible, so it won't take much to (accidentally) send the warehouse up in a giant fireball that could be seen from all across town.

BRETHREN RITUAL TRANSCRIPT

[*New Orleans PD Detective commentary: Chief, so…this one's, uh, probably a little out of our league. After an anonymous tip, we found this…artifact left behind at crime scene #35281-2A. Forensics determined that the parchment it's written on is made of human skin, and the words written on it were inked in human blood. I've never seen anything like this before…and I think I might need to take a few days off. Spend some time with the kids and take my mind off this for awhile.*]

O Master Darque, holder of the keys to salvation, we offer to thee this sacrifice—flesh of our flesh, blood of our blood—that thine own will be done. May thy servant grace us with thy presence, that the path to thy freedom may come nigh. Shower this sacrifice with thy blessing, O Breaker of the Wheel! Show us thy will, O Righter of Wrongs!

From the bone, take the resolve of our will. May it reinforce the bridge between the dead and the living.

From the flesh, take the strength of our commitment. May it steer thy path ever closer to this world.

From the blood, take the energy of life itself. May it empower thee and grow thine influence upon this realm.

Bone and flesh, and flesh and blood, and blood and bone: we bind thee together in service of Master Darque! We bid thee: arise! Take shape and pave the way for the advent of the Breaker of the Wheel!

ARISE!

Dox's Journal
Jack, Alyssa, and I foiled the Brethren's schemes once before, and it was a near thing. But these clowns are dug into New Orleans like a swamp leech on an open patch of skin, and by the time we pluck one off, we'll have two or three more attached. And it's bad enough that they're all over this city—winding up and down through the upper echelons of politics and business. That just makes them even harder to get rid of.
Just because we ruined one scheme doesn't mean they've just given up. Knowing them, they've already got a backup. The problem isn't finding out whether they're up to something: that's a foregone conclusion. We need to focus on finding out what they're up to before it comes and bites us in the rear. That Mr. Twist caught us with our proverbial trousers down, and I don't want to see that happen again. I almost didn't walk away from that monster, and Jack's still trying to wrap his head around the whole Shadowman thing. He might be a little more focused, but am I? Could I survive being drained of necromantic energy like that again?
Fool me once, shame on you; et cetera.
So we hunt down the Brethren. Lather, rinse, repeat.

Suggested Characters: Shadowman, Dox, Alyssa

OBJECTIVES

- Discover what the Brethren are up to
- Interrupt the ritual
- Stop the sacrificial creature

CUES

- second verse, same as the first ● Feels like someone walked over my grave
- suspicious activity ● They're always up to something ● It's far too quiet

TAGS

- police investigation ● the Brethren ● ritual ● secret meeting
- sacrifice ● necromantic energy ● uninvited guest

THE SETTING

The Abettor's safe house in the Lower Ninth Ward has a lab, a library filled with magical and historical tomes, and places for everyone to crash. It's not much, but it beats risking the night at Dox's house in the French Quarter, which is likely still swarming with Brethren. The police seem to be out in force, which means the Brethren are definitely up to something. And it's better to do something about it than just sit around and wait for something else to go wrong.

ENEMIES/OBSTACLES

Scene 1: *Suggested NPCs: Brethren Goon*

There are a number of ways the team can go about searching for clues to the Brethren's next move. Some possible solutions are to wander the Ninth Ward to look for signs of activity, finding and shadowing a suspected businessman (who may or may not be a Brethren), the Brethren can come to the team, or the team might catch wind of some strange rumor that will point the team in the right direction.

Scene 2: *Suggested NPCs: Brethren Goon, Lionel Devereaux, Mr. Twist*

Once the team has found confirmation of Brethren activity in the area, the team should find its way to an abandoned warehouse that has some Brethren on guard in the area. The approach to this scene is up to the players: they can go in, guns blazing, or they can keep quiet and try to observe what the Brethren are up to.

The Brethren have gathered some sacrificial remains here, and Lionel Devereaux is leading them in performing a ritual within an arcane symbol drawn on the ground. If the team tries to interrupt the ritual, they will be too late: after two rounds of Narrations, things take a turn for the worse as the sacrificial remains knit themselves together and form a monstrous flesh golem that calls itself Mr. Turn (use the Mr. Twist NPC Dossier). Mr. Turn positively glows with necromantic energy.

Scene 3: *Suggested NPCs: Master Darque*

If Mr. Turn's Health ever reaches fewer than 4 Health pips, the necromantic energy inside of the monster releases, and it loses its Regeneration Power. Also, this release of energy tears open a partial rift into the Deadside, and a partially formed Master Darque tries to break through this tear.

Use the Master Darque Dossier, but to represent his intangibility, subtract –1 from all of his die rolls and disregard his Luck stat.

If Darque reduces a character's Health to Knocked Out, then Darque becomes fully tangible but is still tethered to the Deadside through the half-formed portal. If this occurs, Darque no longer suffers roll penalties, and his Luck Stat functions as normal.

When Master Darque is Staggered or Knocked Out, he vanishes and returns to the Deadside.

WDSU BREAKING NEWS

This is Henriette Cienfuegos with a WDSU Breaking News update.

Just moments ago we received official confirmation that the daughter of New Orleans City Councilman Pierre Jourdain has indeed gone missing. Isabel Jourdain, seven years of age, was last seen taking the bus to school yesterday morning near her home in Edgelake, but she reportedly has not returned home since. A missing persons report has filed with the New Orleans PD. Isabel has not been found at or near any of her friends' houses, and the search parties currently scouring the area near the Jourdain home and Little Woods Elementary School have found no trace of her.

According to New Orleans Chief of Police Simon Williams, no foul play is suspected in this disappearance. Neighbors and friends of the Jourdain family believe the councilman's daughter may simply have run away from home, and claim she will likely turn up on her own within a few days. However, Councilman Jourdain claims his daughter did not run away from home, and he asks the people of New Orleans to look out for his daughter.

Isabel Jourdain was last seen wearing a blue denim jumper and a red-and-white Pokémon backpack. If you have seen the girl in this photograph, please call the New Orleans Police Department's Missing Persons Hotline at 1-555-MPR-NOPD.

Email from Doctor Mirage

I'm sure you've probably heard about that New Orleans city councilman's daughter that went missing, so I won't bore you with the details. Councilman Jourdain contacted me about his daughter and asked for my help to find her. Now, you know I'm not your standard police detective, so here's why he hired me.

For reasons he won't go into, Jourdain believes his daughter may already be dead. Me, I'm not so sure, but I told him I'd look into it for him. I know some crazy stuff has gone down in New Orleans since I was last in town, and I've got this nagging suspicion that this case might be connected. If that's true, then I'm thinking you might want in on this investigation.

If you want to put our heads together and help me out on this case, maybe we can kill two birds with one stone.

I'll be in town tomorrow. If you're interested in collaborating, meet me at Bourbon and Toulouse at 7 PM. I know a great little place in the area, and we can discuss this further over dinner.

Shan Fong
thedoctor@doctormirage.com

Suggested Characters: Shadowman, Alyssa, Doctor Mirage

OBJECTIVES

- Locate the missing girl
- Free the children
- Disrupt Brethren operations

CUES

- missing persons report ● extremely potent batch of soma ● Too much spirit noise here
- spirits can show us the way ● distilled nightmares ● Can someone literally die of fright?

TAGS

- missing children ● Bourbon Street ● spirit guides
- abduction ● soma ● nightmares ● ransom

THE SETTING

Bourbon Street is *the* place to be in New Orleans after dark. The heart of the Big Easy seems to come alive as the sun sets. Dazzling lights and neon signs invite the many passersby to shop or grab a drink or a bite to eat. People about town are wandering up and down the street, and the sounds of dinner and drinks and friends can be heard from all directions. A few blocks further down, neon signs advertise dive bars, burlesque shows, and dance clubs.

ENEMIES/OBSTACLES

If normal New Orleans policemen are involved in this Event, use the *Security Guard* NPC instead but replace the Stun Baton weapon with a Police Baton (Damage 1, Close OK, Near —, Far—).

Scene 1: *Suggested NPCs: Deadside Ghost, Jaunty*

At dinner, the team needs to decide how they will go about trying to find Isabel, whether by supernatural means or more mundane methods. A few possible options involve asking spirits about the missing girl or traveling to the Deadside to see if the girl's spirit can be found there. Summoned spirits (or Jaunty, if in the Deadside) can also give clues or try to point the team, but Deadside ghosts might get confused and attack if the team asks the wrong questions.

Bourbon Street is brimming with spirits (specifically the dead kind), so the team may need to wander to separate out one or two specific spirits from the spiritual "white noise" of the area.

Scene 2: *Suggested NPCs: Brethren Goon*

By asking spirits, doing some old-fashioned police work, or questioning the locals, the team will learn that the Brethren have been lurking around the area where the councilman's daughter was last seen. Tracking one of the Brethren goons will lead to a previously unknown soma den, where sleeping children on gurneys have strange helmet-like apparatuses covering their heads. The children are shuddering and murmuring due to nightmares, and these nightmares are distilled to create the drug soma. The den itself is guarded by Brethren thugs.

The councilman's daughter is not at this soma den, but the team is on the right track.

If any character drinks a vial of soma or gets injected with a soma syringe for any reason, apply the following effects for the remainder of this scene: the affected character feels like the weight has been lifted from his or her shoulders, and everything feels right with the world. At the beginning of each of the affected character's Narrations for the duration of the effect, he or she must pass an Intellect Challenge in order to take any action apart from reveling in the drug's euphoric effects.

Scene 3: *Suggested NPCs: Brethren Goon, Parasite Monster*

After the first soma den attack, the Brethren will try to move Isabel around to stay one step ahead of the team. The team's persistence should eventually lead them to the soma den where the Brethren are holding Isabel and making soma from her nightmares. Isabel was abducted to convince Councilman Jourdain to vote along Brethren lines on a particular city issue. Instead, the councilman voted his conscience, so when Isabel disappeared, he initially hired Doctor Mirage to confirm whether Isabel was already dead.

The soma den where Isabel is being held is guarded by Brethren goons, and Isabel herself is guarded by Parasite Monsters recently created by a sacrificial ritual.

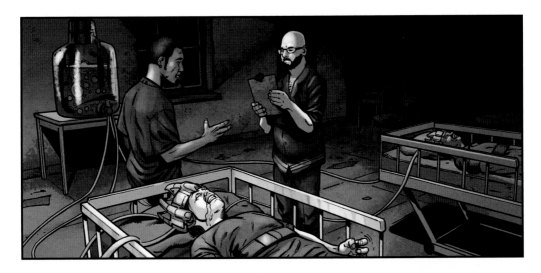

VINE GATHERING

Vine High Council Representative: <We grow tired of delays, Mr. Clement. When will the sacred armor of Shanhara be in your possession?>

MI-6 Director Patrick Clement: <Not to worry, High Council. I have Her Majesty's best agents on the job. You will have the armor back sooner than you think.>

Council: <This is what you promised us before, and we have yet to see results. We grow impatient.>

Clement: <I assure you, there is nothing to worry about. If what you've told be about this thief is true, the man controlling the armor doesn't even know what *millennium* he's in. I doubt he could even fire a gun if someone handed it to him. Trust me, we'll get the bugger.>

Council: <For your sake, you had better produce results. If we do not have the armor soon, we will be forced to destroy the population of your miserable planet. None but the Vine can be permitted to witness the majesty of our race's salvation. Understood?>

Clement: <Yes, Council. We have a strike team en route to Caracas to address the problem. You will have the armor in a matter of hours.>

Conversation with Alexander Dorian

Okay, that should do it: Clement thinks the armor is thousands of miles away from here. That should slow him down for now, but we can only misdirect MI-6 agents for so long. If we want to be able to move freely and address the Vine's desire to wipe out all life on this planet, we need to make this fast.

To buy ourselves some time we need to make the Vine blind to what's happening here on Earth. The best way to do that is to clean out MI-6—my boss, my associates, and anyone else who's still in league with the Vine. I can vouch for a few good people still there, but that's about it.

The building's heavily guarded, so this isn't going to be easy. But then again, MI-6 doesn't have a suit of nearly indestructible alien armor and an über-assassin on their side...

Suggested Characters: X-O Manowar, Alexander Dorian, Ninjak

OBJECTIVES

- Defeat or evade Vine operatives
- Plan attack on MI-6
- Destroy anti-aircraft guns
- Defeat MI-6 Director Patrick Clement
- Cleanse MI-6's Vine infestation

CUES

- I don't like the way they're looking at me ● Let's do this quiet-like ● advance warning
- security station ● cleaning Her Majesty's house ● MI-6 penthouse ● After him!

TAGS

- the Vine ● plantings ● MI-6 ● infiltration ● sentry guns
- security cameras ● intrusion countermeasures ● Patrick Clement

THE SETTING

The safe house on the northern side of the Thames looks out across the river at the headquarters for the Secret Intelligence Service—MI-6, to those in the spy trade. The rest of London lazily dozes as cabbies and night buses escort people home.

A small group of people are hanging around on the street. They look normal, but something about them doesn't sit quite right.

ENEMIES/OBSTACLES

Scene 1: *Suggested NPCs: Vine Planting (Minion)*

The team has found a safe house within sight of the MI-6 headquarters. From there, they will formulate their plan of attack on the building. Three general options are available: full frontal assault, stealth infiltration, or a combination of the two.

During the planning, a few people are loitering on the sidewalk in front of the building. These are among the many Vine plantings that MI-6 has stationed around London to act as the Vine's eyes and ears. The plantings will recognize any other Vine plantings (such as Alexander Dorian) or any Vine technology (such as the X-O Manowar armor or a Vine weapon), alert MI-6, and then attack—making the attack against the MI-6 headquarters all that much harder. If the team identifies these plantings and defeats them, no warnings go out and MI-6 will be unaware of the team's plans.

Scene 2: *Suggested NPCs: Vine Planting (Minion), Security Guard, Soldier*

The MI-6 headquarters is positively crawling with plantings, both among the intelligence staff and the security forces. To determine whether any NPC inside the building is a planting or a human, roll a D6: a result of 6 means the NPC is a human.

This scene can play out in different ways depending on the alert status inside the base:

No Alarms: MI-6 personnel will attack any unknown individuals on sight, but any Vine planting characters (such as Dorian) and known MI-6 agents (such as Ninjak) can enter the building and traverse the halls without being hassled. However, if one if the MI-6 personnel passes an Intelligence Test, they will grow suspicious and sound a silent alarm.

Alarms: All MI-6 personnel will attack anyone on sight, including any Vine planting characters (such as Dorian). Sentry guns on the building's rooftops will be active.

In addition to security personnel and Vine-loyal plantings, the base features the following security measures:

Sentry Guns: The three rooftop sentry guns are only manned when the base's alarms have been triggered. These guns are controlled by an operator via remote in the base's security center. The guns have the following weapons stats: Armor 10, Action D8, Damage 3, Close −2, Near OK, Far OK. The guns can also be disabled by taking out the operator (a standard Vine planting), hacking into the computer network, or destroying the guns' control console.

Security Cameras: Security cameras are located inside the entrance and in other sensitive areas. The cameras' facial recognition software will trigger an alarm if it detects a face that doesn't belong to a known MI-6 operative (or anyone else cleared for access).

Scene 3: *Suggested NPCs: Vine Planting (Minion), Vine Planting (Overlord), Security Guard, Soldier*

The director of MI-6, Patrick Clement, is somewhere in the base. His location will be dependent on the alarm status. If the alarm is inactive, he'll be in the penthouse with his security staff; the penthouse windows have emergency shutters (Armor 12 each). If the alarm is active, he will be sequestered in the security center; this area is protected by a blast door (Armor 15). To fully eradicate the Vine infestation of MI-6, the team needs to kill or capture Clement.

ACROSS SPACE AND TIME

<...>

<... ric...>

<... Aric...? Aric, can you hear me through the Gathering? It is I, the High Priest of Shanhara. I pray to you, hear my plea!>

<You have been away from Loam for some time, and I fear matters are no longer in the same state you left them. Though you left the Vine homeworld under my stewardship, many of my fellow Vine do not subscribe to my authority. A large group of dissidents within the military has broken away and found a way to exclude us from their personal Gatherings, so we cannot discern their plans or intentions.>

<They have taken hostages. Many of them are Vine—some young, some old, some childbearing— but the rest...I am sad to say that the many races our people enslaved but freed upon the High Council's downfall have been enslaved yet again.>

<Dalgan and I have attempted to rectify this situation ourselves, but the rebels are just too strong, too organized, and too devout in their cause. Though General Axil died for clinging to belief of you fulfilling the prophecy, many of his soldiers did not share that sentiment. Our efforts to quell the rebellion have thus far been in vain, and just today Dalgan was taken prisoner. I have tried to contact him via the Gatherings, but he is not responding. I fear he may already be dead.>

<Before our beloved paradise becomes reduced to a cinder once again, I beseech you: lend us Shanhara's aid. Grace us with your presence and help me set things right on this planet! I will endeavor to assist you in any way I can, even if it means fighting these rebels head on...>

<...>

Conversation with Alexander Dorian

I know what you're thinking: You're from Earth, not Loam, and you don't owe the Vine anything. But you do. They made you what you are, and you turned their civilization on its head. Whatever you may think, you are responsible for these people. They are going to war over you, and only you can stop all of this.

I don't agree with some of the things the Vine have done, but they're under new management, so maybe I can forgive enough of it to lend a hand. And it sounds like you might need my help.

Plus, at a very young age I was told I'd never see my real homeland: only "true" Vine ever get that privilege. I think it's high time we correct that.

Suggested Characters: X-O Manowar, Alexander Dorian, High Priest

OBJECTIVES

- Travel to Loam
- Infiltrate the Vine rebels
- Free enslaved races
- Destroy rebels OR convince rebels to stand down

CUES

- Vine homeworld ● The planet is wounded once more ● the Chosen of Shanhara
- What are their demands? ● How are they hiding? ● Take no prisoners ● Let me handle this

TAGS

- the Vine ● Loam ● distress call ● rebels ● General Stoma ● slave races
- Sky Array ● Petros Bouldermen ● Klunn diggers ● Grifan flyers

THE SETTING

The Vine homeworld is a lush paradise filled with greenery—mostly. Vast forests and orchards of gargantuan trees sprawl across the land, but the craters and scars from the last war between the Vine and its slave races still dot the landscape like a rash. Vegetation has slowly begun to grow over some of the craters, but more traces of brutal fighting have replaced them. Smoke from recent battles drifts to the sky.

The planet appears still and quiet. This, however, is not the silence of peace. This is the silence of fear. Vine people—young and old, civilian and military—appear defeated before the war has even started to begin.

ENEMIES/OBSTACLES

Scene 1: *Suggested NPCs: Vine X-O Commando, Vine Wolf-class Armor*

As the team meets in the Hall of the Council, the building comes under attack from General Stoma's rebels. The rebel forces have learned that the High Priest's help has arrived, and they are determined to end the priest's stewardship by any means necessary. If Stoma's troops gain control of the Hall, they will gain even more public support, which will make the team's goals more difficult to accomplish.

Scene 2: *Suggested NPCs: Vine Slavemaster, Vine X-O Commando*

After the Hall has been defended or abandoned, the team needs to discover where General Stoma's base of operations is located so they can strike back. This can be done a number of ways, one of which is to try to discover how the rebels can block the High Priest from their Gatherings. If the team gains access to the rebel Gatherings, they can listen in on General Stoma's planning.

At the outskirts of the base are massive cages in which Stoma has imprisoned many of the Vine's former slave races. These prisoners railed the most against Stoma's coup attempt, and many of them have been tortured as an example to the others. The cages are minimally guarded, but commotion will draw out the bigger guns. The cages have 8 Armor, and freeing the inhabitants will earn the team a distraction in the next scene.

Scene 3: *Suggested NPCs: Vine X-O Commando, Vine Wolf-class Armor, Vine Commander*

At the rebels' base, General Stoma pulls out all the stops. In addition to his ground troops, he also commands giant walker pods (Armor 20, Might D12, Action D4), which can attack with one of their legs (Damage 4, Close OK, Near OK, Far −2).

Stoma reveals all of the hostages he has taken, which include members of the Vine priesthood and Dalgan, one of the High Priest's staunchest supporters. He also reveals that his agents have infiltrated and taken control of the Sky Array, an orbital weapon platform that is trained on the battleground. If the team cannot find some way to disable the Sky Array, General Stoma will try to fire it on his next action after losing his last Armor pip.

If the Sky Array is fired, all combatants in the scene—both player characters and NPCs—will suffer 6 unavoidable damage that cannot be reduced by Powers; no die rolls are necessary. Due to the length of time it takes to recharge and reload, the Sky Array can only be fired once during this scene.

"Everything carries within it the seeds of its own destruction." That little saying of mine has been hijacked many times over the years, but I meant it in a broader sense: every living thing in the world will eventually undo itself. The Greeks understood hamartia, even respected it, but their idea of a "fatal flaw" was flexible. It could be something you did, something that happened to you, or something you simply *were*.

Did my brothers and I err? In lives as long as ours, our mistakes outnumber the stars. Have we experienced the vagaries of random misfortune? The answer to that question exceeds my strength to write it.

No, the fault is buried in the very fiber of who we are. Our love caused my fool brothers to unleash the Boon upon the world in a foolhardy attempt to bring me back—but it afflicted Telal as well, twisting him in unnatural ways. Our sense of justice and mercy let him live, but should we have been coldhearted beasts and snuffed out the poor soul instead? Our arrogance led us to challenge the demon, at the cost of many more innocent lives.

Throughout the ages he has hunted us and those like us, seeking to consume the spark of our immortality to rectify his own warped rebirth. We have struggled to oppose him, but now the time has come to face what we have wrought, to confront our hamartia with open eyes. Now, at last, the seeds must bloom.

Note: "A Hunt for the Ages" is a campaign intended for characters who are either immortal (Armstrong or Gilad Anni-Padda), capable of time travel/displacement (Timewalker), extremely long-lived, (Xaran or Geomancer), or characters who become immortal through some other means (LN's discretion). The use of mortal characters is possible, but their counterparts in each successive Event will likely be their descendants.

THE SCROLLS OF GILAD ANNI-PADDA, ETERNAL EMPEROR

Aram once told me that the first moments after the Boon's energy rushed into him were horrendous. I can't imagine what that must have been like for Telal, half-formed and twisted as he was by his distance from the Boon and by hovering between life and death when it activated. Despite all his degenerate actions that followed, the madness, pain, and horror he experienced in those first moments is almost enough to make me feel pity for him.

I awoke to a changed world. No, not changed—destroyed. Barely visible were the outlines of the market in which I played with my brothers in our youth. Most of the town's homes and buildings were annihilated, the surrounding fields were afire. Even the mighty ziggurat from which we triggered that infernal device had all but crumbled around us.

Still adjusting to our new states, we staggered from our makeshift tombs and attempted to aid the handful of souls not claimed by the Boon. The fires raged for days, and we found more bodies than survivors. Even Ivar seemed to return to sanity, though most of those we found viciously refused our help.

I remember when we exhumed my brother's men Telal and Sakkat—or what was left of them. Even now, recalling what the Boon did to their bodies, I feel fortunate. We assumed they would not be long for this world…but we were not that fortunate.

Telal's Musings

The fools Anni-Padda…they have finally done it. They have destroyed the world.

When they returned from the Faraway, I and a few true believers among the city guard vowed to follow Ivar in his mission to restore his noble brother. Even when Ivar slew the king and seized power for himself, we refused to believe he had gone too far.

The woman-slayer Aram felt otherwise. He attempted to betray his older brother, and when Sakkat and I tried to stop him, he dealt us both mortal wounds. I lay in a pool of my own blood, ready to meet my ancestors. Then the light…the endless, consuming light.

Sakkat and I woke screaming, our bodies horrifically pulled apart and rearranged. They left us alone in a small shelter to prepare for death. But I could feel the power shifting, sliding around inside me…and more importantly, I could feel that same power inside Sakkat.

OBJECTIVES

- Search for survivors
- Begin rebuilding efforts
- Confront Telal

CUES

- What happened? ● This is all your fault! ● Did you hear that?
- Please…please help me… ● Behind you! ● What is he? ● We've all been changed

TAGS

- ancient Sumer ● rebirth ● city ruins ● fallen civilization
- relief efforts ● the Boon ● the Anni-Padda brothers

THE SETTING

What was once a bustling ancient metropolis has been gutted and devastated by the Boon. Even the sturdiest buildings have been virtually blown away, and the streets are choked with ashes and half-incinerated skeletons, especially around the ziggurat at the center of the city, where many residents gathered to witness the activation of the Anni-Padda brothers' mysterious device. All seems lost, but the moans of a few gravely injured townsfolk are borne along on the hot, dry wind.

ENEMIES/OBSTACLES

Due to injuries from being half-buried in the rubble atop the central ziggurat in the aftermath of the Boon's activation, the players begin the Event with D6 Health damage. However, they should be surprised to find that their newfound Powers heal their injuries quickly.

Scene 1: *Suggested NPCs: Telal*

The players must extricate themselves from the rubble of the chamber from which they triggered the Boon, and find a way down the ziggurat. The destruction at ground level is extreme, and bodies are everywhere. No signs of life are immediately present, but a thorough search of the area and successful Intellect Challenges will reveal that some residents survived the event and are buried underneath piles of rubble.

The newborn immortals will find that helping these people won't be easy: the same buildings that shielded the victims boast the equivalent of 8 Armor and must be moved carefully to avoid crushing those underneath. Any conscious victims will react with immediate hostility toward the Anni-Padda brothers and may attack them with rocks or other simple weapons.

Eventually, the group will unearth two individuals they recognize as Sakkat and Telal, guards loyal to Ivar Anni-Padda. The two appear to have been blasted clear of the ziggurat to their current location and, more horrifyingly, have been horribly twisted and mangled by the blast. The players must decide whether to reveal these men to the other shell-shocked survivors or hide them away.

Scene 2: *Suggested NPCs: Telal*

As the first night falls after the apocalypse, only a few dozen survivors—from a city once numbering the in the thousands—have been recovered. They begin erecting rough shelters and forming a new ruling council. The players can approach this council and work with them by succeeding in a Charisma Test at a –2 modifier (–3 if Ivar is doing the talking).

At some point, an ear-piercing shriek calls the players to where Telal and Sakkat are being held. Upon arriving, they witness Telal horrifically "consuming" Sakkat—the exact manner in which he does so is left to the players to narrate, but his grievous disfigurements are clearly healing as Sakkat dies.

If the players attempt to engage Telal, they will have one round of Narrations to do so before flees with superhuman speed into the night, vowing to return and claim the brothers' lives as well.

TELAL, DEMON OF UR

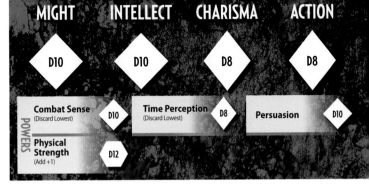

	MIGHT	INTELLECT	CHARISMA	ACTION
	D10	D10	D8	D8

POWERS

Combat Sense (Discard Lowest)	D10	Time Perception (Discard Lowest)	D8	Persuasion	D10
Physical Strength (Add +1)	D12				

Health track:
-1 TO MIGHT ✖
-1 TO MIGHT & ACTION ✖
STAGGERED ✖✖
KNOCKED OUT ✖

ARMOR (BOON'S CURSE)

HEALTH

WEAPONS

	DAMAGE	RANGE Close	Near	Far
Sword	2	OK	–2	—
Sword	2	OK	–2	—
Machine Pistols*	3	OK	OK	–2

*Events 3 and 4 only

EQUIPMENT

Chemistry Gear	Tactical Maps
Ritualistic Knives	Sumerian Texts

CUES

I am the Demon!

Your time is at an end.

I have consumed the ages.

THE SCROLLS OF GILAD ANNI-PADDA, ETERNAL EMPEROR

My brothers and I dabbled in war throughout the centuries. I had my mission, Ivar had his curiosity, and Aram…well, I think Aram took up arms when he was bored, thought there'd be women or vice in it, or—once in a rare while—if the cause moved him. He was never comfortable with slavery in ancient Ur, and when the American Civil War broke out over the same issue, he got both of us involved, on what he believed was the right side.

Enlisting as a soldier was much easier in those days, and as long as we didn't encounter the same unit we got "killed" out of, staying out of the way wasn't too much trouble. Always the enthusiast, Aram practically dragged me in front of a Union recruiter as soon as the first shots were fired at Fort Sumter, and we received front-row seats to the farce that the North's early campaigns became. Case in point: the Battle of Fredericksburg. Forget the strategic problems, if you can. After a dozen charges up Marye's Heights, I was prepared to arrange an accident for Burnside and just take command of the Army of the Potomac myself, but Aram did everything he could to stop me.

Out of respect for the brave, shell-shocked men with whom we retreated from the battlefield, my brothers and I kept our analysis of the conduct of the battle—and our compliments for Lee—to ourselves. It was just another army, just another battle—until that first flaming wagon crashed down to block our path, the Sumerian word for "devil" written in blood on its side.

Despite four days of battle we'd just endured, that's when the first chill ran down my spine.

Telal's Musings

Once again they involve themselves in the affairs of the beings we once were. To what end? To make a difference? To entertain themselves? To study the insects? They have lost sight of what it means to be eternal. But not I.

In the millennia since we last faced each other, I have not been so idle. They and I are the same, but the process that created us was not. They endure, but I decay. After I Consumed Sakkat, I enjoyed life...for a time. But age set in, injuries did not heal, and I raged against the end that appeared nigh, learning all I could about the Boon and my unlife.

Finally, a breakthrough: I discovered I could turn one of my foolish followers into a pale shadow of what I was—and then Consume them. It was enough to knit my frayed organs and give me power to Consume those who might give me the permanence I truly seek—the Brothers.

OBJECTIVES

- Fight off Telal
- Evacuate soldiers and escape

CUES

- Bring them to me! ● We have to get these people out of here ● It can't be him…can it?
- It's a trap! ● I consume what I need ● I can't see him ● He's too strong!

TAGS

- Battle of Fredericksburg ● an old foe ● the perfect ambush
- cultists ● chaotic battle ● flaming barricade ● breakthrough

THE SETTING

The date is December 14, 1862. The Union army has reached a turn in the road amid a deep ravine, with steep rocks on both sides preventing easy ascent. The aurora borealis shimmers brilliantly in the sky overhead, a rare phenomenon at this latitude—and perhaps an ill omen.

ENEMIES/OBSTACLES

Scene 1: *Suggested NPCs: Telal Cultist*

Marching in retreat from Fredericksburg, the road sharply dips and continues through a steep ravine. To detect the ambush, someone in the group must succeed in an Intellect Test. If they are unable to sense the trap, the group will suffer a –2 to all rolls for the remainder of the scene once the ambush begins.

When the bulk of the troops are in the deepest part of the ravine, a series of flaming wagons will crash down both behind and in front of the column, cutting it off. Moments later, hidden Telal Cultist sharpshooters in the brush above will begin firing down on the troops with rifled muskets.

Scene 2: *Suggested NPCs: Telal Cultist, Telal*

The initial hail of bullets quickly subsides, and the true threat is revealed. A wave of Telal Cultists descends on the players. In the middle of the cultists

is Telal, appearing mostly human, though clearly ravaged by injury and time. He lets his acolytes clear out the area of Union soldiers and joins the battle after the first round of Narration.

As the players damage Telal and attack his followers, they will see him disengage to crouch near a fallen acolyte and Consume him or her in the same way that the players witnessed in Part 1. The act takes a full Narration, during which the other cultists will attempt to keep the players at bay. Each time Telal Consumes a follower, he appears more hale and healthy, with a corresponding bump in his abilities—he ignores the first 4 damage suffered after doing so, and he inflicts 2 additional damage on his next successful attack.

When one of the players is Staggered, or when they realize they will run out of time before Telal runs out of cultists, the group may decide that retreat is the better option. By that point, most of the Union soldiers trapped inside the ambush with them have either been killed or are injured and begging for help.

The flaming wagons have 5 Armor and deal 2 damage per round to anyone attempting to interact with them at Close range. Once the players have broken through or found some other way out of the trap, Union troops on either side of the barricades begin assisting the survivors, allowing the players to attempt an escape.

TELAL CULTIST

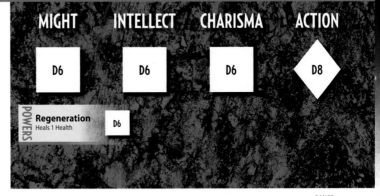

	MIGHT	INTELLECT	CHARISMA	ACTION
	D6	D6	D6	D8

POWERS

| Regeneration | Heals 1 Health | D6 |

WEAPONS	DAMAGE	RANGE Close	Near	Far
Sword	2	OK	—	—
Rifled Musket*	2	OK	–2	—
Pistol**	2	OK	OK	—

*Civil War setting only   **Modern setting only

EQUIPMENT

Tattoo Equipment

Sumerian Artifact

-1 TO MIGHT

-1 TO MIGHT & ACTION

STAGGERED

KNOCKED OUT

ARMOR
(THE DEMON'S GIFT)

HEALTH

THE SCROLLS OF GILAD ANNI-PADDA, ETERNAL EMPEROR

The turn of the second millennium—what a nightmare.

I saw little of my brothers in that time, consumed as they were by their own interests. We should have pursued Telal immediately, regrouped and pressed the attack. Instead, we bickered. Ivar wanted to study how the demon gained strength from his followers. Aram drifted, as he always does. For me, there was no shortage of conflict, war, and strife to navigate.

We finally reconnected early in the new millennium, when I reached out to my brothers for their help in defeating our old enemy. A contact in San Francisco told me her brother Nathan inexplicably began learning ancient Sumerian and frequently ranted about "the heart of a warrior" and "the power of eternity." My fears were confirmed after she noticed that he and several of his friends got matching tattoos of the Sumerian cuneiform for "demon."

Our ancient mistake had found a new home somewhere in that city and was gathering new followers. Finding the beast's lair required a subtler approach than we usually take, but what we found in those catacombs beneath the city was the very stuff of nightmares. The devastation wrought by the Boon was a fading memory, and the clamor and gore of a thousand battlefields no longer reached me, but the visceral, personal horror we witnessed down there…it was unforgettable.

Telal's Musings

The sheep gather to me with an ease that even my ageless mind struggles to comprehend. It was not so easy, once. Communities were more closely knit and less trusting of outsiders or deviations from the norm. Families knew where their children were and with whom they associated. Those I could turn, and thus Consume, were the outsiders, the lost, the damned. Now they are fools trying to prove they are special.

The Brothers eluded me a century and a half ago because my followers were too few, my resources too sparse. Now, finally, I have all that I need to change these mortals into something useful and begin to build something that can crush the Brothers Anni-Padda for all time.

OBJECTIVES

- Locate the cult member
- Follow the cultist back to Telal's hideout
- Disrupt operations

CUES

- How are we supposed to find him in all this? ● I'm just here to party
- No, I'm not looking for your phone number ● Bartender!
- This place smells like a sewer ● These experiments are inhuman
- Don't leave anything in one piece

TAGS

- Mission District ● City by the Bay ● Mission Street Tavern
- underground headquarters ● cultists ● no one home ● stealth mission ● horrors

THE SETTING

The Mission District is one of San Francisco's most vibrant and oldest neighborhoods, boasting a variety of cafes, theaters, arts venues, and bars. One of these is Mission Street Tavern, a frequent haunt of Nathan, a young man who appears to be involved with Telal. His preferred watering hole is packed with every imaginable denizen of the nightlife, dancing and drinking to loud music.

ENEMIES/OBSTACLES

Scene 1: *Suggested NPCs: Telal Cultist*

Assuming the players can talk, buy, or sneak their way into Mission Street Tavern, the first order of business is to find the cultist Nathan. This requires Intellect or Charisma Tests, as appropriate, when they interact with patrons, staff, bartenders, and other individuals. Eventually, someone will be able to point them toward Nathan, a trim, well-dressed young man with tattoos the players may recognize as ancient Sumerian cuneiform script.

While they may approach Nathan himself, he is just a follower of Telal. An altercation will cause him to flee, and he will gain a +2 modifier to his Intellect Tests in the next scene as he will be aware that someone has taken interest in him. After a time, he will strike out with several girls and leave the bar on his own.

Scene 2: *Suggested NPCs: Telal Cultist*

Pursuing Nathan on the streets is relatively easy, as foot traffic is thick. However, he soon turns into a rundown area and opens a well-hidden manhole cover, dropping into the city's underground tunnels.

While the players trail their target through the underground, any action or Power used at Far range will not raise his alarm; any Near action will cause Nathan to make an Intellect Test. If successful, or if the group approaches to Close range, he will become aware of their presence and flee—but in his panic he will bolt directly toward the cult's chambers. If this happens, the cult will begin the next scene ready for the players to arrive.

Scene 3: *Suggested NPCs: Telal Cultist*

When the group arrives at the cult's base, they will have either succeeded in staying quiet or managed to raise the alarm. In the case of the former, they will have the chance to explore the series of small, connection chambers. In the latter, they'll be forced to immediately begin fighting a series of cultists.

The chambers contain typical common areas, living quarters, and an odd, out-of-place storeroom. A successful Intellect Challenge will locate a hidden door. Behind it lies Telal's laboratories, a half dozen chambers of grotesqueries and horrors. One room is stocked with shelves of a luminescent blue liquid, the serum Telal has been feeding to his followers.

The players can decide to break as many objects as they can, kill or capture as many cultists as possible, and/or gain information on Telal's actions. However they proceed, the group's nemesis is clearly not here.

THE SCROLLS OF GILAD ANNI-PADDA, ETERNAL EMPEROR

Even immortals are not immune to the changing world. Time is a wave we ride for eons, but it carries us along on its own path, taking us where it will. So it has been these last millennia, as death and change raced across the world, mocking our plans to forge our own destiny.

I have carved out what stability and happiness I can, stepping to the fore again as a protector. My brothers have dealt with the forty-first century in their own ways, and finally, I have stopped judging their choices. What more could it possibly matter?

Still, there remains some unfinished business, a thread stretching into our past that has once again brought us together. Telal. The warrior, the demon. Certainly the two millennia since we last faced our old nemesis must have been no kinder to him than they were to us. But this world feels more like his world, and if the rumors from the north are true and a war band using old Sumerian names and trappings does exist, they can answer to only one master.

With what strength we have left, it is time to face our demon, accept our mistakes, and never stop until the world is free of his darkness.

Telal's Musings

At long last, I can step from the shadows and take my place as ruler. Ah, but perhaps it is too late.

Consuming no longer appears to bestow the same benefits it once did. I am aging, fading. So too must be the Brothers, our time drawing out along its final beats. I doubt Consuming even them will be enough to change my fate now, but that no longer matters. My followers will carry my name and my lessons forward.

Joining this final battle serves a higher purpose: I will settle an old wrong and enter oblivion knowing that the Brothers arrived first.

OBJECTIVES

- Approach Telal's headquarters
- Defeat the Demon

CUES

- The time has come ● Nothing can save you now ● It's been too long
- Time to die, Demon! ● Do you remember? ● There is no hope ● that must be his home

TAGS

- 41st century ● the fallen world ● evil ascendant
- Boulder, Colorado ● true believers ● warlords ● final showdown

THE SETTING

The Earth is poisoned, wracked by centuries of war, nuclear weapons, famine, and death. Wildlife—not all of it native to old North America—has reclaimed the wilderness, and the few people left cling tightly to their villages. Technology is a thing of the past; it is kept alive only in rumors and whispers of murderous techno-beasts that descend upon villages without warning.

Most American cities of old have turned into overgrown ruins, full of lurking dangers and artifacts of the world that was.

ENEMIES/OBSTACLES

Scene 1: *Suggested NPCs: Telal Cultist*

As the players move north, they will have to speak to other travelers and villagers to gain information about Telal's cult. The cult is not keeping a low profile in their search for the players, and eventually the group will be steered toward the ruins of what was once Boulder, Colorado.

Along the way, the players may encounter roving bandits, mutated creatures, and other hostile entities (feel free to modify NPCs—such as Roanoke Tribesman, T-Rex, or other appropriate Dossiers—to represent these threats). Earth of the forty-first century is a savage wasteland, and players can let their imaginations run wild.

As they near Boulder, the group will notice regular patrols of cultists carrying Sumerian-style weapons and dressed in an approximation of ancient Sumerian armor. They can attempt to avoid these guards or fight them.

Scene 2: *Suggested NPCs: Telal Cultist, Telal*

Entering the ruins of Boulder, Telal's home is immediately apparent: in what was the center of town stands a large ziggurat similar to that in ancient Ur. Few others besides cultists are present, and as the group approaches, a fight breaks out. Shortly thereafter, Telal will enter the fray.

Telal once again seems to be aged and falling apart, and while he can Consume a cultist (see Part 2), doing so will allow him to only ignore the next 2 points of damage, and he does not gain any attack bonuses. After taking 4 points of Health damage, Telal will attempt to flee, triggering a desperate chase through the ruined streets.

AFTERMATH

If Telal is defeated

Gilad Anni-Padda: The Demon is no more, and for the first time in millennia, I will sleep in a world no longer stained by his evil. The poor souls converted to his cause are beyond saving, and perhaps that is for the best: the name of Telal will sink into the sands of time, unremembered.

Ivar remembers the man who was once so loyal that he watched his king's murder and let the Boon be triggered. Aram said little, just something about having to kill Telal twice. As for myself, I am tired, but glad to leave a monster in the past, where he belongs.

If Telal escapes

Telal: Once more, the Brothers have challenged my power, and once more they have been found wanting. My defeat of the Eternal Emperor will only draw more followers to my cause, and perhaps they will be enough to sustain me. If not, I will spread my power as far as I can before the end, uniting the world in the name of the Demon.

VITAL FACTORS

Name: _____

Affiliation: _____

Character Level: _____ **Event Points:** _____

Tags: _____

_____

HISTORY

_____

_____

_____

_____

_____

_____

_____

PERSONALITY

_____

_____

_____

_____

MIGHT	INTELLECT	CHARISMA	ACTION	LUCK

POWERS

CUES

_____   _____
_____   _____
_____   _____
_____   _____

ACTION CUES

_____   _____
_____   _____
_____   _____
_____   _____
_____   _____

DISPOSITION

_____   _____
_____   _____

-1 TO MIGHT

-1 TO MIGHT & ACTION

STAGGERED

KNOCKED OUT

WEAPONS	DAMAGE	RANGE		
		Close	Near	Far

EQUIPMENT

ARMOR **HEALTH**

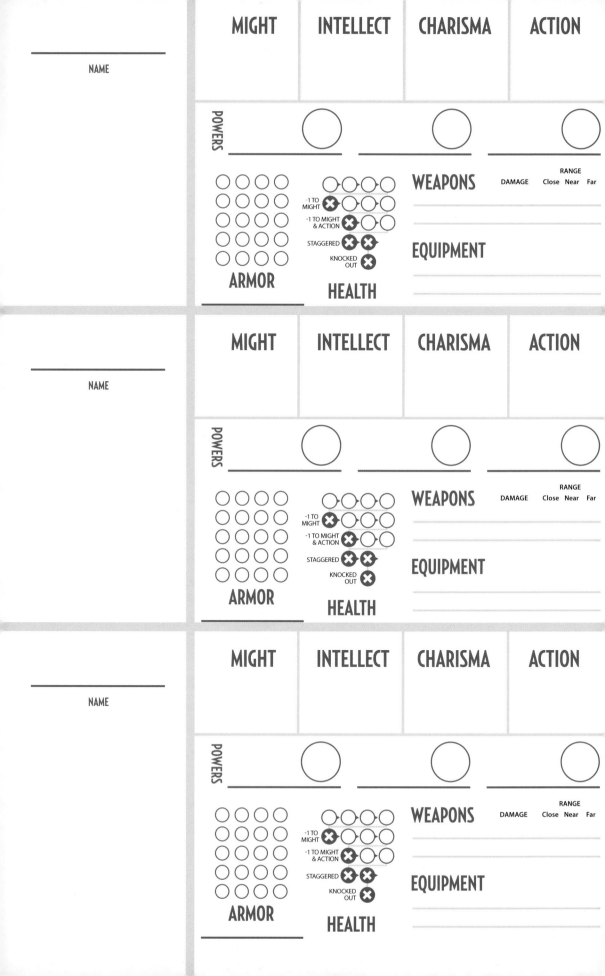

RANDOM EVENT GENERATOR

If you're having a hard time creating ideas to flesh out a blank Event Brief, just roll on each of the tables (see p. 72).

THEME: TIME

Roll D6	Result	Examples
1	Prehistory	Sumeria/Mesopotamia
2	Known History	402 AD, American Civil War
3–4	Present Day	—
5	Future	41st century
6	Outside of Time	The Faraway, the Deadside

THEME: SETTING

Roll D6	Result	Examples
1	City	San Francisco, New Orleans
2	Countryside	Roman Empire, African savannah
3	Facility	PRS "Nursery," Area 51
4	Compound	Anti-government militia
5	Vessel	Aircraft carrier, Vine battlecruiser
6	Extraterrestrial Locale	The moon, Loam

OBJECTIVES

Roll D6	Result	Examples
1	Protection	Alexander Dorian, Timewalker
2	Extraction	Pull a scientist out of a MERO facility
3	Distraction	Capture ERA clones
4	Demolition	Eliminate a PRS outpost
5	Delivery	Pass Vine tech to highest bidder
6	Evasion	Escape H.A.R.D. Corps team

PLAYER CHARACTERS

Roll D8	Result	Examples
1	Archer & Armstrong	Archer, Mary-Maria
2	Bloodshot/H.A.R.D. Corps	Bloodshot, Disciple
3	Eternal Warrior	Eternal Warrior, Xaran
4	X-O Manowar	Aric, High Priest
5	Unity	Ninjak, Livewire
6	Harbinger/Renegades	Peter Stanchek, Harada
7	Quantum and Woody	Quantum, Woody Henderson
8	Shadowman	Shadowman, Alyssa Myles

NON-PLAYER CHARACTERS

Roll D8	Result	Examples
1	Archer & Armstrong	Sect Security Guard, Green Dragon Lama
2	Bloodshot/H.A.R.D. Corps	PRS High-Tech Soldier, Chainsaw Operative
3	Eternal Warrior	Sword of the Wild, Berserker of the Dead
4	X-O Manowar	Vine Commander, Vine Wolf-Class Armor
5	Harbinger	Eggbreaker, Torquehalla Troll
6	Quantum and Woody	Crone-Clone Soldier, Nightmare Brigade
7	Shadowman	Deadside Ghost, Brethren Goon
8	The Faraway	Quetzalcoatlus, Roanoke Tribesman

VALIANT

CONTEXT

_____
_____
_____
_____
_____
_____
_____
_____
_____
_____
_____
_____
_____

OBJECTIVES

_____

CUES

_____

TAGS

_____

THE SETTING

_____

_____

_____

_____

_____

_____

_____

_____

ENEMIES/OBSTACLES

_____

_____

_____

_____

_____

_____

_____

_____

_____

_____

_____

_____

_____

_____